... AND OTHER
DIRTY STORIES

OTHER BOOKS
by Larry L. King

CRIME AND PUNISHMENT

HUCKLEBERRY FINN

A TALE OF TWO CITIES

THE DEERSLAYER

AN AMERICAN TRAGEDY

THE ONE-EYED MAN*

WINESBURG, OHIO

HAMLET

FOR WHOM THE BELL TOLLS

YOU CAN'T GO HOME AGAIN

THE GREAT GATSBY

THE BOOK OF JOB

DR. ZHIVAGO

* Especially recommended

... AND OTHER
DIRTY STORIES

by Larry L. King

Foreword by Willie Morris

An  *Book*

The World Publishing Company
NEW YORK   CLEVELAND

FOR ROSEMARIE:

my agony & my ecstasy

Published by The New American Library, Inc.
in association with
The World Publishing Company
2231 West 110th Street
Cleveland, Ohio
Library of Congress Catalog Card Number: 68–18256
Printed in the United States of America

Foreword

Larry L. King is the product of a violent, isolated, impoverished heartland of America. It is a land of jangling country tunes and limitless spaces, of fierce personal politics and cutting loneliness, of bloodletting fundamentalism, and secret poetry. "Men would spray asphalt over the long, prairie-straight wagon trails and throw up brick siding against the stabbing sand," Lawrence Goodwyn wrote in his *South Central States*. "But the effect on the people would be the same. The wind, endless, unengageable, would still haunt the women and leave the men feeling strangely diminished. The plains wind would intimidate, as in the earlier time, and restless people would feel a need to proclaim their own identities." In Larry King's lifetime this West Texas country would superimpose upon itself an aggressive new wealth that gave the region a strangely disjointed and unpredictable character; its modern-day contortions and cruelties would still be undergirded by an extravagant, gleeful humor. To appreciate King's writings, one need know that the land of his youth was a reluctant civilization, and that to escape it was to come a very long way indeed. He has escaped with a rollicking old-style prose reminiscent of the early Mark Twain and Mencken, but as more than one writer from the same area has commented, he owes as much to a fellow Texan, one W. C. Brann, a cantankerous reforming editor of the nineteenth century who was murdered in a journalistic rivalry. Brann's freewheeling prose touched a whole generation of aspiring writers from the Southwest; in a provincial context this prose may seem rather old-fashioned, but in the hands of a talented journalist attuned to our contemporary American existence it is a perfect instrument for expressing the nihilistic madnesses of our age.

But what King has brought to our magazine journalism is much more than a feeling for the eccentric, the irrational, and the unpredictable. Even at his most cutting, I think, his writing has been characterized by a deep and abiding commitment to America and to authentic American values—almost to an older and vanished America whose expressed ideals of democratic justice and humanity touched somehow the unsophisticated young men in its provinces and shaped them into maturity: a belief that poverty could be overcome and that one would be the better for having experienced it; a belligerent regard for the underdog, for the wayward tramp, for the homeless lost brother; an allegiance to free expression and a hope that in the clash of strong voices some truth might prevail; and an almost mystical country boy's faith that this nation was the last great hope of the world.

All these qualities, in the most human and unrighteous way, run through the essays in this book; what King never loses sight of is the essential fascination and sadness of individual human beings in all their joys and failings, nobilities and cruelties. The new Federal expressway may have destroyed his hometown in "Requiem for a West Texas Town," but it failed to destroy his memories of its people three decades ago. Congressman Joe Pool of Dallas may have made the front pages with his unusual demagoguery on the House Un-American Activities Committee in 1966, but after several drinks in a Capitol Hill bar he was just another small-town politician after big-town glory. "My Hero LBJ," a classic in its genre, holds Lyndon Johnson to the untarnished idealism of a boy at a country crossroads in 1941, and "God, Man, and William F. Buckley" is an outrageous exercise in juxtapositions: Yale vs. Texas Tech, Skull & Bones vs. West Texas Boosters, oilman-financer father vs. dirt-farming daddy. It is the unforgettable and slightly insane incident which always stands out: a Honda ride up Park Avenue with the conservative icon; a minor-league pro football team pushing a stalled bus up the Gulf Freeway; a flamboyant county judge getting a "three minute lecture in virtue" from a future President of the United States; a Negro cabdriver expounding the wonders of America's space program; a fundamentalist's dialogue on education; a jazz musician's demonstrations on how to cure all the diseases known to man.

It is at the end of King's marathon bouts with bourbon and Swiss Kriss in the company of Louis "Pops" Armstrong that these two strange companions paused at the end of a pier jutting into the ocean at Atlantic City:

"Pops lit a cigarette and leaned on a restraining fence to smoke. For long moments he looked up at a full moon and watched the surf come and go. The glow from his cigarette faintly illuminated the dark old face in repose and I thought of some ancient tribal chieftain musing by his campfire, majestic and mystical. There was only the rush of water, gently roaring and boasting at the shore. 'Listen to it, Pops,' Louis said in his low, chesty rumble. 'Whole world's turned on. Don't you dig its pretty sounds?' "

Larry King's work has captured something of the rhythms, roarings, and boastings of the place we inhabit, and in doing so he has become one of the finest of our magazine journalists. We at *Harper's* are proud to have him.

—Willie Morris
New York City
April, 1968

*The author wishes to genuflect before the several
publications permitting in this collection use
of materials which appeared earlier under
his by-line in their pages, though sometimes
in slightly different form.* "My Hero LBJ,"
"Requiem of a West Texas Town," "God, Man, and
William F. Buckley," "The Battle of Popcorn Bay,"
"Bob Jones University: The Buckle on the Bible Belt,"
"Yesterday's Heroes in the Mickey Mouse League,"
"Joe Pool of HUAC: McCarthy-in-the-Round,"
and "Everybody's Louie" *all originally appeared
in* Harper's Magazine. "Making the Scene
at Mailer's" *and* "On the Rocks & with
a Twist of Lemon" *appeared in* The Texas Observer.
"Hedy, Ecstasy and Me" *was published in* The New
Republic *under the title,* "Poème d'Extase."
"Waltz Me Around Again, Sugar . . ." *first appeared as*
"Sugar: Down But Not Quite Out" *in* Sports Illustrated.
"Notes of a Native son: An A-B-Z Primer of Texas" *first
appeared in* Venture. *The remainder of this book has not
previously appeared anywhere in the world, and very
possibly should not be appearing even now.*

CONTENTS

Introduction

to you your book is important. to doubleday and doran it is number 702.
—*Fred Allen to H. Allen Smith*

I don't like to write. I like to have written.
—*Gloria Steinem*

There was this magazine (Today's Woman) which conducted a survey to discover which fiction writer was most popular among its readers, and I won. They never bought another piece.
—*Charles Bonner*

If you write a book that is full of pressures and comes out of your very center, it will sell twelve copies. People from Hollywood will call at three in the morning to say, "Hate to bug you at this hour, baby, but I just finished it and all I can say is like War and Peaceville. Go back to bed and sleep easy. Tomorrow it goes over to Marlon and then I want my people to chin with your people." You never hear from them again. You then write a book that is meant to tide you over and hold the fort until you think up another that has all of the original pressures. And, of course, sales go through the roof. It is crap shooting and it is action and the dream is always there and I doubt that you can get it this way in children's ready-to-wear although I met a man on a train who said you have the same thing in shingles.
—*Bruce Jay Friedman*

To members of the writing craft those little quotes above are about as funny as Christmas Eve at Parris Island. I don't mean writers whose books sell like hula hoops did a few years back or like Harold Robbins does now. I mean the peripheral thousands of us who haven't the foggiest notion where our next quarterly income tax payment is coming from: we sour legions who pay the rent by knocking out first-person confessionals for *The Hub Cap Thieves Review* or *Female Impersonators Monthly,* hoping that Johnny Carson will accidently hold our "serious" works up to the camera between spiels for dog food and odorless body sprays, so that all the folks out there in Television Land will go galoomping down to the bookstore as if running a Chinese bank.

Hardly a day expires but what some slide-rule authority proves that if all the books sold last year were laid end to end they would reach from here to the valley of the dolls. Authors are said to be more prosperous than supermarket owners. Teddy White's never more than four years away from Making Another President. Ralph Nader's buying a car.*

This literary prosperity has escaped me. Apparently it has eluded my publisher as well. He wore a sad face the day he told me how nonfiction collections won't sell for sour apples, saying how proud and happy I should be that he had placed Art before Greed in consenting to bring this book out so that it might live to lose its way among the 30,000 tomes that will assault America's eyes and senses this year.

I said: Look, there will be gobs of new material in this book. Even the old material isn't too doggy, I said. This book will tell all about such diverse folks as Lyndon B. Johnson, Sugar Ray Robinson, Louis Armstrong, and William F. Buckley, Jr. It will reveal what life is like at a Bible Belt school where every dorm elects its own prayer captain, and of the time I almost whiskey-drank with the late Senator Joseph McCarthy, the famous witch-hunter. There will be in this book valuable information about the House Un-American Activities Committee, football, Texas, making the scene at Norman Mailer's, and what grand bastards one may encounter in the writing game. My publisher said he didn't care if it revealed that Martin Bormann is an Israeli jet pilot, that if word got out it was a nonfiction collection then I am done the same as burnt offerings.

Success and I are strangers. Failure and I are such old friends he drops by the house for coffee. I have wearied of his company and bid the stranger come in. So it's really neither my fault nor my publisher's

* And in strange or inventive ways. After this book was promoted for one year under the title "My Hero LBJ and Other Dirty Stories," guess who decided not to run for President again this year?

that a few low-born types who peep windows, stay up late, and talk filth may consider my use of the word "dirty" in this work's title to be an outright act of deceit, trickery, and untruth-in-packaging. I would remind those base creatures that you can't judge a book by its cover.

This sad fact emerges from the swindle: a few loosely used cuss words aside, you may never know an opportunity to read a cleaner book than this one, Mother. Just try to remember that most of this is much more serious than it looks.

... AND OTHER
DIRTY STORIES

CHAPTER 1

Confessions of
an Obscure Famous Arthur

I suppose that to some, "writing" is just another occupation like hustling insurance, pumping gas or helping to build hydrogen bombs. For me there was always a special magic in the craft: something like the glamor that goes with being a jousting knight or a circus clown, transcending time clocks or the award of a thinly plated gold watch after thirty years' tedious loyalty at the Glue Works. Though I hatched the usual number of boyhood fantasies (saving Shirley Temple from a wicked witch, quarterbacking SMU to the Rose Bowl), my special dream was to be A Writer: one of God's Chosen, pursued by panting editors wanting to give me money and by buxom beauties who perhaps wanted to give me something, too.

The itch to write seems, in retrospect, to have been an ancient urge beating in the blood: some ancestral calling, perhaps, from the tomb of David who wrote his singing Psalms, or at the very least an echoed command from some lost band of kinsmen in the Shakespeare family. One might say that such notions are fanciful, though it would better serve accuracy to label them pure bushwa. For I descended not from Davids or Shakespeares but from a poor band of village blacksmiths, dirt farmers, cattle traders, country storekeeps and brush arbor preachers. No men fought the land harder, or weighed your goods on more honest scales, or with more passion tried to snatch you from the certain fires of Hell. Neither, however, did they waste motion through picking up books or quills.

In all my traceable family lineage, from Texas back through Indian Territory to a half-dozen deep Dixie states where the trail grows so suddenly cold that genealogy becomes no more than a wildly speculative game to bolster family reunions sagging on the second day, no one ever put pen to paper unless it was for the practical purpose of making a grocery list or for the necessary one of signing next year's crops over to mortgage. No scholars, poets or philosophers clutter the branches of my family tree with a lot of fiddlety-diddlety grand notions or fuzzy theories. The only even marginal scholar in my line (a great-uncle who from the age of twenty affected a walking cane, waist-length whiskers and delicate health) quit his schoolteaching gig in favor of lounging in the shade of an old Texas farmhouse, moving only with the sun, where he gave his days to chewing tobacco and pounding his walking cane vigorously against the packed clay at his feet unless his meals got served on time. This sole ancestor, who might have been cogitating his way toward new visions, sciences or forms of Art, died unrecognized and unmarried, and in a way that even our poets cannot make ennobling to the human experience. Uncle Rube simply choked to death stuffing himself from a gift basket of grapes.

Uncle Rube was called to the Great Vineyard Up Yonder long before my time. Much of what I learned of him was contraband information hijacked as it passed from adult to adult in scandalized whispers: how he chewed vile plugs, cursed lavishly, manufactured his own wet goods, bought on credit if credit could be had, and was sometimes suspected of quoting poetry. Even so, I secretly fixed on him in my childhood as the family member to emulate. For Uncle Rube toiled not in the fields, nor kept this world's dusty shops or grubby ledgers. He entered no pew on the Seventh Day, there to plead with Heaven for special favor or to offer hypocritical thanks when the cow went dry or an infant died a-borning. He neither cut his hair nor took excessive baths. He was, altogether, quite a heroic figure and I feel cheated of his instruction. You must remember that somebody thought well enough of him to give him grapes.

The family library at our old homestead held but two books: the Bible and a battered reference work called *The Volume Library*. I almost wore the latter out thumbing through it, poring over the pictures while wondering what mystic secrets might be contained in all those strange letters strung together to form words. Did the words tell all? What dying was like, or how much money the rich folks had and how high was the moon? My mother recalls that before I was out of diapers I would bring that book to her, dragging it across the floor by its hard cover, signaling by grunt and gesture that it should be read.

One illustration particularly sticks in my mind. A line drawing

depicted one of the Kaiser's meaner Huns impaling a Belgian infant
on a bayonet while the helpless mother swooned and hysterically
pounded herself on or about the mammary glands. The text told even
more terrible tales on the Kaiser. I honestly believe that my one con-
scious ethnic prejudice today—an unfortunate suspicion of Germans
ranging from Marlene Dietrich down to a beer-garden keeper I know
named Scholtz—stems more from that old book than from revelations
of the mass mischief to follow at Auschwitz and Dachau.

The Bible was read to me, though not often at my urging. I found
it a horrid collection of inhuman tales—yarns that prompted feverish
dreams of Daniel at the mercy of the ripping lions, of an angry God
who on losing His unholy temper would turn fun-loving wives into
pillars of salt, send floods and famines, or even permit His only son
to be strung up on the cross. Very early did I conclude that such a
petty, short-fused God (who had created rattlesnakes, the multiplica-
tion tables and castor oil as well) was not the kind of fellow I wished
to spend the weekend with, much less Eternity.

We had little money to squander on books, magazines or newspapers. I was born on the first day of the year of the Great Depression—1929. Our worn-out farm, never having known crop rotation,
irrigation or the sweet purr of a tractor, produced precious little in
the way of profit whether feast or famine visited the cities. No matter
how hard my father drove himself or his lone team of horses there
was always something to frustrate his hopes: a broken plow point,
crop-killing late frosts, droughts, flash floods, a strange malady of
blackleg to snuff out the cattle, or epidemics of what my father called
"limberneck disease" that caused chickens to drop dead on their
roosts. The most money clear that I remember my father having at
any one time in those early years was $88 after he'd sold an unusually
good crop of turkeys. He was on the fringe of solvency for exactly
two hours before some city slicker from Cisco picked his pocket of
every last dime. It was a scramble each year just to raise enough
money for seed crops or school clothes.

For one short span we somehow subscribed to the magazines *Progressive Farmer* and *Farm & Ranch*. Once we accepted for thirty days
a "free introductory gift subscription" to the Fort Worth *Press*. For a
month I was lost in the adventures of Barney Google, the sports
pages where heroes sprouted with each new paragraph, and a serial-
ized saga, entitled "Fifteen Dollars a Week," starring that ward of
Heaven, the poor working girl. Otherwise, except for week-old news-

papers handed down by neighbors, or an infrequent pulp Western from the same source, we simply knew nothing of the printed word.

In those formative years Dad sometimes wanted to hold me out of school to pick cotton, fence-mend, pitch hay or perform other of the endless tortures afflicted by agrarian life. I hated such enforced absences—not because I loved school so much, but because I despised labor more. The few quarrels that I recall my parents having always seemed to hinge on whether I would be plucked from the schoolroom and replanted in the fields. "That boy"—my mother predicted—"won't amount to a hill of beans without an education. I aim to see that he gets one."

My father took a rather cavalier attitude toward school. He had dropped out of necessity at age twelve—after his own father had been shot to death in one of the backwoods disputes not uncommon to the region—to scratch out a living for his widowed mother and her brood of nine. Older than his siblings, he grew up never knowing the joys inherent in one-act plays, football, school-ground romances or the learning processes themselves. Faced with a life sentence of poverty and with no hope for parole, I see now where he might have thought me more useful in the canefields than the classroom. At the time, however, I was not so considerate a son. It dawned on me early that the best way to avoid hard labor was to strike for high marks in school. For this not altogether altruistic reason I stayed near the top of my class.

In the summer sandwiched between my first and second years of school, I came into the prideful ownership of my first book as a reward for having survived whooping cough. *The Adventures of Tom Sawyer* was read to me perhaps a dozen times; I fought my own way through it more times still. The following Christmas I got *The Prince and the Pauper*. These books inspired my first literary efforts. Printing in huge block letters on a five-cent Big Chief lined tablet, I began works-in-progress entitled *The Adventures of Hap Hazard* and *The Rich Man's Kid and the Poor Boy*. Mark Twain can be imitated just so far, however; like most beginning novelists I finished neither work. I did finish a poem required by my third-grade teacher. "The Indian Squaw" won first prize for Grammar School Original Compositions at Putnam, Texas—but somehow begat malicious rumors of plagiarism.

These dark rumors were not stilled even when the weekly Putnam *News* printed the prize-winning doggerel with my own wonderful by-line over it. Eventually, my teacher felt constrained to inquire—in front of the whole class—whether I had perhaps "had help" in writing my little masterpiece, or, maybe, if I had read a poem "something like it" in a book or magazine. My choking tears of frustration were immediately interpreted by classmates as an admission of guilt equal to a confession signed in blood. Having already fought every boy in the class for the folly of being a poet, I now had to re-fight them for the crime of literary theft.

Ultimately, my father learned of the accusations. He sternly demanded to know whether I had cheated. I had by this time worked up such righteous indignation that even Heaven could not have questioned me with impunity, and I came damn close to saying so. My father called for a copy of the poem. For long moments he studied it in the small circle of light from the kerosene lamp at his elbow, his lips moving soundlessly over the words. At length he said, "Yeah, I reckon you wrote it. Can't think of anybody *else* that would."

One might think that such an experience would kill whatever remained of the literary instinct. And for a long time it did. Periodically, however, I came back to the pen: haltingly, fleetingly, to no immediate purpose. Still, when adults amused themselves with their eternal game of whatcha-gonna-be-when-you-grow-up?, I seldom failed to answer "a writer." Sometimes I rather haughtily pronounced that Destiny had it in mind for me to be "a rich Famous Arthur."

Wouldn't you know that I wrote the freshman play? It was all about a talented, sensitive boy whose own freshman play had been greeted by boatloads of scorn by his contemporaries—until it suddenly sold to the movies, Broadway and (somehow) to the Federal Government for sums slightly in excess of six million dollars. After this low farce was received with more high glee than I thought seemly, I waited for weeks at the mailbox for vindication from Hollywood, Broadway or Washington.

Vindication was so long coming that it hasn't come yet. But if I have not become "a rich Famous Arthur" pursued by well-endowed publishers and impatient ladies-in-waiting, I have, at least, become a writer of sorts. True, writing has yet to bring me the whole goodie bag I envisioned in more innocent times. I drive an old car that suffers from mechanical bronchitis, scuffle every 120 days to meet my $600 quarterly income tax payments, and buy the less exotic cuts of meat. My wife and I live in a well-appointed but tiny apartment which we get a little cheaper than the standard rate because we let them keep the brooms in here. Some weeks there is barely enough money to pay for her gin and my dirty books. Yet, even when the rent's doubtful I would not change places with the Rockefellers if it meant leaving my craft and the foolish wife who still believes that one day she will be the lady of a rich Famous Arthur without having to run off with Truman Capote. We are consoled by the knowledge that Ian Fleming made only $613 off his first James Bond book and we are sustained by encouraging words from high places: only last week my editor wrote, "One of these days, fella, you are certainly going to get yours." Until we "get ours" we are content to traipse around the country in pursuit of the Muse, not really minding the carry-out cheeseburgers or the motel rooms with old-fashioned black-and-white TV.

It was not all smooth sailing for Columbus; neither is it on the literary high seas. Though I would have rejected the notion in the generous ignorance of my youth, writers have toothaches and head colds and days when they drop things on their toes the same as mere mortals. Nobody excuses us from fits of melancholy, tax audits, census snoopers, or front-stoop sermons by Jehovah's Witnesses at dawn. We know the same serpents that slither around in your Eden—plus such exotic snakes as editors who wouldn't recognize a sure-fire best seller if they caught one sneaking over the transom, agents who always remember to rake their 10 percent off the top even if they can't remember your first name, literary critics who don't love their sweet mothers and never had fathers to love.

Writers know a variety of special terrors. Though I am such a neophyte in the game that when my agent once told me he was sending my manuscript over to "the Little, Brown people" I thought he meant the Filipinos, I have been baptized in fire. I had a lone magazine credit when an uppity lady whom I knew only because she once insulted me at a cocktail party years before I had published, sent around a shoebox full of poems, composed without rhyme or reason by her funny maiden aunt, with curt instructions to have them published in the upcoming issue of *Saturday Review*. One barnstorming wing walker, nine dime-store Congressmen, two osteopaths, a blind watchmaker now retired, a fellow who played the Bad Breath Man in mouthwash commercials, and an old lady whose hobby is collecting funeral wreaths are among those proposing deals where I would write their life stories and we would split the profits. I have been the red-faced guest of honor at autograph parties where the only person who showed up was a fellow hired to tinker with the cigarette machine.

Each time a writer publishes a new book total strangers walk in off the streets to demand their free, autographed copy; nobody believes that you get only ten freebies and have 137 living relatives not counting second cousins. I don't know why writers are supposed to give their talents away any more than a doctor is supposed to pass around free Christmas appendectomies, but Society somehow expects it. (One writer friend swears that in just such circumstances he was once called a stingy son-of-a-bitch by a lame nun.) When advance orders indicate you may break 100 in golf before you do in book sales, your best friends presume to console you by saying they'll "wait and get it in paperback." Ancient debts you had long assumed wiped out by the statute of limitations are resurrected in the courts the day after your first book ad appears in *The New York Times.* Some fig-eater in Hollywood is going to buy the screen rights for Lancaster and then Newman and finally Ginny Simms. The can't-miss deals fall through only after extracting the last ounce of hope from your liver.

Meanwhile, that pride which goeth before a mighty fall forces you to encourage publicly the fiction of your new wealth even though your banker knows that if you've got a quarter you shortchanged a hawker of Girl Scout brownies. Hardly has your mother apologized to her friends for what you wrote until your prideful work lands on the remainder table at fifty-nine cents. I think I shall never learn to enjoy seeing my books in heavy repose on what is called "the bargain counter" alongside such titles as *How to Eat Chili with Chopsticks* or *The History of Pot-Bellied Stoves in South Dakota.*

Then there are days when the words just won't come.

Often when I sit at my typewriter staring googley-eyed at the whitest piece of paper in the world, I think in tandem of an unlikely pair: the late Adlai Stevenson and my late Uncle Rube. Only a few hours before his death Stevenson spoke what my Uncle Rube might have said, given less gluttonous instincts and more articulation: "I want to sit on the sidelines for a while, with a glass of wine in my hand, and watch the people dance."

The writer is a sideline-sitter and dance-watcher, too. Only he goes on to tell everything he has seen or heard at the ball: how the dancers were dressed, the joyful noise their feet made shuffling or scraping or stomping across the floor, the merry tunes that were played. And if he is worth the carbon that cakes his keys, he will tell not only of the exhilaration of the dancers as they whooped and circled to and fro, but of the secret fears and vain hopes of the bucktoothed wallflower as she hid in the shadows, alone, while the music came to her bringing both a faint touch of happiness and a sharp stab of pain. . . .

CHAPTER 2

Requiem for a West Texas Town

I don't know how 1936 was for wine, but it was my best vintage year.

Maybe you remember 1936 because Spain's Civil War erupted, or because Alf Landon proved—at least until Goldwater came along—that there was no way a Republican could botch up Maine and Vermont. Maybe you remember it only because it's the year wedged right in there between '35 and '37, but it was the year in which Social Security started and Edward VIII quit. The Texas State Centennial in Dallas opened that year and furnished pulpit fodder for many a naysaying parson by presenting the daring fan dances of Miss Sally Rand. The only one of those events I remember is the opening of the Texas State Centennial—and then only because my Cousin Kenneth, who got to go, taunted me with the reminder that I'd have to wait "a hunnert years" for the next one. I remember 1936 so favorably because that's the year we moved to Town. The world throbbed and was freshly green.

We had moved away from Putnam, Texas, my birthplace, when I was too young even to remember its milk and honey. We left in mid-1930, in a burdened-down T-model Ford. I was still in diapers. For the next two years we followed the cotton harvest on the sandy high plains of West Texas. I think Steinbeck had the Kings in mind when he wrote *The Grapes of Wrath*. We were all-too-typical of the nomadic, washed-out domestic D.P.'s who vainly sought that elusive prosperity Herbert Hoover told us was just around the corner. Perhaps we took the wrong turns.

My initial memories of life go back to the small village of Meadow, Texas—a wide spot in the road in cheerless waste country that must be related by blood to the dark side of the moon. No doubt Freud would have a certain number of pointed comments to make about the three incidents that are so clearly etched in my mind as infantile recollections. In the first, I am sitting on a small potty in front of the propertied man's converted garage where we live, my parents and one sister jolting off in a wagon to pick cotton while Libby, the sister in whose charge I remain, urges me to do my business like a big boy. My second memory is of the day when the propertied gent's small daughter, a dutch-bob hairdo hussy with a runny nose, conned me into drinking a cup of sand, which, with cunning native to Eve, she had convinced me was water. Quite naturally, I choked. The third recollection is of that fearful, noisy day when the world ended both with a bang and a whimper: Dad had to shoot my rabid collie dog. I could not have been more than three years old when those visions passed.

We next moved to a farm—my father's "Old Home Place" in Eastland County. He had first come there with his parents as a small boy in the early 1890's, crossing Indian Territory from Arkansas in a covered wagon. Though it was the taproot land of my people, I hated that farm. It was graveyard lonely and as barren as those Depression times. The old house had long stood vacant. Somebody had once stored potatoes under it, burying them for protection against frost and freeze. For months the place reeked of the rotten, acrid odor of those potatoes gone bad. The foul cache was a haven for rats. I remember hearing them rustling around under the house at night, and how I slept with one small arm crooked into a protective inverted V, then thrown across my face in case the rats grew tired of stale potatoes and came in the dark to make their supper off my eyes.

The drafty house required back-breaking work to become even marginally livable. After each day's toil in the fields, the woods or the cow lots my parents worked well into the night at their task of reconstruction. Dad cut and planed new boards to go in the floor. Where the old wood was judged good enough to keep he rigged up an apparatus of wires and woodblocks designed to draw the gaping floorboards back together and thus shut out, if not the howling wind, at least the rats. Mother papered over the bare plank walls in an effort both to beautify and winterize them.

Except for the wood-burning kitchen stove, our only heat came from an open fireplace in the living room. Our bedrooms were achingly cold. We slept under a heavy burden of quilts and blankets that made movement next to impossible. Mother heated cumbersome hand-irons each bitter night, wrapping them in layers of cloth before inserting them in our beds to give our feet warmth. If the cloth slipped and your foot touched the bare iron too soon you'd have a blister to show for it. Conversely, by the wee hours of morning a foot touched to the chilled iron was like making contact with a block of ice.

It seemed always to drizzle rain or sleet. My father would come shivering from the cow lot after his pre-dawn milking chores, blowing on his numb hands, stomping his feet to restore circulation, and hurrying to throw more wood on the fire. The wood had to be cut and horse-drawn from distant pastures, just as our water had to be hauled by the barrel or painfully toted bucket by bucket from an old man-made earthen tank. Since livestock had free run of the tank, our water had to be boiled before use. (Even so, we were subjected to typhoid fever shots each summer in the name of health safety. My sister Estelle lived in mortal fear of needles. This gave rise to my one sport: tantalizing the poor girl for several days before each scheduled in-oculation, saying how her arm would bleed, describing the way a needle felt biting the bone, telling of the thousands who died from typhoid shots and were slipped silently into unmarked graves each year. By the time the country doctor came—my Uncle Floyd, by the way—she was understandably hysterical. She had to be chased down the same way we'd chase down a horse to saddle for the eight-mile ride to Cisco.) Often, in the winter, water would freeze in the gal-vanized buckets we kept in the kitchen and required thawing before you could wash the sleep out of your eyes.

If this sounds suspiciously like a Poor Boy Story—well, then, I guess it is. I never noticed many loose diamonds kicking around the place. I don't claim to have walked barefoot in the snow nine miles to school each day and that it was uphill both ways; I realize I didn't have it as tough as my father, left to fend for a large family at age twelve, or my brother Weldon, who during the Depression left school to work as a cafe "pearl diver" (dishwasher), short-order cook, stump grubber, WPA laborer, CCC worker, cotton chopper, or what-ever he could dredge up in the way of a paying job. Even so, it wasn't exactly the Riviera from my own point of view.

More than the poverty and the endless farm demands, however, I recall those eternal days of rain and cold with nothing to do but huddle by the open fireplace where your front roasted while your rump grew icicles—or vice-versa, should you turn around. The awful, grinding boredom was the primary agony: nothing to read, no radio, nobody to talk with. The isolation was close to maddening.

But how one digresses! For here I would speak not of the joyless solitude of that wretched farm but of the magnificent time when we abandoned it in my seventh year to return to the marvelous city of my birth.

We moved to Town because of mother's determination that I would have the best education it was within her limits to give. Until the year I was scheduled to begin school there had been a one-room schoolhouse at the crossroads settlement of Dan Horn, just a hoot-and-holler from our farm. That year, however, the school was by public referendum "consolidated" with one at Scranton some several miles distant. Scranton, having more voters than Dan Horn, was naturally chosen as the new site of the combined schools. The losers were predictably sore. Dan Horn's blooded gentry made brags that when the Scranton school bus came by, it would be greeted with guns: nobody was taking *their* school, by Ned, or hauling their kids half-way across the county to teach 'em that man had sprung from apes or to make 'em sing in some glee club so sissy the boys wore bow ties.

Sure enough, the Dan Horn gents formed what they called a posse (and what Scranton called a mob) and they emptied the school bus at gun-point the first day around. They also scrambled the bus driver's features for him and sent him back to Scranton as a half-living testimonial to their temper. New blood feuds, criminal charges, civil lawsuits and threats of sudden death were among the several varieties of hell there was to pay. Mother decided that no son of hers could be properly educated in that atmosphere of wild passions. Nothing would do but that we move to civilization. To us, that meant Putnam.

Putnam was one county and some twelve or fourteen miles away. It seemed, however, as distant as the Big Dipper—and as unattainable. It had stores with fragrances that even the finest perfumes have been unable to duplicate; sidewalks, electric lights, running water, indoor plumbing—and, wonder of wonders—*people!*

Dad hired a man with a cattle truck to move our few household goods. I shall never forget the joy with which I quit the Old Home Place, nor my great expectations. When at last we saw the Putnam water tower I burst into tears. Aunt Ethel, who had come from Putnam to fetch the family, knew my history of car sickness. The triumphant entry into Mecca was maddeningly delayed while every-body circled up and encouraged me to upchuck so that I'd feel better. How to tell them I was sick only with joy?

For a boy who had walked a quarter mile to an old dirt road each morning the weather permitted just to receive the rural route mail carrier's "Hi, son," there was so much action in Putnam it seemed a crime to sleep. After school there were vacant-lot football games, rubber gun fights, friends to join in assaulting the dizzy heights of Harper's Hill. I was permitted to join the Secret Wolfs, an order of the brotherhood as ritually clannish as anything ever thought up by Tom Sawyer, The Sons of Italy, or the Woodmen of the World. We met in the storm cellar in my cousin Kenneth Gaskins' backyard, burn-ing pilfered candles, chanting mumbo-jumbo, declaring war first on our schoolteachers and then Japan, while swearing never never *never* to like girls.

Sometimes we prowled the cemetery, Kenneth and I, pausing at the grave of our Grandpaw Clark to see if we might commune with his spirit. I was originally dubious that contact could be had with the Other World, but Kenneth (who had lived in Town all his life and therefore knew about such matters) assured me that he'd seen it done in at least a jillion picture shows. So we talked to Grandpaw Clark, asking his bones whether the streets of Heaven were really paved with gold, and was George Washington up there with him, and how long had it taken him to learn to play the harp, and did he know Jesus well enough to call him by his first name or did he have to address him as Mr. Christ? Sometimes we begged for a Sign that we had been heard. Alas, we lacked Hollywood's technique or sources. Unless you count the time when Kenneth swore he saw the leaves move on a nearby tree in a special way on a day—he pointed out—when not a breath of air stirred, Grandpaw Clark sent his earthbound descendants no Sign from among the stars. Still, the cemetery was a joy. Often I spelled out the names on the headstones, noting when their subjects had lived and died, and tried to speculate what life must have been like for them. Other times I merely enjoyed the philosophical, if ungram-matical, messages ("There are no parting in Heaven") or the tributes ("A Precious Mother and Loving Wife") or the carved angels, cherubs and crosses so pleasing to the eye.

Life among the living was fun, too. I shall never forget the pleasure of eavesdropping on Grown-ups at the post office—a form of recrea-tion discovered as a bonus after Kenneth and I had gone there to read the faces of the latest bank robbers and murderers sent down by the FBI for Putnam posting. (This was Kenneth's idea. He lived in the certainty that he was always just one captured bank robber or grisly killer away from a $5,000 reward. One whole summer he insisted that a certain moon-faced flour drummer who called on his father's grocery store was Pretty Boy Floyd. He was incensed when Uncle George wouldn't go along with his scheme to rap the drummer on the head with a Coke bottle, tie him up with packing cord, and call for the G-men.) I was often forced to hang around the post office alone because Kenneth held grown-up chitchat to be duller than Sunday school. "All they ever talk about," he scoffed, "is who's dying or who's gonna get a baby or who backslid on the church." I recall asking what else was there?

We lived in what the family still refers to as Our Yellow House, though it was long ago sold and removed to parts unknown. When I was but a few months old an uncle, Bob McLemore, a carpenter by trade, came to visit. Jobs were scarce; Uncle Bob stayed a year. He was not, however, in the useless tradition of the man who came to dinner. Uncle Bob built one of the finest homes in all Putnam for us. He used the best lumber from our old house along with new materials my father had accepted in lieu of cash for blacksmith services rendered. Our Yellow House was a palace by all available standards, having as it did concrete steps in front, a set of gleaming French doors, a sink, gas heat, polished hard floors and that beautiful coating of bright yellow paint. Waking in Our Yellow House, I would stretch my young legs and exult in the luxury of it all: the rotten potatoes and nocturnal rats had been beaten at last.

Just as Cinderella knew her midnight, however, I was all too soon reconverted from city dude to country bumpkin. After little more than a year in Town my father wearied of scratching for cash at part-time blacksmithing or odd jobs, and of walking four miles each day to a little plot of land he lucklessly tried to sharecrop on the side. We left the natural wonders and routine miracles of Putnam for a farm two miles outside what I grandly thought of as "the city limits" —i.e., the point where Dock Smith had established his goat barns and rabbit hutches. This remained a vast improvement over the isolated Old Home Place, however. For three more years I was to enjoy at least the fringe benefits of Town.

Eventually, we retreated back to the Old Home Place. From there, not long after World War II broke out, we moved to New Mexico where my father worked for an oil company at the princely sum of a dollar an hour. I have since lived, among other places, in New York City and Washington, but nothing has been as grand as Putnam was in that wonderful year 1936—and I know that nothing ever will be again.

Some three years ago, flying in the face of Thomas Wolfe's best advice, I went home again. My journey was a sad one. My purpose was to write the . . .

REQUIEM FOR A WEST TEXAS TOWN

It was a very special place, and those of us lucky enough to live there felt somehow set apart. Many signs ratified our suspicions.

Didn't visiting politicians confess that reaching our town was the high point of their peregrinations? Of all the towns on the Texas & Pacific railroad, wasn't ours the only one through which the westbound Sunshine Special clattered through at exactly 4:14 P.M.? The Stamps Quartet, Clyde Beatty's Circus, Toby's Medicine Show—none dared pass us by. We had the word of our preachers that the Devil himself placed the highest premium on earthbound souls whose mail came addressed to Putnam, Texas.

Life had its absolutes: the World Domino Championship was settled behind Loren Everett's icehouse each Saturday afternoon. An aged citizen of ours had perfected the telegraph only twenty-four hours behind Thomas Edison. On evidence collected from all quarters of the town, no rational resident could doubt that in the tomb of the Unknown Soldier there slept in honored glory a Putnam boy.

If Notre Dame had its Four Horsemen, the Putnam Panthers had Jiggs Shackelford, Turkey Triplett, Tuffy Armstrong, and Hooter Allen. Where Bernard Baruch advised Presidents from Washington park benches, Ole Man Bob Head, perched on the ledge of sidewalk-level windows in the Farmer's State Bank, warned of hogs expiring of cholera and of our delivery to the Soviets in gunnysacks before FDR had completed the mischief of his first term. Even in our recreations we proved superior. Summer visitors were almost always treated to a "snipe hunt"; many an outlander, given the honor of holding the sack while other hunters fanned out to flush the "snipe" and drive it to him, figured out the game in strange pastures at dawn. More than one boy, taken by a carload of Putnam contemporaries to pick up his blind date—a bucolic beauty named Betsy, whose loose charms had been carefully advertised in advance—bolted for the woods in panic when Betsy's angry "father" fired a stream of oaths and a double-barreled shotgun into the night air.

Putnam was on Highway 80. Cisco was a dozen miles to the east, Dallas 159 miles in the same direction; New York was rumored just a little beyond that. To the west, Highway 80 curved around Utility Hill before winding eleven miles through wooded rangeland offering protection from our natural enemies in Baird, running thence to a mysterious land called California where Tom Mix, Tarzan, and my Aunt Dewey lived. Nothing much was to the immediate south or north of Putnam, though Mississippi presumably occupied acreage somewhere over Harper's Hill, and if you struck out toward the water tower you'd eventually stumble onto the North Pole.

It was here I had discovered the magic little Ulysses Macauley knew in Saroyan's *The Human Comedy*, when upon finding a hen egg he presented it to his mother, "by which he meant what no man can guess and no child can remember to tell." Here I had known the pains and pamperings attendant to that universal distemper, whooping cough; shivered at my first funeral; and roamed rocky foothills in search of Indian arrowheads and in honest fear of God.

I was born in Putnam on New Year's Day, 1929. The oil boom had peaked out a few months earlier, yet the familiar sound of hammer-on-anvil could still be heard in my father's blacksmith shop. Roadwise drummers in straw boaters and polka-dot bow ties still brought their sample cases into our two hotels to stay the night. The cotton gin ran in season a dozen hours a day, during which a good gin hand could make three dollars. On Saturday nights, when the feed-store turned into a magic palace by the mere hanging of a bed sheet, addicts of the silent flicks came with their dimes. Though Ole Doc Britton had owned the town's only automobile in 1910, dozens of Tin Lizzies were backfiring in the streets by the time of my bones. For some five thousand salts-of-the-earth Putnam would still be standing when Rome had only a general store and an old stadium.

That was almost forty years ago as the life flies. Now the faded sign pointing vaguely north of Interstate Twenty proclaims: *Putnam. Pop. 203.* But even this is a gentle fiction. "You might dredge up that many," old-timer Ellison Pruett says, "by countin' chickens, dawgs, and Republicans." Probably no more than a hundred survivors could be mustered for all-day singing with free dinner on the grounds.

The new slab that is Interstate Twenty, down which traffic thunders at terrible speeds, rises thirty feet above what once was the familiar town square with its pick-up baseball games, mineral-water wells, and ancient hitching posts. I had always assumed a stone monument would one day be raised there to commemorate my triumph as All-Pro Quarterback, America's Most Decorated Marine, Famous Arthur, and Richest Man in the World. But the square is gone, along with those vain dreams, and so for that matter is most of Putnam. The skeleton that is the business district—a dozen sad, sagging buildings, half of them wearing padlocks—faces bare dirt walls serving to underpin the overpass forty yards away.

Putnam had been sick for more than twenty years, but it took Congress to kill it. The Federal Highway Act did it in. Supposedly the Interstate System prevents congestion in our towns and cities, speeds commerce, and strengthens national defense. Perhaps more money will be made faster, and bigger bombs hauled over better roads, with Putnam out of the way. But I have wind of darker plots involving jealousy in high places, and possibly Castro's land reforms.

Whatever the motive, some invisible bureaucrat with an operable slide rule (but with no operable heart) decided an imposing overpass, or viaduct, would look good at a given point on proposed Interstate Twenty. He laughed madly, no doubt, as he made his fatal mark on the map. Four-fifths of my birthplace rested under the mark he made.

One day two years ago the growling machines came. An iron ball swung its fist, and bulldozers with metal jaws took bites from the earth. The barbershop, that exciting Istanbul of spicy tonics, racy stories, and old shaving mugs—where my Uncle Claude cheerfully and for two bits skinned young heads before drenching them in Red Rose Hair Oil—fell under the assault. So did the offices of the weekly Putnam *News,* where my first literary work appeared—a bit of doggerel called "The Indian Squaw." The wonder that had been, in turn, the Hotel Carter-Holland, the Mission Hotel, and finally the Hotel Guyton was reduced to rubble along with its splendid sunken rose garden. DeShazio's Variety Store, famed for its square deals on pocket knives, Halloween masks, and sacks of shiny marbles, came down. Pierce Shackelford's Farm Implements, the corner "filling station" where you could pump up your bicycle tires with free air or flag the Greyhound, my father's blacksmith shop, the telephone exchange where my Aunt Flora was the friendly Central who answered when you cranked out one long ring—all are no more. When the bulldozers were gone so was the town square, and everything to the east, west, and south of it. All for an overpass.

Alton White, suspecting his hometown held little future for grocers, moved twenty-two miles down the highway to Eastland. When progress wiped out Charlie Davis' service station, he moved to Cross Plains. Mrs. Bess Herring went 225 miles west to live with her widowed sister. The Sandlin Brothers sold their farm and used the money to buy another two counties away. You can't boss a ranch or tend cattle by long distance, so it became R. D. Williams' lot to suffer the greatest indignity. He moved to Baird.

The government man sent to pacify the survivors told them the town was lucky to have held losses to a minimum. This is roughly comparable to congratulating Whitey Ford should he lose only three fingers on his pitching hand. Local citizens were gratified when they learned the government man wasn't one of our leading diplomats, Averell Harriman, perhaps, or Henry Cabot Lodge, but a representative from the Bureau of Public Roads.

I. G. Mobley thinks Putnam is coming back. Richard Nixon may come back, Khrushchev conceivably could, and some say Jesus Christ surely will. But Judge Crater is not coming back, nor Benito Mussolini, and neither is Putnam.

Sitting in I. G. Mobley's air-conditioned living room on a modern farm near Putnam a few months ago, I could not tell him that. His roots go deep in home. He pays his debts, lives by his labor, and keeps his barn painted. He has served his neighbors as county commissioner and member of the school board.

Mobley sat on the edge of a rocking chair, tensely unfolding his slender hands and long legs. "I tell 'em," he said, "that it's up to the people of Putnam whether we have a town here or not. We're the only town *on* Interstate Twenty from Fort Worth to Cahoma and—why, that must be over three hundred miles! Other little towns are *off* the highway by a right smart. Folks are gonna need gasoline, food, rest rooms. Maybe they'll want to mail a letter." I thought of how, earlier in the day, I had clocked traffic speeding along Interstate Twenty at an average of 72 miles per hour, and of the small sign warning of Putnam's decaying carcass down there beneath the slab.

I. G. Mobley took no note of these facts. Miracles were like buses: if you missed one, you simply caught the next. "The gloom merchants have prayed over Putnam's remains before," he said. "When I was a small kid things were slow as winter molasses. Then the mineral-water boom hit."

That was in 1908. People swarmed in to bathe their tortures— lumbago, gout, arthritis, rheumatism. The Carter-Holland Hotel was built: a mission-style palace of forty-six rooms, and a polished ballroom for dancing if you weren't bedeviled by lumbago or Fundamentalist parsons. For three dollars a day you could bathe in Putnam's miracle waters, have meals in your room, and take treatment from the well-known "rubbing doctor," Doc Milling. By 1912 completion of three red-brick buildings of two stories each—a bank, Yancy Orr's drugstore, the new school with its imposing bell tower—gave the town a slight case of skyline fever. An Opera House was opened over the protests of the preachers, and traveling shows took away dollars Heaven had earlier designated for the collection plates. When, almost without warning and for no obvious reason, the mineral-water craze ended in 1916, nobody had to ask why. The preachers told them.

For a year or two Putnam was in the doldrums, though crops were generally fair. Then came the drought of 1917–18. Creeks, tanks, and cisterns dried up. Water was hauled twelve miles from Cisco by wagons and teams. But May of 1919 brought a new miracle. "It rained frogs and fishes," I. G. Mobley recalls. Wheat made fifty bushels to the acre that year and each bushel sold for $2.75. The following season Putnam's two gins handled 5,000 bales of cotton. On top of the agricultural prosperity came the oil boom of 1922. Wildcatters fogged in to drill shallow wells, and the rocky foothills around Putnam seemed loaded. Once again the hotels were filled. Tom Davis operated a flourishing wagon yard; in my father's blacksmith shop fires were seldom banked. Yancy Orr got competition from the new Black's Drugs, and the Putnam Supply Company was founded.

I. G. Mobley had put himself through Draughton's Business College in Abilene through clerking part-time in one of the hotels, before a few producing wells blessed his acres. "Everybody was drilling for oil and swinging big deals," he recalls. "We had more paper millionaires than Carter had little liver pills."

The boom had almost everything associated with booms—inflated prices, muddy streets, the tents and shacks of nomadic "boom hands." Everything, in fact, but open saloons. Saloons weren't really needed; drugstore counters did a booming business in a patent medicine of high alcoholic content said to cure nagging coughs, chest colds, and other convenient ailments. Old heads recall that one of the parsons who fought so fiercely against the Opera House developed the most persistent cough in town.

In 1928, with no more warning than might be given by the rattlesnakes on Harper's Hill, the boom went bust, and the Depression followed. Oil dropped to thirty cents a barrel, a lease pumper was grateful to keep his job at $30 per month, and fly-by-night oil operators left town by the dozens even if their unpaid bills didn't. My father could only sigh and write off the $10,000 due him for blacksmith services rendered. Putnam Supply Company and Black's Drugs folded, and the movie house cut its schedule to Saturday Nights Only. Men who had swarmed to town for good-salaried jobs, or to wheel-and-deal in oil speculation, went back to farms long lying fallow where they could at least grow food for their families. Some left for good, riding the rails in search of jobs or dreams, or joining the westward migration of jitneys laden with household goods in the manner of Steinbeck's Joad family.

Putnam had one more opportunity to snap back. About 1932, as New Deal pump-priming measures brought faint signs but great hopes of relieving the misery, a stranger came to town from "across the waters"—though no one seems to have pinpointed his sources better than that. The foreigner charmed Putnam's ladies with deep bows, pretty speeches, and hand-kisses. Somehow he also charmed the town's businessmen. Within a few months he promoted money from hard-pressed Main Street merchants to finance what he envisioned as "the largest automobile dealership in Texas." The daughter of a prominent citizen consented to be the go-getter's wife. She sold her diamond rings and persuaded her father to add $5,000 to her fiancé's venture. After hot excitement and speeches at the depot, the promoter left by train to arrange for the first shipment of cars. He was slightly delayed to the extent that he has not been heard from again. Even I. G. Mobley gave up hopes of his coming back about three years ago.

Not all Putnam natives share I. G. Mobley's optimism for the future. "She's about dried up and blowed away," grocer Charley Odom says of the town. Some worry about losing their churches. On a typical Sunday there had been eight, nine, and eleven worshipers at the Campbellite, Methodist, and Baptist Churches, respectively. One recent collection plate at the Methodist Church brought in $3.48. You can't keep a preacher on that.

Miss LaVerne Rutherford has worked in the post office almost since graduating from high school in 1943. She was appointed Postmaster by John F. Kennedy, and she now worries over the possibility of the office being closed. She would be transferred to a larger office, reduced to clerk, forced to live away from Putnam for the first time. Hopefully she says, "These people have to get their mail *somewhere!*"

The title of chief optimist of Putnam, and maybe of the world, must go to Jim Meador, a newcomer. He opened J. E.'s Steak House, at a reported $5,000 investment, *after* the bulldozers had done Putnam dirt. The J. E. Steak House sign is new, orange and green, made of a glittering substance which dazzles the eyeballs in the sun. It cannot, however, be easily seen from Interstate Twenty.

Putnam cannot fairly lay all its troubles at the feet of Washington. Its alternating cycles of boom and bust are common to many of the nation's small towns. Census figures show the startling migration from rural to metropolitan areas. In 1940, some 43.5 percent of Americans lived on farms or in rural hamlets. By 1960, only 30.1 percent did.

Rural America is full of towns dead or dying. In Texas alone there are examples without end. Take Thurber, for instance. In 1887, after the discovery of a rich bituminous coal vein, it grew into a city of 10,000. For several years it supplied almost all the coal or building bricks used in the state. Thurber grew its own Nob Hill of haughty homes, a spacious Opera House, a man-made lake stocked with fish or suitable for boating. The local Pooh-bah of commerce and industry tooled about in his own plush railway car and handpicked his mayor. When the coal supply and brick orders ran out, so did Colonel Pooh-bah and everyone else.

The death blow fell in 1933. General offices of the Texas & Pacific Coal and Oil Company were ordered to Fort Worth. Stocks were sold from store shelves; buildings were wrecked and moved away; wires and poles came down; water and gas mains were removed. Where in 1930 Thurber had almost 6,000 people, it was virtually gone by

1935. The population in 1960 was eighty. Today it is exactly zero. All that is left is the remnant of an old smokestack bearing a bronze marker saying in twenty-five words or less that Thurber once knew glory.

Shafter and Terlingua, in the Big Bend Country, were booming mining towns as recently as the mid-1940s. Now they are ghost towns, too. Wink, in the western sands of what has been called "the Texas Sahara," was born with the oil strike of 1926. Little more than two years later it was a shack-and-tent Baghdad of 7,000 people, mud-bog streets, and open saloons serving up red-eye whiskey and sudden death. It knew a decade of stability, during which its Wink Wildcat football teams earned the reputation of being meaner than your ex-wife. But oil production petered out. By 1960 the federal government decided to restore Wink as a model city in the new urban-renewal program. At a cost of only two million of your tax dollars, planning geniuses replaced rusty tin pool halls and dilapidated sandwich shops with modern, sanitized miracles of glass, brick, and fluorescent lights. The scheme didn't work. Too many of Wink's 1,863 remaining citizens used profits from condemnation proceedings to hightail it to where the action is.

Ranger, in Eastland County, reached 16,205 in 1920. Old-timers swear its oil boom of that era pushed it 5,000 higher than that. Drinking water fetched ten cents a glass in restaurants, and special policemen who dealt in mayhem were hired to handle street rowdies. Long on the wane, Ranger today claims only 3,113 residents.

Even home bogs of Great Men and their ladies have declined. Only one member of Lyndon Johnson's 1926 high-school graduating class chose to build a future in Johnson City. The President has said, "I go back to my hometown and I find difficulty locating anyone under twenty-one years of age that has finished high school. They have moved on."

Jefferson, a bustling seaport of 38,000, was Texas' second-largest city from 1867 to 1873. Then Jay Gould, the genius of the T & P, incensed when he had trouble getting right-of-way through the town, ran his railroad tracks *around* it. Jefferson started to wither. Soon the natural dam that backed the water up and made Big Cypress Bayou and the lakes navigable was removed. Jefferson is now a sedentary village of 3,000. The biggest attraction is the birthplace of a local girl everyone remembers as Claudia Taylor, now Lady Bird Johnson.

Putnam, too, knows the loss of its young. In the words of one old nester, "Every kid with good sense and the price of a bus ticket leaves." Figures back him up. Where Putnam High School graduated twenty-six seniors in 1941, it conferred degrees on only eleven a decade later, and the Class of '64 consisted of Doris Lee Donaway, Charlie Ivie, and Farrell Thorp.

The bottom dropped out of Putnam for good about 1942. The peak population of 5,000—reached during the oil boom of the 1920s—shrank to less than half that figure by 1936. In 1940, the census counted only 1,403 people. When World War II came, Putnam had no munitions factory to brighten the times and nobody looked after it when military bases were passed around in Washington. Following Pearl Harbor Putnam boys answered the call to arms; fat paychecks lured their elders to shipyards and factories. Seventy-five houses moved away in the single year 1942, and a dozen more were shuttered. A dozen cousins of mine joined the military that year, Uncle George Gaskins sold his grocery store and moved to California, and my father took a job with a New Mexico oil company. The exodus was on.

It was a broiling-hot day when I went home again last summer. My head was full of memories and my car full of kinfolk. The air conditioner was on full volume, while on the car radio T. Texas Tyler sang "When I Look Up My God Looks Down On Me."

We flashed by Baird (Pop. 1,633) at a high speed, and it seemed but a couple of minutes before my father said dourly, "You better slow this thing down to about a thousand. It's right down yonder."

But we had gone past the sign pointing north to *Putnam. Pop. 203.* Seeking a spot on Interstate Twenty to turn around, I noted Harper's Hill with shock. In my youth it had towered over the countryside, and probably no man had scaled it, even if Lem Harper did grow peaches and apples up there. I recalled when a committee of jelly-smeared faces had solemnly judged it three million feet high. But now. . . .

"Look at Harper's Hill," I said. "Somebody's sawed the top off."

My father chuckled. "Naw, it never was anything but a little ole mound of dirt."

Where the depot had been was only the wooden platform on which it had rested. The platform seemed no bigger than a life raft. I complained that not only was the depot gone, but part of the platform as well. My father enjoyed another laugh. No, the depot had been that exact size. I didn't dispute him, though I clearly recalled when dozens of us—Benny Ross Everett, Bobby Gene Maynard, Kenneth Gaskins, Humph Weeks, Buck Yarborough, a barefoot army—had stood on that platform with acres of wooden boards running in all directions, and the yellow depot looming grandly behind us like Convention Hall in Atlantic City.

As I U-turned on Interstate Twenty, my mother fretted how this was the exact spot where so-and-so got killed turning *his* car around in March of 1926. There was little point in reminding her this particular highway had not existed then, for my mother is blessed with an infallible memory for tragedy. Nobody got killed this time, much to her surprise and, perhaps, slight disappointment. I followed the highway signs as we tooled under the viaduct and drove by sixteen strange white pillars supporting it like sentinels of an enemy army.

That couldn't be Putnam there! Not that collection of frayed little buildings, bare and huddled against the sun, where once had been a proud line of stores grandly sending forth all the world's good smells. There were skips between buildings: vacant lots overgrown with weeds and Johnson grass. Grass poked up through the sidewalks, cracking and crumbling them. A patch had burst through almost at the exact spot Ole Man Bob Head had angrily scuffled his feet while warning that grass would grow in the streets should FDR be much longer tolerated. In the silence my father said, "It was a purty good town, once."

On this hot Saturday afternoon only two cars, one ancient pickup truck, and absolutely no human beings were visible on the single, one-block business street. In Putnam's salad days the sidewalks would have been crowded with round-eyed urchins, women sampling cloth bolts in Norred's Dry Goods, farmers hustling to sell their butter and eggs in time to sweat the domino matches. While my father conducted a door-to-door search for friendly natives, I explored the short stretch of sidewalks in pursuit of memories.

Orr's Drugs was padlocked. Peering through the glass I could see, under layers of dust, the marble soda fountain with its brass-headed spigots, three marble-topped tables with wire wicker chairs, the cumbersome upright scales that for a penny had given your weight and the bonus of a small trinket. Long, narrow shelves held ancient concoctions Putnam mothers had sworn by: Dr. Caldwell's Syrup-of-Pepsin, a bitter brew called Al-Da-Reka (once assumed more vital to health than sunshine or surgery), and I wondered if in the clutter there remained that miracle cure for coughs, Jamaica Ginger.

I walked over to the lonely site of Uncle George's grocery store, where the Candy Bandits of 1936 did their work. Cousin Kenneth would enter a rear storeroom, banging among crates and boxes, whooping like an Apache until his father rushed back to deal with the menace. With the candy case unguarded, I would scoop up jaw-breakers, peanut brittle, chocolate bars, and peppermint sticks in quantities that would have foundered all the inhabitants of Boys' Town. We divvied up in a jungle of back-alley weeds after each successful foray. But the community's leading busybody entered the store one day to buy some baking powder and caught the bag man of the duo. The flogging administered by the village blacksmith to his youngest son was painful, though less so than Cousin Kenneth's bawled denials that the conspiracy involved him. The final indignity came when my blood cousin publicly forgave me for swiping from his daddy's store, then led the First Baptist Church Sunbeams in loud, pious prayer for my long-range rehabilitation. This act of charity was enough to win for Kenneth the Jesus' Little Helper Award. I was delighted when his prize proved to be nothing more interesting than a New Testament.

My father's return interrupted this reverie. He complained over having recognized three people who had not recognized him. Nor had he found any of his old cronies. Morosely we ambled toward Tood Cunningham's service station. As a battered pickup truck rattled down the street my father bellowed in a bass key that was stunning for lungs pushing eighty years' service: "Ellison!" The truck faltered, zigzagged, and stopped. The driver gazed out suspiciously.

"Don't set there with egg on your face," Dad called. "Get down outta there."

The old man didn't budge from the truck. "Says who?" he demanded.

"By durn, says I."

That seemed to settle something. Ellison Pruett climbed stiffly down, a large, raw-boned, red-faced man who probably tended his own fractures with cow-chip poultice. He wore a Western-cut shirt, khaki pants, scuffed boots, and the cattleman's coiled hat.

"You know me?" my father demanded.

Ellison Pruett studied my father's face. He probably recognized that it had known hard work and the outdoors, but that was all.

"Naw." Then his shotgun-eyes moved over and got the drop on me. He jerked a thumb like Randolph Scott uses in warning bad-hat gunslingers to hit the road.

"Don't know the feller with hair on his face, neither."

"That's my son." The beard needed some justification. "He's a writer."

"*Hell* he is." Ellison Pruett examined me down to the skin pores. He nodded, slowly and with stern sympathy. He watered the dusty earth with a golden stream of tobacco juice. "He use a name when he writes?"

"Yeah," said my old man. "Same one I do. Leastwise, the *last* name." He chortled in delight, slapping his knee. Ellison Pruett grinned, shoving his hat to the back of his head. Knowing when he'd met his match he said, "Thunder, I give up. I couldn't name you if I was a-gonna be hung."

"Well, I worked for you once upon a time."

Light dawned in Ellison Pruett's old eyes. "You ain't Clyde *King?*"

"I reckon I am. What's left of me."

"Naw. *You* ain't Clyde King!" This time it wasn't open to question. "Why, Clyde King weighed over two hundred pounds and was stout as a mule. He wasn't no little ole dried up nobody like you!"

They gurgled in delight, embracing in the street. "Clyde King!" Ellison Pruett repeated. "By *damn!*" He slapped his old comrade on the back, then whirled on me. "Boy, I seen this man lift a whole barrel fulla water from the ground and set it *flat-dab* in the bed of a wagon without straining hisself."

My father grinned. "Can't do much anymore. I'm kinda like Putnam. Too old and wore out."

"Why," Ellison Pruett said, "this burg never amounted to much, anyways." Then his eyes walked slowly along the solitary main street, as if he'd noted its diminution for the first time. "Things change," he said. "I don't care for some the changes, neither. Do you, Clyde?"

"No," my father said. "I'll betcha there's one thing hasn't changed, though."

"What's that?"

"I'll bet you still can't play dominoes!"

"Why, I'm *teachin'* dominoes. Got a beginner's class you might be able to get in." They whooped and hoo-hawed, and when the mirth died down Pruett said, "We been playin' all afternoon up in the old Odd Fellows hall."

My father was chagrined. "Why, durn it! Who all played?"

"Same ole bunch. Me and Lee White. Elmer McIntosh, Walter Caldwell. Feller named Truman Blaylock, from over at Scranton."

"I sure wish I'd knew it," Dad said. "It wouldn't of taken much to clean *that* bunch's plow."

They talked then. Of crops and the Bible and men a long time dead. When Ellison Pruett took his leave my father watched the dust of his pickup as far as the eye could see.

Though the school house was locked for the summer, an official yielded to my attack of nostalgia and provided a key. "Look around," he said. "Likely there's not much in there you'd have."

Yet the place held many treasures. In a glass display case was the silver-plated trophy won by the Bi-District football champions of 1937. Misshapen and deflated but awesomely majestic was the historic football Oliver Davis had romped with for the 65-yard touchdown that had brought Putnam its championship—and, far more important, a 13 to 6 victory over the loathsome Baird Bears. Had I not feared the grip of Superintendent R. F. Webb reaching from out of the past, I might have copped it like Murph-the-Surf.

The grandfather's clock in the principal's office had ticked off doom while I once awaited judgment for having talked in assembly. President Johnson's portrait was next to the one of Franklin D. Roosevelt, hung when Federal Emergency Administration of Public Works Project No. 1295, more commonly known as Putnam High School, had been dedicated. We had been proud when we moved into the shining new palace of cream-colored bricks in 1937. It was a showplace. Even ill-at-ease farmers had shuffled in to view the Central Sound System (*i.e.,* a public-address hookup to every room) dedicated at a cost of $200 by the Class of '37 to give "our Beloved School access to the diffusion of knowledge that will aid pupil advancement." Some of the charm wore off when school authorities failed to pipe Jack Armstrong or Amos 'n' Andy into the classrooms.

It wasn't a showplace anymore. Cracks ran through its bricks in several places, the summer grounds were a jumble of grass and weeds, a disreputable car with three flat tires sat near the bare flagpole. The auditorium, where I had played Grumpy in a very swinging one-night production of "Snow White" to the applause of several thousand people, now seats only a couple of hundred and doesn't need half that. They have lowered the drinking fountains three feet each. The walls of my old classroom have been moved in by several feet, and the wall lockers are scaled for midgets.

Nor were outside objects in their rightful places. The pine-board lunch stand, where I had violated home training by first buying on credit, is no longer there as a temptation to hungry schoolboys. The football field—where I played two heart-bursting minutes in my first "real" game as the Putnam Grammar School Pussycats routed Scranton, 28 to nothing—is grown over with alfalfa. Missing, too, was the clump of trees where ranch boys had tied their horses and fed them bundled roughage during the noon hour. My father counted the absence of nineteen houses he recalled near the school. In a growth of mesquite bushes stood the concrete steps which once led to the house where I was born.

Was Putman just another of man's experiments gone bad, no better than those tens of thousands of isolated villages where people had dandruff and gas pains and warts on the nose?

What we had produced in the way of native sons and daughters would not cause the earth to move. Statesmen? Billie Mack Jobe had served two terms in the Texas legislature and called the Governor by his first name, but his name appears in no histories I have read. Athletes? Stanley Williams played pro football with Dallas and Baltimore, but his name became a household word only in Putnam. The arts? Lewis Nordyke published a couple of books and several articles in *Saturday Evening Post,* not quite enough to rank with Sartre or Faulkner. Most ex-Putnamites were safe in the anonymity of our society, working for a weekly wage in undistinguished jobs, watching "Bonanza" on television, and fretting over income-tax forms. This knowledge was painful for me, and altogether new.

Our town had not been a complete one—not even an "average" one by national standards. No Negroes lived in Putnam within the range of my memory, nor Jews, and the only Catholics had been Mexicans who lived in converted railroad boxcars for a few weeks each year when their work as itinerant section-gang hands brought them briefly our way. We were, I could now acknowledge, a bigoted town. I remembered the despair of local people when Joe Louis knocked out Jimmy Braddock to win the world heavyweight championship in 1937. I had learned of this the morning following the fight, when a gentle Putnam lady remarked to a companion in the post office, "Well, the ole nigger is champion." And the other woman answered, "I guess they'll be pushing white folks off the streets and into the gutters now." In November of 1937, when the Japanese seized an American vessel, tore down our flag, and tossed it in the Hwang Pu River, many of our natives said the U.S. could "whip those little brown monkeys in ninety days"; Japan wasn't even as big as Texas. We were narrow in politics: you were a Democrat because Daddy was, and his father had been before him. Our theology fell just short of teaching a flat earth, and in some cases it did teach that eternal damnation followed infant baptism. Sin had meant the strict idea of the word: drinking spirits, dancing to music, or wearing lip rouge. The more destructive sins—gossip, bigotry, indifference to injustice, oppression of free thought—were cheered in the streets.

Man being the weak creature he is, no doubt Putnam had known its share of commerce in Prohibition dew, its backstair romances, small larcenies or other transgressions that I had always assumed to be the property of New York, Washington City, or Baird. We were not rampant with wrongdoing, but for the first time I questioned whether we had been creatures of Utopia.

We left in the late afternoon. I stopped by the only business house open, J. E.'s Steak House, for cigarettes. Four men in work clothes sipped coffee while on the jukebox a cowboy singer urged us to "Cross the Brazos at Waco." I wondered how long it might take Jim Meador to get his $5,000 investment back at ten cents a cup.

As I drove away into the sun, the loss of the town saddened me beyond the telling of it; it may not have been anything unusual, but it had been home. Suddenly I was angry—at Congress, the Bureau of Public Roads, the Depression-makers on Wall Street, the greedy oil speculators, the foreigner who had failed to open the biggest automobile dealership in Texas. How could a place be allowed to die?

But the anger passed, for I knew I would not find the answer—not this side of whatever Heaven there is that has rewarded all Putnamites who lived by the code. And even then the answer would probably lie on the farther slope of the last holy hill, guarded by a mean old dog.

I sweated blood over that piece— not because I feared that my facts were wrong, but because I feared they were too brutally accurate. Some of my relatives and a few old friends still live in the wreckage of Putnam. Others live in such close proximity that ancient ties, new cars and blood dictate their frequent return. The erosion of the place, I feared, might not have been readily apparent to them. They would not see my old hometown as my stranger's eyes had seen and recorded it after a long absence. I remembered how Wolfe was hounded, reviled and virtually stoned from his North Carolina birthplace following the appearance of his autobiographical first novel, *Look Homeward Angel*.

My wife and I were wintering in Florida when the article hit the newsstands. Reading it anew I was sick all over again: this cousin would be offended, that aunt furious beyond forgiveness or the grave, a certain old chum would sue or possibly break my jaw. Mother's first letter after publication carried a single economical comment that was —coming from my own flesh—terrifyingly ominous: "I thought the Putnam piece was interesting." A few days later my brother messaged that had he known the *kind* of article I intended to write, he could have been helpful. This implied boatloads of failure by my paranoid interpretation.

Then tragedy struck a double blow. I learned that grocer Charley Odom, quoted in the article ("She's about dried up and blowed away"), had fallen dead on the street the very day the Putnam article went on sale. Less than two weeks later my old superintendent of schools, R. F. Webb, who also had been mentioned, met with the same sad fate. Maybe nobody else knew why—but *I* did. My wife, a very rational human at the most unexpected moments, berated me for being sillier than the words to "Mairzy Doats." I am not being flippant when I say that I could not be dissuaded: the agony was real. One night, no longer able to stand the screaming silence that shouted of my guilt, I telephoned my-cousin-the-lawyer, Lanvil Gilbert, in Austin. He is at once a literate, honest and perceptive man; more than once has he dealt patiently with my attacks of artistic lunacy. At my request he made the long trek to Putnam for purposes of soliciting comment on the article from townsfolk.

Most of the grumbles, it turned out, were in a minor key. Some folks thought I had leaned too much on I. G. Mobley for recollections when this old graybeard or that old-timer could have added to the big picture. My father's old friend, Ellison Pruett, grumbled that I'd written of his watering the earth with a splash of tobacco juice "when I never chewed tobaccer in my life." ("I don't know what he seen me spit," the old man said emphatically, "but it wasn't tobaccer juice no more than it was cod liver oil.") The reigning school superintendent wrote *Harper's* in anger, challenging my claim that cracks exist in my old school building and also telling the world that Putnam's students had rated above average in some sort of nationally based student tests. (I'm sorry: the cracks in the building *were* there, and may be found on the south side of the west end. No comment had been made on the scholastic worth of PHS students: I was delighted, in fact, to learn that modern-day Putnam students are as brilliant as were my contemporaries.) No other complaints reached my ears. So I had not defamed a town, or several generations, and nobody suggested that I had blood on my hands.

Several of the relatively few living Americans aware of my work have called the Putnam piece my best writing. Willie Morris, who edited it, went so far after two pre-luncheon martinis as to claim, "People will be reading that piece fifty years from now." (Willie, however, thought Goldwater might win and still insists that 3-D movies can make the right man a fortune.)

I might have got a bad case of what we called "the big head" back in Putnam had not columnist Katharyn Duff of the Abilene *Reporter-News* written me: "Will you drop me a note telling a little bit more about yourself? A number of ex-Putnamites have come in or called saying they loved the article and remember a lot of the incidents in it—but nobody remembers *you*."

CHAPTER 3

My Hero LBJ

Writing candidly about Presidents of the United States, like courting widow women or taking sides in barroom brawls, entails a certain amount of natural risk. Politicians as a breed are thin-skinned creatures prone to bleed great gobs when stabbed by the slightest journalistic pen-prick. The higher they climb up the national ladder the more their heads swim in dizzy outrage at the gross irreverence of wordsmiths who presume to chronicle their deeds. Presidents come down with "political hemophilia" as readily as three-for-a-nickel Congressmen or your local Inspector of Hides & Ticks.

For all John F. Kennedy's self-deprecating wit (and despite his wry public remark about "reading more and enjoying it less") there came a day when he pettily canceled all White House subscriptions to a critical newspaper. On another occasion, he more seriously urged *New York Times* executives to recall their Vietnam correspondent, David Halberstam, because he did not approve of Halberstam's coverage of the war. (Which, for the record, was only good enough to win the Pulitzer Prize.) Harry S Truman, author of that now-infamous S.O.B. letter to a music critic who thought that daughter Margaret sounded like less than a nightingale, and said so, possibly railed against "the one-party press" in his slumbers. Franklin D. Roosevelt once awarded, in ceremonies remembered for a complete lack of hilarity, the Iron Cross of Nazi Germany to a journalist who had incurred his displeasure. The mere mention of one particular female reporter was said to add a dozen strokes to Dwight D. Eisenhower's golf score and several points to his blood pressure reading. Then there was Richard Milhous Nixon's sour—if premature—swan song to the press following his defeat for governor of California, a performance of such self-righteous blame-placing and stuck-pig squealing that for the first time Mr. Nixon showed me at least one Presidential quality.

So much for the amateurs. My nomination for the all-time, revolving, indoor, outdoor, and bare-knuckle professional champion of press clipping sensitivity is Lyndon Baines Johnson. He is capable of breaking out in clusters of choice invective, if not exotic skin rashes, when displeased with the way words have been strung together in linkage with his name. Medical science has not yet found a magic potion strong enough to serve as a vaccine against LBJ's particular strain of Presidential Red-Eye, and if you will forgive a small excursion into prophecy, then I will here predict that when the common cold, cancer and mumps have been banished from the earth, *that* particular malady will continue to ravish its victim.

This is not a malady Lyndon Johnson caught from standing in drafty White House halls, nor from sleeping in Lincoln's bed—though both may have worsened the condition. Presidential Red-Eye may be contagious to a degree, but most of its victims seem to have brought the germ to 1600 Pennsylvania Avenue with them. Lyndon B. Johnson showed early symptoms as Senate Majority Leader. Johnson did not exactly dodge around behind marble pillars trying to keep his name out of the papers. Reporters whom the Leader felt deserving of his larger confidences were made gifts of private scoops and helpful little inside stories that would prompt their editors to think of them as seers and sorcerers. Those who wrote of LBJ without revealing a proper appreciation of his legislative hocus-pocus, or without otherwise discerning how lucky the Republic was to have secured his special services, were alternately wheedled, lambasted or shamed. The same cranky female reporter who upset the Eisenhower metabolism once prompted Senator Johnson to remark that "that woman" obviously wasn't getting what she needed, and to suggest to a young staffer—only half-jokingly—that the hired hand could do the woman, the Senate Majority Leader, and very probably the NATO powers a favor by taking care of the situation. When a Dallas *News* reporter wrote a flattering feature story about LBJ's brother, Sam Houston Johnson (then serving on the Senator's staff), the Majority Leader, far from being pleased, griped that his brother had "hogged the headlines." Michael Davis, in *LBJ: A Foreign Observer's Viewpoint,* tells of his subject's response to a reporter who, thinking to break the conversational ice, began an interview with a trivial question. "Why do you come and ask me, the leader of the Western world," President Johnson grumbled, "a chickenshit question like that?"

One need not understand bushels of politics nor five acres of Freud to quickly discern why public men are so sensitive to the journalistic pen-prick. That dratted, overworked dingus the politician calls his "image" is largely fashioned by what the public reads of and about him. Naturally, the politician wants to help his image along. Even if his press is as favorable as J. Edgar Hoover's was until somebody mentioned wiretapping and the bangtails, the politico can no more resist gilding the lily than you could resist Miss Universe alone in a Turkish bath. Rare, therefore, is the public man without one or more staffers whose primary duty is to manufacture press releases giving the Boss the nod in direct comparison with Solomon, Colin Kelly, Dr. Schweitzer, Will Rogers, jolly ole Saint Nick, and—according to personal tastes and geographical expectations—either Lincoln or Lee. (I have heard it said that some Border State politicians demand both.)

Then an amazing thing happens. I, myself a reformed flack for several statesmen of well-advertised talents and no faults at all, have seen it with these old eyes: the politician develops a simple, childlike faith in the accuracy of his own campaign tracts. Never mind that they were written by men who, if they were not paid $15,000 or more annually for writing them, very well may have been inspired to write something else. Never mind that the statesman's small molehills of virtue were turned into mountains by committees formed for the purpose, or that his paid authors never once lost a midnight struggle to the Truth. Is it not down there in black and white how he, Hon. Prominent Whoozits, can turn water into wine? Can he not make the lame walk, the dumb talk, and the blind see in Technicolor? Once the politician has gorged his soul on such sweet, subsidized poetry he is never again satisfied with the plain-vanilla prose of the independent journalist.

In ten years of happy serfdom on Capitol Hill, the harshest private criticisms I heard members of Congress make were not against Godless Communism, Those Bastards in the Opposition Party, or even their own bothersome constituents who sent postcards demanding that we not launch space rockets because we might somehow release poisonous moon gases upon the earth. Nosir, the really blue-ribbon invectives, the kind to make little ole ladies leap in alarm for their prayer books, were reserved for inveighing against the Goddamn Press. The average professional politician greets each new morning armed with the same irrefutable Absolutes: (1) he was destined to be, and has become, a Great Man, and (2) not a one of those peckerwoods of the Goddamn Press has tumbled to this most obvious of universal truisms.

Working at the spear-carrier's level in Congress, however,

taught me that jackassery knows no partisan or ideological bounds. Some of the most liberal men I know thrill me to jig-dances with their votes, but I would not trust them with my billfold or with your wife. Conversely, some real Regular Fellahs vote on the side of Satan so often their persons seem to harbor a faint whiff of brimstone. I am quoting this neither as the exception nor the rule—merely stating that it is sometimes so. No Great Man is quite as grand as he believes himself to be or his ghost-writers claim; yet, even the sorriest slob in the last row of the Mississippi legislature is possibly considered by God to be a little better man than his enemies describe him. It is this simple knowledge that leads me to be able to admit in print that some few of my own old champions are capable of using the wrong fork, scratching where they itch when they itch, or telling official whoppers without cracking a smile. (If you think every writer can make this distinction, just find a kind word about LBJ in a William F. Buckley, Jr., column—or an unkind word about him in the writings of William A. White.)

The working politician, however, cannot conceive of being admired only 66 percent or 92 percent or by any other fractional measurement. If you are not with him 100 percent, up to and including the breaking out of star-spangled bunting or the crashing of cymbals at the mere mention of his name, then you are walking picket in the enemy camp. You cannot write of his altogether human tendency to curse when his toe's been stumped, to blow his cool when he sits down on flypaper, or even hint that he has less hair than he did a year ago, without stirring up his lust for vengeance.

That is especially true of those of us who once hired our typewriters out to public officials but who have since repented of that particular venality. Politicians who once slipped us the secret handclasp of the brotherhood somehow assume that we are forever bound to protect them from being revealed as mere earthlings. We have belonged to the same lodge (their reasoning runs) and we have no more right to reveal the secrets thereof than we would have, upon turning in our Shrine fezzes, to expose the private rituals of the Masonic Lodge to a bunch of Knights of Columbus. If we *do* give History the benefit of our special insights, then we are thought of in high places as somebody named Gerald Ratfink. Rumors are started that we have taken up with stray blondes, or sold atomic secrets.

Similar rumors came to flower after original publication of the article to follow, "My Hero LBJ." There are politicians in Congress, and lobbyists without number, who still turn pale at the thought of being reported in my social company. One highly placed White House staffer berated a *Harper's* editor for printing my work, an inner-circle spy smuggled out the intelligence that President Johnson's reaction to the article was "sort of grim," and good citizens from all over America wrote in to accuse me of new and inventive forms of subversion. One vexed midwestern lady, who apparently does not know her President personally, flatly insisted that Lyndon B. Johnson would never have used some of the more colorful expressions credited to him in my article. Others, who may have known the President better, did not question the accuracy of the quotes but did fault my judgment for having used them.

In defense of another in a long line of poor boys just trying to get along, I can only say that if it is not the independent journalist's duty to tell it like it is then it *should* be. I did make the point, in a side-bar to the LBJ article, that "I personally think that no President has done more for the country in the way of progressive domestic legislation," and otherwise copped my bet with conciliatory declarations, but these apparently did me about as much good as Brutus did Caesar. This happened because I chose to chroncile select remembrances and glimpses of . . .

MY HERO LBJ

If anything set me apart from my boyhood contemporaries in the parched and impoverished area of West Texas where I grew up, it was a precocious interest in politics. My father, a small dirt-farmer and lay preacher, took me to a political pie supper when I was nine. I fell completely under the political spell. The idea of being applauded by a crowd for bragging about yourself, and maybe getting paid for it besides, fascinated me. A county-commissioner candidate from our mud-bog precinct, one Arch Bent, was the Devil's instrument in my case. He paid me the highest compliment a child may receive from a practicing adult by solemnly shaking my hand, soliciting my vote as if I had one, and asking if I'd like to help him campaign. Then he gifted me with a fistful of campaign cards. For days I walked barefoot on the dirt roads of Eastland County on behalf of Arch Bent. Arch Bent's victory sealed my fate. Someday—somehow—I would hitch up with a big time political hero.

My first recollection of Lyndon Johnson dates back to 1941, when I was twelve. Johnson, then a Congressman representing a district many miles to the southeast of us, was running for the U.S. Senate. One morning I walked the quarter-mile from our shabby old farm-house to the rural-route mailbox. There I found what even then I recognized as the literature of a political pitchman. The candidate was frozen in the poses I would later get to know so well: smiling from a platform as folks reached up to shake his hand, serious as he talked with a rural pharaoh, radiating cheer in the traditional family photo where hair was slicked down, dresses starched to a fault, and every-body looked as if he'd stepped out of a bandbox. What made this campaign pamphlet especially memorable for me was a red-letter pledge across the top in triple banners:

THE DAY LYNDON JOHNSON MUST VOTE TO SEND YOUR SON TO FOREIGN WARS, THAT DAY LYNDON JOHNSON WILL LEAVE CONGRESS AND GO WITH HIM.

With Japan warring on China and Hitler's panzer divisions smash-ing through Europe it was a dramatic pledge; to a small boy who saw only glory and medals in the bloodletting it was a heroic one.* Stand-ing barefoot by that mailbox a quarter of a century ago, I became an instant LBJ man.

Johnson did not win the Senate seat in 1941. He lost by only 1,200 votes to W. Lee (Pappy) O'Daniel, that sprightly demagogue and hillbilly singer who had emerged from a flour salesman's obscurity to the Texas governorship by shouting radio hosannas in the name of the Old Folks, the Alamo, and Jesus Christ. The Texas Election Bureau prematurely announced that Johnson had won. When a flood of O'Daniel votes came in from the boondocks and pine thickets two or three days later, the reversal came as a bitter disappointment to me.

At this point I had not only never seen Johnson; I had never even heard the sound of his voice. I knew LBJ only as a face smiling from posters nailed to fence posts and from stories in week-old newspapers

---

* Johnson fulfilled his promise. Obtaining leave from the House after Pearl Harbor, he served in the Southwest Pacific for eight months, until President Roosevelt ordered all Congressmen on active duty to return to Washington.

cadged each Sunday from our more affluent neighbors. Yet these so impressed me that once, while helping my father harvest corn, I was prattling enthusiastically about Lyndon Johnson and turned a team of horses so short the flatbed wagon flipped over and very nearly maimed me. "Boy," my father asked, "don't you never think about nothin' but Lyndon Johnson and football?"

I would not see Johnson for another thirteen years, when he was campaigning for reelection to the U.S. Senate in 1954 (he had been first elected in 1948 by his memorable 87-vote margin). I was then a newspaper reporter deep in oil-and-McCarthy country. Senator Johnson came to West Texas to give a speech. It was a conventional one: service to the good folks of Texas, love of country and faith in the free-enterprise system, the soil, and Heaven's Plan. There were the usual homelies, the same hoary political jokes, the same cardboard poses I had gotten to know in other candidates. I left disappointed by my first glimpse of The Great Man. Besides, boyhood idolatry has a way of vanishing, and Johnson by this time had two strikes against him in my book: he had given Adlai Stevenson only token support in 1952, and he had remained too long silent while the McCarthyites treated us to their national spook show.

But Johnson's Democratic opponent in the primary reawakened my allegiance. Douglas T. Daugherty campaigned in a red fire truck and made speeches that would have frightened George III. He favored quitting the UN, going back to the Hoover Dollar, making deep knee bends to King Oil, and cleaning "the Godless Commies" out of the State Department. I went straight away to County Democratic headquarters to enroll again in Lyndon Johnson's cause. Through that summer I tacked posters, sealed envelopes, and spoke for Johnson to vest-pocket rallies of ten-folks-and-a-rooster in remote villages like Wink and No Trees.

I went to Washington in late 1954 with a freshman Congressman who, after noting my talents in menial tasks, had chosen me for his administrative assistant. Johnson was Texas' senior Senator and blossoming as a national figure. I arrived in Washington assuming that I would be the frequent companion of Speaker Rayburn, Senator Johnson, Mr. Justice Tom Clark, and other Texans who had preceded me to the sources of power. I did not know that "the help" is "the help" in Washington much as it is in the kitchen pantry.

Though I didn't drink coffee at the White House or socialize with Johnson after work, I did see a great deal of the Senator's staff. A neophyte in Washington could have done worse. As Majority Leader, Johnson had great powers—many of which he had created or assumed for himself. He kept a sensitive finger on Texas politics. He could bestow grand favors. Consequently any Texan who needed to plead a special cause for his constituents or for himself naturally went to LBJ. Since most such matters are handled at the staff level, I worked in those early years with Walter Jenkins, Arthur Perry, Booth Mooney, Sam Houston Johnson, Bill Brammer, Harry McPherson (Bill Moyers was still in college and unknown to any of us), and other Johnson staffers on a thousand routine chores. I was beer-drinking close to some of them.

I knew of the Lyndon Johnson who hired man-and-wife staff teams because as one of his secretaries quoted him to me, "I don't want some wife at home cryin' about the cornbread gettin' cold while her husband's busy doin' somethin' for me." Often he drove his employees to the limits of their physical endurance or to drink. He sometimes showered staff workers with gifts, praise, and promises of greatness. He might in anger banish an employee from his sight forever, later to pay thousands of dollars for the same man's hospital bills, with no prospect of reimbursement. Once he ordered several new white shirts for George Reedy, on the eve of an extended trip, because "that boy's always runnin' out of white shirts." And he overruled Mrs. Reedy on what size he should buy. He could reduce a secretary to tears because she had failed to locate some airborne Senator by telephone within two minutes, or because she had served him an inferior cup of coffee—later apologizing by saying, as one of the young ladies told me, "Honey, you go to the best beauty shop in town, get the full treatment and tell 'em to send me the bill." This was the Lyndon Johnson who once tossed a speech back to his writers with the instructions to "Put somethin' in there that will make me sound goddamn *humble!*" Another time he asked Bill Brammer, "Can't you brag on me a little more in that?" "Well, Senator," Brammer responded, "it's awfully hard to brag on you when you're making the speech yourself." Ego? There was a time when LBJ gifted any Texas baby named after him with a calf from his ranch. His office walls were festooned with pictures of infants named Lyndon Johnson Schultz, Lyndon Baines Garcia, or Lyndon B. Washington. Once a man joined LBJ's staff, however, he would be judged a quisling if ever he spoke of his employer in any but the most flattering of terms, or if he groused about working overtime.

Once in a while I encountered the Senator in the Capitol Building, and if he saw me we might exchange quick nods or a rare smile. Generally, however, he would have another Senator in tow: leaning into his companion's face and speaking with some dreadful urgency that blinded him to mere earthlings. The Johnson who rattled the Capitol's staid walls with mad hoo-hawing and aimless goddamning, crowded you like a pickpocket while he poured on the persuasive goose grease, or who threatened, cajoled, or compromised his way through the political jungles was still to me a shadowy myth composed of corridor whispers, poker-table legends, and newspaper photographs.

Sometime in 1958 I began to see Senator Johnson a bit more frequently. At one meeting in his office, representatives of a half-dozen executive agencies spent an hour enumerating to several of us the reasons why a new international bridge between the U.S. and Mexico could not be built at El Paso. Johnson crossed his long legs, feet propped up on his desk, and drawled, "Now, boys, you-all spent the last hour tellin' me why we *can't* open up another international bridge. Now I want everyone of you to give me one reason why we *can*. Then I want you to get the hell out of here and *open it!*" (They did— and LBJ cut the dedication ribbon.)

I had drinks a couple of times in the Majority Leader's suite in the Capitol along with Texas Congressmen, other administrative assistants, and favored Johnson staffers. In these sessions LBJ's conversation ranged broadly: a current political problem in Texas, chances of passing a Reciprocal Trade bill, an anecdote about Franklin D. Roosevelt, a stinging parody of Dwight D. Eisenhower. (He would screw his face into a frown, mimic Eisenhower's flat, clipped speech, and give us his version of the Eisenhower syntax: "Now, I may not know everything there is about this bill, Senator, and I might make what you might call a *mistake* now and then, but I am what you might call *sincere* about this . . .") Suddenly he would bark a question at an aide about tomorrow's schedule, turn his head abruptly to ask a Congressman "what you're gonna do to help me and the Speaker when that Education bill comes to the Floor," or grab a telephone to dial another Senator. Sitting under a life-sized oil portrait of himself that was illuminated by indirect lights, his in-the-flesh person looking down on us from his subtly elevated executive's chair, Senator Johnson was invariably jovial and full of hope. I enjoyed these performances hugely.

I saw the famed Johnson temper for the first time in 1959, during a three-day tour of duty that seemed a century.

Senator Johnson came to my home district as part of a state-wide tour designed to solidify the political base in Texas from which he would seek the Presidential nomination the following year. It fell my lot to act as "advance man"—the nearest thing the Western World has to a Chinese coolie. The advance man arranges for halls, podiums, luncheons, or dinners, keys to the city, press conferences, hotel accommodations, rendezvous between the visiting pooh-bah and his local political underlings, or a pitcher of water for the dignitary's bedside table. He referees disputes over who will sit where at ceremonial functions, and tries to discourage bores or potential troublemakers who might embarrass the Official Presence. Johnson's own staff attended to many of these details, but as resident coolie I was responsible for being on hand to guide everyone through the proper jig-steps.

At his first appearance, on the mezzanine floor of a downtown hotel where he spoke to about a hundred local leaders and their wives, Senator Johnson's performance could have served as a blueprint for the Compleat Cornpone Politician. He was charming, relaxed, and lean. He slouched on the podium, grinning boyishly, pulling at his ear, saying how grand it was for "me and Lady Bird to get out of the steel and stone of the cities and come back here to feel the soil of home under our feet, and draw close to all the things we hold dear while we gaze on the Texas moon." He invited all hands to "drop by and see us when you're in Washington." He reported that the coffeepot was always on, and added that "sometimes Bird bakes a buncha little cookies in the shape of the State of Texas to go with the coffee." (This earned a standing ovation and Rebel yells.) He confessed to vast stores of humility, giving credit for "whatever I may amount to" in equal measure to Celestial Beings, his mother, and everybody present. When he had finished he ambled off to mingle with the crowd, pressing flesh, cooing low, kissing old ladies on the cheek as if he had flushed a covey of favored maiden aunts. Then the party broke up and the Senator's official group retired toward his suite for a brief rest before the evening's scheduled dinner.

With the closing of the elevator door LBJ's sunny smile gave way to thunderstorm expressions. "Goddammit," he said by way of openers, "nobody told me I was supposed to make a *speech!* Didn't know it until I saw the damned podium. Up till then I thought it was just gonna be coffee, doughnuts, and bullshit!" He stared at me down to the blood. "Why in hell didn't you *tell* me they expected a speech out there? You think I'm a mind reader? Hah?" I didn't think "Yes" was the proper answer, but I was mortally afraid to say "No."

Within the next twenty-four hours Senator Johnson had berated me and his staffers because (1) his hotel bed was too short and "I have to scrootch my legs up until I fold up like a goddamn accordion"; (2) nobody could locate Senator Dick Russell of Georgia on the telephone at the snap of a finger; (3) we were late for three consecutive appointments because "half of you are crawlin', half of you are walkin', and *none* of you are runnin'," and (4) he couldn't immediately find his reading spectacles. In another town where a press conference had been scheduled (and to which I had clearly heard Johnson agree the day before in a rare cheerful moment) the Senator claimed knowledge of it only as he entered the hotel where local reporters waited. He blew up in the lobby and threatened not to appear. He was finally steered into the hotel ballroom, but not before his histrionics caused passersby to congregate and investigate the commotion. One reporter repeatedly baited Johnson with hostile questions. Finally, ignoring him completely, Johnson silently pointed to somebody else. When the heckler persisted the Senator snapped, "That's it. Thank you, boys." He plunged out of the ballroom, the rest of us chasing along, though handicapped by not having heard the starter's gun.

In the elevator the Senator's first words were: "Which one of you do I thank for *this* little lynching?" No one stepped forward to claim the medal. Those were Johnson's last words for the next fifteen minutes as he brooded silently, staring at the television set in his room. The rest of us stared and brooded with him. I was terrified that I might have to sneeze.

Maybe there is something about Lyndon B. Johnson and elevators not apparent to the eye. Some of his greatest conniptions have been thrown there. Likely, however, this is true because elevators happen to be the first place he is able to drop the necessary public poses and give vent to human frustrations. At any rate, my one head-to-head battle with Johnson started in an elevator the night before he would mercifully leave our district. Following a dinner where he had flashed his usual mixture of country charm and worldly knowledge, the Senator barked directly at me: "Who was that redheaded son-of-a-bitch set two chairs down from me?" I groped for the red-headed S.O.B.'s identity, but at that moment I could not have read my own name off a billboard. "Who*ever* he was," Johnson said, "I don't want that goofy S.O.B. sittin' in the same room with me again. Ruined mah whole night . . ." He trailed off into mumbles, glaring.

The hour was late. I was tired, and just about one more harsh word away from tears or running off from home. In his room the Senator was unhappy because a delegation of local citizens required entertainment. I would have gladly done the job. It required nothing more strenuous than pouring a little whiskey, laughing at the punch lines of old jokes, and massaging shriveled egos. Senator Johnson, however, assigned this choice duty to his own permanent staff people. He thrust a slip of paper in my hand. Just before plunging into the bathroom he said, "I want these people in that *exact* order." The note required two telephone calls to Washington, one to New York, one to Austin, and two or three more to small Texas towns. There wasn't a telephone number on the slip. I sat on my hands and let my juices boil. When the Senator entered the room he gave me one quick glance. Then he asked the room-at-large to whom he had given the note. Eventually all eyes turned my way. It was like standing in front of a firing squad.

I'm sure my voice trembled as I said, "I'm tired of being your lackey while your staff people sit on their rumps and drink whiskey. I've got *my own* man to lackey for." (The last sentence was spoken with some strange, hot pride—which shows what being a second-banana politician will do for your sense of values.) I have the vague recollection that somebody dropped an ashtray. One of Johnson's staffers suddenly snatched the note from my hand and whisked it away, presumably to the nearest telephone.

I am unable to recall the Senator's immediate reaction to the mutiny. Everyone seemed frozen in place. My ears throbbed blood as I plunged from the room. A friend stumbled out behind me, eyes wide and face pale. I would hesitate to quote him exactly, but I think he called on his Lord in a hoarse voice and asked if I had lost my goddamned mind. While I raved about holding Senator Johnson's hat, carrying his bags, and being treated like a stepchild, my friend made frantic shushing sounds and waved his hands as if he might be flagging the Greyhound. He desperately begged that I go someplace to "get a beer, cool off, and for God's sake stay out of Lyndon's sight."

I cooled off enough to worry about whether I'd lose my $16,000 a year job, then returned to a night of feverish sleep. About daylight the next morning the telephone in my room rang.

"You had your coffee yet?"

I said no.

"Come on up and have some," he said.

The Senator was in a figured robe. The morning newspaper was scattered about the floor and on the coffee table. He greeted me with a grunt that sounded half-friendly, then poured some coffee and handed it over. Just as I took the cup he said, "You can get kinda salty, can't you?" Then he grinned. My mumbled response consisted of mere sounds without any form resembling known words. The Senator took my arm and stood nose-to-nose, breathing on my eyeglasses. He talked about how "young fellas" like me make big politicians tick. He himself had been secretary to a Congressman, he said, in 19-and-32.

Then he settled on the couch and for perhaps the next half-hour entertained me with memories of New Deal days, and of his Texas boyhood, and praise of my boss. He spoke of how dedicated his staff was to him, and of how very much he loved his staff. He offered free advice ("You oughta get a law degree, young man like you. Come in handy no matter *what* profession you follow"), asked my opinion on whether a local politician had Congressional ambitions "enough that it won't let him sleep nights." Then he so adroitly maneuvered me out of the room with a darting little of series of back-pats, soothing clucks, and handclasps that I was in the elevator before I fully realized the audience was over.

I soon came back, though. For when the Senator departed for the airport, I found myself struggling with the bellhop for the honor of carrying his bags.

Some admiring newspapermen, many Southern Congressmen, and almost all Johnson staffers thought LBJ would be nominated for President in 1960. I disagreed. Unwisely I said so a few times. When the word got around, one of Johnson's key advisers met me over lunch to suggest a little more diplomacy. "You're from Texas," he pointed out. "It couldn't help the Senator, it couldn't help your Congressman, and it couldn't help *you personally* if you went around saying 'Johnson can't win.' " Though this sounded a little like a threat, it also sounded a lot like the truth.

In early 1960, Johnson-for-President headquarters opened in Washington's Ambassador Hotel. Walter Jenkins, Johnson's long-time administrative assistant, solicited my "volunteer" help at the campaign headquarters at nights and on weekends. The Senator, Jenkins said, would not be a candidate of record. He might even issue statements from time to time disavowing Presidential ambitions. Meanwhile, the Humphreys, Stevensons, Kennedys, and Symingtons would hopefully knock themselves off in Presidential primaries. The Johnson-for-President headquarters was ostensibly to be a volunteer citizens' group with no official LBJ connections, Jenkins said, but clear everything with him.

I was but one of many "volunteers," many of them from Capitol Hill and almost all of them with Texas roots, who pioneered the Johnson Presidential effort. No doubt I had more inner conflicts and reservations than most. I did not believe the Senator could be nominated because of sectional limitations, and I was personally attracted to Jack Kennedy.

By 1960 my feelings about Johnson were ambivalent—I admired him on the one hand and couldn't tolerate him on the other. As a working politician I admired his art in steering legislation through Congress at a time when he could have frustrated President Eisenhower by tying up the legislative machinery. But he refused the obstructionist role, saying that "any jackass can kick down a barn but it takes a carpenter to build one."

In fact, he saved Eisenhower's legislative chestnuts time after time. It seemed apparent, however, that many of Senator Johnson's shows suffered from overdirection. Often I was amazed that the national press (to say nothing of Republicans) didn't blow the whistle on his more obviously staged dramas. He seldom called a record vote until his pulse-takers had determined that he had enough votes to win. He often stashed two or three or four "safe" Senators away in the Senate cloakroom, rushing these loyal reserves in to win a cliff-hanger at the most dramatic moment. LBJ knew that the more powerful and effective he could *appear* the more powerful and effective he would *be*.

Politicians, like sleight-of-hand artists, must create certain illusions: there is simply not enough legitimate, workable magic to satisfy the customers. Any show—however well-staged or smoothly presented—requires a lot of honest toil behind the scenes before it approaches perfection. Johnson's did.

But in the matter of exercising national partisan leadership, or in performing real political services in Texas (emotionally, I confess unashamedly, almost as important to me as all the Senate productions in the world) my boyhood hero was sadly disappointing. It was not merely that he failed to be liberal, not even that he had voted against anti-lynch legislation in the late 1940s, or that he sang praises to the 27½ per cent oil-depletion allowance under which the rich get richer and the poor pay taxes. As a working pol, I could understand his dilemma. He represented a state largely oriented toward the Southern viewpoint, a state where schoolboys are taught that oil is the backbone of the economy and is, therefore, sacred. What disappointed me most about Johnson was that he threw his considerable weight and prestige into the camp of mossbacks who held Texas as if it were their own grand duchy.

The Texas Establishment has opposed social reforms to the extent of perpetuating oppression, ignorance, and poverty. Even today, Texas ranks at or near the bottom of the fifty states in aid to the blind, aged, and mentally ill, and in almost all social services. Texas Governors have routinely vetoed appropriations to improve hospitals, libraries, penal institutes, and old-age pensions. They have cheerfully signed "right-to-work" laws and harsh segregation measures. Legislators have urged soak-the-poor taxes on bread, work clothes, and medicines. They have permitted loan sharks to charge usurious rates and have refused to enact any laws protecting the state's thousands of migratory farm laborers who are carted from farm to hovel in open cattle trucks. They have openly cavorted with the fat-cat lobbyists. They have damned the federal government for foreign aid, aid to education, the antipoverty program, and the Peace Corps. I am not speaking here of John Birch Republicans nor even of Eisenhower ones, but of Tory Democrats who have made the wheels of influence go in Texas.

If any man had the power and finesse to move Texas toward a more moderate, enlightened political climate it was Lyndon Johnson. He chose not to use his talents in that direction at all. He did not stay on the sidelines while the liberals fought desperately for survival (as he might have done) but he invariably cast his lot with the Tories. He saw the labor-liberal bloc as a rising threat to his grip on Texas. Time after time he fused patchwork coalitions that effectively crushed liberal hopes of gaining a voice in the Democratic party. Working within the framework of the Establishment—*i.e.*, the Governor, the State Democratic Executive Committee, and local political bosses— Lyndon Johnson got what he wanted. What he wanted was, simply, control.

A typical display of Johnson's tactics occurred at the Democratic state convention in Fort Worth in 1956. As in past years, Johnson and crusty old Speaker Sam Rayburn arrived from Washington like visiting feudal barons. They received in their hotel rooms, and if you had business to transact you sought them out with a smile on your face and your hat in your hand. They brought along a coterie of Texas Congressmen to use in the same way that they used office runners and legislative aides in Washington. The Congressmen, taking to heart Speaker Rayburn's advice—"the best way to get along is to go along" —fanned out to their respective home-district delegations to act as Johnson's eyes and ears. Most of them were so conservative they did not fully approve of indoor plumbing.

These Congressmen were on friendly, first-name terms with the yahooing Main Street merchants, bankers, oil barons, labor-hating farmers, and xenophobic ranchers who were delegates to the convention. If the Congressmen heard rumors that a certain delegate was flirting with "the Red Hots" (LBJ's private name for the liberals) they rushed to pass the word. More than one delegate who had "flirted with the Red Hots" found himself confronted by his banker, preacher, lawyer, Congressman, brother, or anyone else who might hold some financial or emotional claim on him. Most were happy to scurry back into the fold after being exposed to "The Treatment."

In 1956 numerous counties sent contesting delegations to the state convention—liberal and conservative groups both claiming to be "official." The handpicked credentials committee invariably, of course, certified the conservatives.

El Paso County Judge Woodrow Wilson Bean was chairman of a liberal delegation. No stranger to ambition, he badly wanted his delegation seated, but knew this would take some special miracle. He set out to fashion one. Judge Bean went to Johnson and propositioned him: See that my El Paso liberals are seated and I'll deliver their votes to you. Senator Johnson saw the opportunity to woo away a delegation everyone considered firmly committed to the liberals, and at the same time acquire a pipeline into the Red Hot camp for future purposes. He told Bean that a floor fight was in prospect over whether to seat the huge Houston liberal or conservative delegation. Would Bean's liberals be willing to vote for the Houston conservatives as the price for their own seats? Judge Bean said they would. Johnson picked up the telephone, and very shortly the credentials committee certified the El Paso liberals.

Judge Bean had outpromised himself. Deeply committed to liberal causes, the El Paso delegates balked at opposing their Houston counterparts. One angrily stormed, "I didn't come down here for the pleasure of being Lyndon Johnson's rubber stamp." In a turbulent session behind locked doors the delegates reminded themselves that their purpose was to rid the state of "Dixiecrats masquerading as Democrats." Bean couldn't deal with the mutiny. He did not, however, pull up lame by rushing to Senator Johnson with a full confession.

He didn't need to. Johnson had eyes in the back of his head, it would soon seem to Bean. Through one of his many agents the Senator learned of the El Paso rebellion. He sent someone to fetch Judge Bean. When Bean arrived, Johnson said, "Judge, I hear you've decided not to go along with me on the Houston delegates."

"I'd like to, Lyndon," Bean said. "But I'm having a little trouble with some of the boys. You know how boys kick up their heels when they get away from home."

"Well, can you deliver 'em or not?"

"I can try, Senator."

"Trying don't count," Johnson snapped. "You with me or against me?"

"Well, I tell you," Bean said, "it looks like we'll be forced to go the other way, Senator."

Johnson poked a finger into the Judge's chest. "Woodrow Bean," he said, "I'm gonna give you a little three-minute lesson in integrity. And then I'm gonna *ruin* you!"

The Senator lectured Bean for approximately three minutes on the virtues of loyalty, courage, dealing honorably, and of being a true friend to Lyndon Johnson. Whereupon he *reconvened* the credentials committee after it had permanently adjourned, a perfect sign of his iron hold on the convention. One hour later Bean's troops had been shorn of their credentials and replaced by conservative delegates.

Judge Bean joined other dissidents in a fruitless "rump session" at a nearby cowbarn.

It was the memory of his home-state tactics that made me the least joyful "volunteer" at Johnson-for-President headquarters in 1960. His preconvention campaign, as it turned out, was a shambles. Nobody seemed to be in charge of Johnson's headquarters in Washington. The co-chairmen (John Connally, now Governor of Texas, and Oscar Chapman, one-time Interior Secretary under Harry S. Truman and now a sugar lobbyist) were theoretically in charge. Perhaps they occupied themselves diligently elsewhere, but they were seldom seen in headquarters. In their absence nobody assumed command. Volunteers milled about without purpose or assignment. A half-dozen of us who had practiced the craft of politics for years sat idly by while "policy decisions" were made—or pretended to be made—by a handful of old biddies I knew largely from seeing their pictures on the society page.

Once I tried to get some direction from the man said to be nominally in charge: Marvin Watson, then a Texas steel executive on loan to Johnson and now a top White House aide. Watson cheerfully confessed that he hadn't much notion of what we might do to help. Then he continued dictating a letter to some agitated Dixie mystic who had written in about "the nigger problem." Watson solemnly explained that Lyndon B. Johnson's "roots are in the South and his heart is with the South." He mentioned the Senator's heroic old Confederate soldier granddaddy.

Eventually, about all I found to do was dictate letters of the same type. Almost all of Johnson's mail came from the South or the flatlands Midwest. Much was written on lined tablet paper or in a palsied hand. Many letters contained Doomsday tracts of the type handed out on street corners by trembling, popeyed prophets. Others were directed against John F. Kennedy as "the Pope's candidate," or railed against plots by the UN to take over the Pentagon, or spoke of Alaskan concentration camps being prepared for the enemies of Hubert Humphrey. Obviously, there was not a delegate vote in a carload of such correspondents. Just as obviously, LBJ was at that stage the candidate of Tory Democrats of the world.

Johnson's advisers mistakenly assumed that tactics successful in Texas would prove workable nationally. In Texas you cuddled up to the Establishment by making alliances of convenience. You used your Congressional influences where they best served, by manipulating young legislators eager for seats in close proximity to the Congressional leaders, or by logrolling with cynical, horse-trading old pro pols. Thus did Johnson partisans set out to form a coalition of Dixiecrats, aging New Dealers whose visions had dimmed even as their paunches had increased, and Congressmen or Senators thought to be susceptible to suggestion because of the vast influence of Johnson and Rayburn.

I suggested to Walter Jenkins that somebody needed to take the campaign firmly in hand. Jenkins listened a bit impatiently to my complaints. Perhaps it is well my advice was offered free, for he seemed not to set a high value on its worth. "The Senator's got a world of faith in John Connally," he said. Then he pointedly added, "I have, too." He blandly said that Johnson would capture all the Southern states, that old New Deal cronies would deliver "a lot of votes in the North and East not apparent on the surface," and that endorsements had been lined up from Congressional powers "all across the nation." (Asked for examples, Jenkins named Representative Ralph Rivers of Alaska and Senator Thomas Dodd of Connecticut.) He said Johnson would "naturally appeal" in Western states such as "New Mexico, Arizona, and Wyoming." He even claimed certain influences for Senator Johnson in California, adding that "the Senator worked out there as a young man for a couple of years—running an elevator in an office building." Thereafter, I privately thought of Johnson's campaign headquarters as "Disneyland East."

Typical of these elusive "supporters" was Senator Gale McGee of Wyoming. In May of 1960, with the national convention about two months away, Jenkins asked me to accompany a Texas Congressman, another from Alaska, and a former Congressional delegate from Hawaii, into Wyoming. Our assignment was to see to it that the state Democratic convention adopt a motion binding delegates to the national convention under a unit rule—meaning that all delegates, regardless of their personal preferences, would be under instruction at the national convention to vote for the candidate earlier endorsed at the state level. Walter Jenkins was certain that in Wyoming that man would be Johnson.

"Go see Gale McGee," Jenkins ordered. "He'll cooperate one hundred per cent." He exhibited the latest issue of *Time* quoting Senator McGee on Senator Johnson: "He'd make a hell of a Presi-

dent."* When I saw him Senator McGee chatted pleasantly with me, praised Johnson, and gave the name of his local campaign manager in Casper who "will give you anything we've got."

In Casper, I asked Senator McGee's man what we might do toward locking up Wyoming's delegates under the unit rule. He was abashed; why, he'd been instructed to be strictly impartial; he couldn't take sides because Senator McGee was adopting a "hands-off" policy. I told him this was news to me and no doubt would be news to Senator Johnson.

After two days of politicking in Wyoming, it was apparent that Washington had misjudged the situation. Almost everyone favored Kennedy, including State Chairman Teno Roncalio, who would control the delegation's fifteen votes. In these circumstances the unit rule could be disastrous to Johnson's hopes.

When we conveyed this news to Jenkins, he suggested that we should reverse ourselves. Rather then seeking to "solidify and harmonize" delegates under the unit rule, we should fight to "preserve the independence of the individual delegate." In that way we might salvage anywhere from four to seven of the fifteen Wyoming votes. Jenkins was especially shocked when he learned that if Senator McGee favored Johnson, he had managed to keep it a secret from everyone in Wyoming—including his campaign manager. Later, after he counseled with Senator McGee, Jenkins called us to say there was no worry on *that* score. McGee would fly in to Wyoming to help us fight against the unit rule.

Senator McGee flew in, all right. But if he did any fighting for us he kept that a secret, too. He also kept a protective cordon of aides and friends about him and, when finally cornered as he left a downtown restaurant, he said smoothly that all the delegates were his friends, that his friends were split up among the numerous good men seeking the nomination, and that he just couldn't find it in his heart to disappoint any of his friends. So he would stay "neutral."

In the end, only the efforts of Governor Joe Hickey kept the Wyoming convention from going for Kennedy under the unit rule. Hickey, we tardily discovered, favored LBJ for the nomination. So we escaped from Wyoming with five firm Johnson votes, two more "possibles," and our scalps.

The last act in this melodrama came two months later on the floor

* Which prognosis many of us would not now quarrel with, and you can take that any way you choose.

of the Los Angeles convention. With John F. Kennedy only eleven votes short of the nomination, Ted Kennedy approached the Wyoming delegation, where his brother was known to have eight and a half solid votes, Johnson had six, and one-half vote remained loyal to Adlai' Stevenson. Suddenly one of Wyoming's leaders broke away from a frantic huddle with Ted Kennedy, hopped on a chair and held up four fingers to the delegates. "Give me four votes!" he begged. "We can put him over the top! *Please* give me four votes!" Hastily the Wyoming delegates decided to write themselves a footnote to history. Chairman Roncalio proudly spoke of honor and glory as Wyoming cast all fifteen of its votes for John F. Kennedy.

In the roar greeting the announcement, I kept my eyes on the man who had begged for four votes. He was jumping up and down, slapping a beaming Ted Kennedy on the back, apparently beside himself with joy. I recognized him as our old friend Senator Gale McGee.

O\nce the Kennedy-Johnson ticket had been nominated, their pre-convention staffs joined for the battle against Nixon and Lodge. With the Kennedy forces in charge of the campaigning, conditions were much improved. Any campaign knows errors that could be authored only by green gremlins. A few boners cropped up after the Kennedy-Johnson fusion of staffs. None, however, was as glaring as those oc-curring among LBJ's preconvention forces. If you had a suggestion, you'd get a full hearing. Nobody attempted to sweep bad news under the rug. We were better organized and more professional.

One of the first stops was scheduled for El Paso, Texas—my home territory. I was sent ahead to assist in local tub-thumpings and physical preparations. Johnson reminded Texas Congressmen that the six-city tour of Texas would be Kennedy's first real exposure in our state. "I've gotta carry Jack Kennedy on my back in Texas," he said. "I don't want anything going wrong down there." One of the Con-gressmen remarked that Johnson appeared more "down-in-the-mouth" than he had ever seen him. Official Washington wondered how LBJ would accommodate his bombastic personality to standing in young Jack Kennedy's shadow. GOP partisans taunted Johnson by parodying his campaign slogan: "Half the way with LBJ."

On the night of Sunday, September 10th, Johnson flew in from an engagement in Detroit. The crowd at El Paso International Airport would have warmed any advance man's heart. We had 20,000 cheering and clacking on cue when LBJ's plane touched down. He was supposedly only twenty minutes ahead of the Kennedy plane, which was flying in from California. Along with my Congressman, local officials, and Speaker Rayburn (who had arrived in El Paso a few hours earlier), I lined up at the foot of the ramp for the official greeting. Johnson was obviously delighted with the enthusiastic crowd. He called to old friends while posing on the ramp, and cracked good-natured jokes to the photographers. Before he could step down to the speaking platform, someone called that Kennedy wanted the Senator on the airplane radio. Johnson disappeared inside. Twenty minutes later he had not returned. I was sent to see what had gone wrong.

Johnson was making it very clear. Kennedy had left California late and would be another hour in arriving. Meanwhile, he suggested that Johnson remain aboard his own plane. Johnson was in an uproar. In poolroom language he fumed because Kennedy was late, because he had been quarantined in his own aircraft, and he predicted that "the damn crowd will be gone when he gets here." Congressman Homer Thornberry and others tried in vain to soothe him. I told Lloyd Hand, a Johnson aide, that local officials were also fearful of losing the crowd unless we got the Vice-Presidential nominee on the platform. Somebody, I suggested, should pass this word. Hand suggested that I pass it. Foolishly, I did. Johnson poked a finger at me in a quick, stabbing motion and barked, "You get outta here!" As I retreated he demanded that the door be closed after me.

Five minutes later the door opened and Johnson led his entourage out. Though he acknowledged cheers with a wave of his hat, his smile seemed strained. Someone had prevailed on Johnson to call Kennedy's plane, explain the situation, and request permission to get out. Permission was granted. Having to *ask,* however, had not noticeably improved Senator Johnson's personality. He fidgeted on the platform while a dozen Congressmen and state officials made war-whooping partisan speeches. When Senator Kennedy arrived he spoke briefly, inviting the crowd to his speech the following morning in El Paso Plaza. Though Johnson's introduction of Kennedy was warmly partisan, he thereafter sat glumly on the platform, apparently in a thoughtful study of his shoes. Leaving the airport Johnson was further unsettled when the crowd spilled from behind restraining barriers, surged against the nominees as they made for waiting automobiles, and almost swept Mrs. Johnson off her feet. She clutched at her husband and said something, her face white. I heard Johnson snap, "For God's sakes, clear a path! Somebody's gonna get killed."

The Hotel Cortez was so crowded with cheering hordes we could hardly force our way into the elevators. I was pushed into an elevator and wedged between Kennedy and County Judge Woodrow Bean. Bean was babbling about the moment being "the greatest in Texas history" while JFK silently smiled and nodded.

The floor where Kennedy and Johnson had been booked proved to be a madhouse. Much of the crowd had eluded special policemen stationed on the stairs. Seeing the confusion Kennedy said quickly to the elevator operator, "Close the door." This done he ordered, "Stay here until they're dispersed." Somebody handed Kennedy an orange. He began to peel and eat it, cupping the peelings in his hand until I relieved him of them. When no one was looking I slipped them into Judge Bean's coat pocket.

Unfortunately, Johnson's elevator operator had dumped him into the milling crowd in the hall and he took another buffeting. By the time we arrived in Kennedy's "Presidential Suite," Senator Johnson was waiting there in a new rage. "Goddammit," he yelled to Lloyd Hand, "where's Speaker Rayburn?" Hand said that "he was in the hall a couple of minutes ago." LBJ said, "I don't give a damn where he was a couple of minutes ago! I asked you where he is *now!*"

Hand disappeared to hunt the Speaker. Kennedy sat on a couch to eat his orange. My Congressman sat down by him. While they talked, I approached to take pictures to be used in the campaign. Kennedy quickly hid the orange behind his back, straightened his posture and his tie, and gave my Congressman his full attention. After I'd finished taking pictures he resumed eating the orange.

A Kennedy staffer began clearing the room, now overflowing with local officials and unknown gawkers. He was pushing me out also (the camera leading him to think I was a newspaper photographer) until Kennedy called, "No, he's with us." I then asked Senator Kennedy to pose with my Congressman, Senator Johnson, and Speaker Rayburn. Kennedy nodded, and called across the room now free of hangers-on: "Lyndon!"

Johnson was in Sam Rayburn's face, crying out some terrible woe and emphatically poking the Speaker's chest with that stabbing forefinger. The Speaker looked tired and faintly agonized.

Kennedy called again: "Senator Johnson!" Still no answer. Lloyd

Hand plucked furtively at Senator Johnson's sleeve. LBJ whirled on him: "Can't you see I'm talkin' with the Speaker, goddammit?"

"We need you for a picture," Senator Kennedy called.

Johnson snorted a pithy expletive.

Kennedy grinned. He said, "Settle down, Lyndon. It's a long time until November."

I saw Lyndon B. Johnson very infrequently during those years he was immersed in the sticky bogs of the Vice-Presidency. The world now knows what many of us knew at the time—that those were restive, unhappy years for him and that he accommodated his personality to his secondary role at a terrible inner cost. Photographs of the period show LBJ standing very much in the background, wearing an expression about halfway between that of a sad-eyed bloodhound and an early Christian martyr being readied for the lions. Except for attending a Texas State Society breakfast at which Johnson spoke, and accompanying a visiting lawyer-friend to a five-minute visit with the Vice-President in his office, and speaking on the telephone with him two or three times, I recall no other personal contact with him in that era. Working on Capitol Hill, however, made me very much aware of a power struggle in which Lyndon Johnson was involved behind the scenes. The struggle was an open secret among Texans in Washington.

From the first, Lyndon Johnson felt ill-suited to the passive role of the Vice-Presidency. Soon he was fretting to friends that he had little of substance to do, that the White House "palace guard" treated him like a stepchild, and he was hurt when a story circulated that President Kennedy, relaxing with his Irish Mafia henchmen in the White House one evening, cast a mischievous eye on the artifacts of power surrounding him and facetiously asked, "Whatever happened to Lyndon Johnson?" Ultimately, LBJ told favored Texas Congressmen that "Bobby Kennedy's out to knock me off the national ticket." Johnson rued the day he'd told a crony, who had advised him against getting trapped in the powerless vacuum of the Vice-Presidency, "Listen, power is where power goes." More than once he muttered that former Vice-President John Nance Garner had been right in his blunt appraisal of the office: "It's not worth a pitcher of warm spit."

Soon Johnson became convinced that his old rival for political control of Texas, Senator Ralph Yarborough, had "thrown in with Bobby's crowd." The Vice-President imagined the strategy of the alleged alliance thus: Senator Yarborough and his "Red Hots" would try to undermine LBJ of his Texas power base by grabbing control of the Texas Democratic Party machinery while he was trapped in a national office. In turn, Bobby Kennedy would use the erosion of Johnson's power base to make the point with his brother that LBJ's political influence was no longer great enough to justify his presence on the national ticket.

Whether because he feared such a coup in advance, whether by luck, or whether by instinct, Lyndon Johnson had feathered his political nest against just such a possibility. He had persuaded John F. Kennedy to agree that (as a condition for Johnson's presence on the national ticket in 1960) he, Johnson, would as Vice-President be permitted to make half of Texas' political appointments—and exercise veto power over Senator Yarborough's half. Such arbitrary powers had never before been granted a Vice-President—or even asked by one. With the benefit of hindsight, we now know that President Kennedy made a mistake in granting the request. For, predictably, the concession to LBJ actually led to a renewal of the old Johnson-Yarborough feud. Senator Yarborough was understandably incensed when the private agreement was tardily relayed to him. He felt that he had been robbed of his traditional rights as senior Senator of his state, and that President Kennedy had crossed into constitutional never-never land in interfering with the prerogatives of a member of the legislative branch. Further, the Senator was humiliated. "Why," he angrily told an associate, "the way they've ganged up on me I can't go to the bathroom unless Lyndon Johnson feels like taking a pee."

Over the troubled months of the Johnson Vice-Presidency this old feud ripened. Governor John Connally, long a confidant and chum of LBJ, increasingly criticized Senator Yarborough in the Texas press. The Senator returned barb for barb. Convinced that Connally was acting at Johnson's suggestion (and, indeed, that the Governor was trying to read him out of the Texas Democratic Party so that LBJ could retain control), Senator Yarborough struck back at the source of his torment. On a weekend trip to Texas, Yarborough made an angry speech against a certain "power-mad politician" in Washington —under the circumstances as obvious a reference to LBJ as if the Senator had added "who grew up in Johnson City."

Meanwhile, back on Capitol Hill, the Vice-President attempted to lure Congressman Jim Wright of Fort Worth into the Democratic primary as an opponent for Senator Yarborough. Wright, a middle-roader with friends in both the Johnson and Yarborough camps, was reluctant to make the race. Johnson pressed an ardent courtship. Despite the fact that President Kennedy reportedly ordered LBJ to back off, the Vice-President continued covertly to encourage Congressman Wright. About one month before the tragedy in Dallas, LBJ spent an entire Saturday morning walking with Wright in the garden of the home he had bought from Perle Mesta and offering reasons why the Congressman should oppose Senator Yarborough.

This bitter family fuss among Texas Democrats has been denied as the motivating factor prompting President Kennedy's last trip by almost all of the participants involved. In the wake of the tragedy, one can easily understand why that should be so. One may even know compassion for the men who feel compelled to make such declarations. One cannot, however, wholly agree. While JFK was interested in a fund-raising political tour of the state, at least five hundred people personally *know* that John F. Kennedy went to Texas largely for the purpose of showing the public a unity among Texas Democrats that simply did not exist.

Following his elevation to the Presidency, Lyndon B. Johnson reversed his field on the question of Wright's running against Senator Yarborough. "It's too late," Bill Moyers relayed. Determined to mend the feud with Yarborough, President Johnson invited the Senator to well-publicized swims in the White House pool and otherwise went out of his way to shower attention upon his old rival—all a part, of course, of Johnson's admirable efforts to bind the nation's post-assassination wounds. Some politicians could not see the forest for the trees, however. Congressman Joe Kilgore, long a Johnson friend and a conservative member of the Texas power structure, announced against Senator Yarborough despite LBJ's advice to the contrary. Suddenly, he found that his expected money sources (oilmen, financiers, the Big Business community) had dried up as potential wellsprings of campaign revenue. Investigation led him to believe that Lyndon Johnson had passed word that he did not approve of Kilgore's candidacy. Kilgore ran to an old ex-college chum for help—apparently a wise choice, since his old chum was Governor John Connally. The Governor, still recuperating from wounds suffered in the assassination (and no doubt harboring emotional scars in the moment) reacted with anger. He telephoned Washington to demand that Lyndon Johnson reverse his decision to bar the Kilgore candidacy.

"No, John," the President said. "I need at least one Texas Senator who'll back my program. John Tower won't do it—he's a damn Republican. And Joe Kilgore wouldn't support me more than 10 per cent of the time."

Governor Connally angrily played what he thought was his trump-card. "What"—he asked his old friend and former employer—"if *I* resigned as Governor to run against Senator Yarborough? What would you do then?"

"Well, John," the President drawled, "I guess in that case I'd have to follow my established policy of going along with the incumbent."

Faced with this threat, Governor Connally drew in his horns—and Congressman Kilgore withdrew from the Senatorial race. At long last, Lyndon B. Johnson had cast his lot with the progressive forces of Texas. I was so thrilled at my hero's sudden recovery of his old glitter and shine that it was months before I thought to analyze his motives.

Unless slavery comes back, I left Capitol Hill for good in May of 1964. On January 20, 1965, when LBJ rolled up to the U.S. Capitol Building to take the oath as President in his own right, I was there as a special reporter for CBS radio. Bands played "Hail to the Chief" and "Happy Days Are Here Again" while Secret Service men nervously eyed the surging revelers.

The President's shiny black limousine stopped within a dozen feet of where I stood at curb-side, chatting with a Secret Service agent. Lyndon B. Johnson hopped out, grinning, to wring the hands of official welcomers. Mrs. Johnson was radiant and sparkling beside him. As the President turned away from the official delegation the last of his smile faded away like an old soldier—and we stood face-to-face. No more than five feet separated us.

"Hello, Mr. President," I said. "Congratulations." I meant, of course, to say more. I meant to say that I would appreciate a quote for CBS radio, and that I was parochially proud of him, and maybe even that I forgave him for several old fits of temper from the past. Perhaps I wanted to tell him all that and a little bit more—sic the Russians or something, I don't know. It's just as well that I didn't. Though the President appeared to be looking directly at me, he gave no sign of having heard what I had said. Indeed, he did not in any visible manner verify the suspicion of my physical presence—merely stared at some ghostly apparition, perhaps, or glimpsed again for one fleeting moment some old and private vision. Without a word or a flicker he turned and walked away.

My hero, washed in cheers, marched up the steps toward his special destiny while the music throbbed, and while I thought of a barefoot boy standing by a mailbox and of a young Congressman who had come out of the Texas hills in 1937—and of how far they both were from home.

CHAPTER 4

Waltz Me
Around Again, Sugar ...

Periodically somebody stands up in the back row to bawl how boxing is the only "sport" where the sole objective is to render the other fellow senseless and how, therefore, we should beat our boxing gloves into potholders and fight no more.

Intellectually, I'll go along with banning boxing right down to my last volume of e. e. cummings. Emotionally, however, I am much against the proposition. I happen to dig boxing, that's all, and if this puts me in the same class with Norman Mailer—well, somebody was bound to suggest the comparison sooner or later.

Among the heroes who stood tall in my youth was one Lew Jenkins. Lew lived at Sweetwater, down the road a piece from my own native Texas diggings. For years he was just another ham-and-egg club fighter who would take you on in the rings of Houston, Gulfport or New Orleans for whatever the promoter could come up with in the way of a purse. Or he would take you on for the pure pleasure in it at the country square dances and roadside honky-tonks he frequented. One night in 1940 they transported Lew Jenkins up to New York so that Lightweight Champion Lou Ambers could make a quick appetizer of him before going on a few weeks later to the main course. Somebody forget to tell Jenkins he was merely the hors d'oeuvre. Ambers did not find the Texan succulent. In less than three wild-swinging rounds Lew Jenkins separated the unsuspecting champion from his senses and his title.

You may have guessed that Lew Jenkins was not one of this planet's gentle creatures. He drank whiskey as if Prohibition had wired him it was coming back on the next train. The reckless way he roared around on his motorcycle might have caused the Hell's Angels to shave, find work and join the JayCees. If you thought you could beat Lew Jenkins at *anything* back in those days—dice or brawling or barking at the moon—why, he would give you a chance to put your money where your mouth was.

The sports writers of my youth tagged Lew Jenkins "The Sweet Swatter from Sweetwater," often hinting that he was about two parts Paul Bunyan and one part God. Had I disagreed at all it would have been a matter of merely reversing the ratio. Alas, Lew's salad days soon turned to clabber. Later on, after he'd gained a different sort of respect as a Philadelphia policeman and a career Army man, Jenkins would admit that he often went into the ring so full of strong ale he might not have been able to hit Man Mountain Dean in the trunks with a matador's weighted cape. It showed: at one stretch the Sweet Swatter lost nine straight. (They say a barroom heavyweight once sneered to Jenkins during this reverse streak, "You ain't so mother-loving much. I seen you fight five times and ain't seen you win one yet." Lew never was much of a hand for debate, but this time he made what was for him an uncommonly long speech. "Well," he said, "you about to see me win one now." Then with one jaw-shattering blow he showed the fellow a winner.) Even when he was losing I was so convinced of my hero's indestructible qualities that one of my first compositions, written at about age eleven, theorized that Lew Jenkins could have licked Joe Louis in a fair fight.

The one drawback to my theory, however, was that Joe Louis did not engage in fair fights. This was Gospel known to everybody in Eastland County, Texas, if not in Las Vegas or Jacob's Beach. The Southern gentry of my youth had scientific proof-positive that a white man could whip a nigger in a fair fight. We were born with this knowledge as a gift of God, never-you-mind Jack Johnson. *Ergo,* there had to be dirty work at the crossroads. Barbershop sages were forever pointing out that a given referee worked a high percentage of Louis's fights. This clearly implied that Joe Louis needed special help in the ring. Since he was knocking everybody cockeyed, I don't know how any referee could have helped Louis short of shooting his opponents in cold blood when they came to center ring for pre-fight instructions. This bit of logic did not occur to me for several years, however, and possibly has not occurred to the barbershop sages or their heirs to this minute.

Among those supremely convinced that Louis had special dispensation from the referee or maybe the Pope and certainly from the omnipotent "They," was my father. "They don't want a white man to whip 'im," I heard him say at least a hundred times. "They got it fixed so no white man *can.*" I considered the overwhelming evidence and agreed: Louis kept winning, didn't he?

We faithfully walked to the neighboring farm of Uncle Tal Horn, who tilled the soil a little, fished the creek a lot, and played the fiddle more, to hear each blow-by-blow radio account of what we hoped would be the black man's comeuppance at long last. We knew as surely as if we had been right there in the $50 ringside seats that Tommy Farr got robbed of the decision after lasting fifteen rounds. We rejoiced when Two-Ton Tony Galento put the champion on the canvas, shaking our heads at the incredible injustice of it all when the referee stopped the fight in the fourth round simply because Galento might have otherwise bled to death. When Bob Pastor went down in the eleventh round, something in the air convinced us that the referee had tripped him. We figured Johnny Paychek had been given the exact amount of dope that would make him faint in the second round, and we guessed that the likes of Abe Simon, Buddy Baer and Tony Musto had variously been hypnotized, splashed in the eyes with ammonia, or hit with a horseshoed glove.

The second Louis-Schmeling fight was the most frustrating of all. We knew that President Roosevelt had publicly wished Joe Louis the winner over Nazi Germany's Herr Max in a fight fraught with international complexities beyond Eastland County comprehension. We were, man and boy, dyed-in-the-wool Rooseveltites. We could not, therefore, cheer for Hitler's man against FDR's—but neither could we bring ourselves to root for "the nigger." When Joe Louis wrecked Schmeling in a shade over two minutes of the first round, my father breathed a sigh of relief merely because the vexation was, at long last, done. (I do believe he had seriously considered turning Republican in the tub-thumping period preceding the fight, solely on the basis of FDR's endorsement of an inferior creature. Probably only the memory of Hoover's Depression, and an old promise to God, deterred him. Dad had strayed from the Democratic fold in 1928 because he suspected Al Smith of chumming with the Pope. Later on, he decided that God was a registered Democrat and had sent the Depression to punish party-bolters. The alternative logic never occurred to him: that maybe God was Catholic.)

On a night in 1941 it appeared that at long last we had Joe Louis beat—crooked referees, ammonia, horseshoed gloves and all. Billy Conn, the handsome Irishman from Pittsburg, stirred our pure Aryan blood. Jabbing, hooking, dancing, Conn built a commanding lead. In the twelfth round, brash Billy had the temerity to slug it out with the best puncher going. Amazingly, he drove Louis into the ropes. Challenger Conn danced to his corner at the end of that memorable round, waving to the crowd and strutting like it was Saint Patrick's Day in Dublin. The radio announcer told us how confused and disoriented the champion appeared. "Boys," Uncle Tal said, "the jig is up!" We roared like it was funnier than anything that had ever been said on "Information Please."

Then, quickly, in the thirteenth round, Joe Louis set Eastland County race relations back a little more by dispatching Irish Billy Conn to where the birdies chirp. We were first stunned and then outraged. Dammit, *They* had done it again! Uncle Tal shook his head sadly and said it beat all he'd seen and some he'd shot at. "Shoulda knew it," my father said. "They don't intend to let a white man whip 'im."

The two men spoke their morose good-byes. We started the dark walk to our farmhouse a half mile away. Halfway there I ventured a heretic's thought: "Daddy, how could They have helped Ole Joe Louis win?"

My father would have been no more surprised had I contended the earth was round. "Why," he said, "They just *did,* that's all. Didn't you hear it?" I said I didn't see how They could do it unless Billy Conn had helped Them do it, and I didn't think he would do that. My father's angry glare came to me through the dark as we picked our way through the cow pasture, dodging scrub oaks and tangles of underbrush. I'm sure the menace in his voice wasn't all imagined when he said, "Whatta you mean, boy?"

I wasn't exactly sure, though I tried to say. "Well, if Billy Conn wanted to win and he had Ole Joe Louis staggering around like the radio claimed he did, then how come They could fix it to where Joe Louis could go out there in the next round and knock his block off?"

"Godamighty," my father said, impatiently. *"I* wasn't there. How do I know *how* They done it?"

We negotiated an unsteady fifty yards. My father steered Mother past unseen menaces by holding her elbow while I swung onto the overall straps crossing in the middle of his back. Dad muttered to my sister Estelle to watch where she was going or she was bound to fall, blundering along in the dark that-a-way. Estelle, who was not the county's leading fight fan, grumbled that if certain people hadn't been in such a blamed hurry to hear that ding-busted ole fight they'd have had gumption enough to bring along a kerosene lantern so a person could see where a person was going. With all the good stories on *daytime* radio—she said—like "Stella Dallas" and "Young Widder Brown" and "When a Girl Marries," we had to stumble around in the dark like a pack of blind fools. Just to hear some ole nigger beat up on a white man up in Detroit or New York or some such silly places where they had a lot of Catholics, dance bands and bank robbers. Mother told her to watch her mouth, young lady, or she would mash it for her once we got enough light.

I stumbled along and belabored the obvious: "If it was a decision, *then* They could have give it to Ole Joe Louis. But it didn't happen that way. He knocked Billy Conn's *block* off."

"I reckon I know what he done to Billy Conn," my father said, stiffly.

"Well, then," I pressed, "don't you reckon that maybe Joe Louis just . . . well, knocked his block off *without* Them helping?"

"Boy," my father said, "what they been teachin' you at school?"

We lurched on through the black void that hid my secret shame: I had become, on the spot, a Joe Louis fan.

Once the racial barrier came down, Sugar Ray Robinson became one of my idols. When the Sugar Man was at his sweetest I knew him only through radio, sports pages, TV, and the accepted legend that he was "the best fighter pound for pound" in the world. Not until the terminal stages of his career, when he was but a travesty of himself, would I see Sugar Ray Robinson in the flesh.

On a June morning some three years ago I read in the Washington *Post* that Robinson would soon be in town to fight somebody named Young Joe Walcott. More, he would go on public exhibition in a training session before the fight. I was just then beginning to sell an occasional story to national magazines. No assignment was immediately in sight, however, though my next child-support payment loomed immediately ahead. Sugar Ray Robinson, I sensed without any special talent for sorcery, was on his last legs. Why not go down in history as the chronicler of the last days of this man who had 199 official fights—and, by his own estimates, probably 200 more bootleg ones?

I had no definite scheme when I approached the Jewish Community Center in Washington where Robinson was to stage what had been advertised as a public workout. Indeed, I had no way of knowing whether the ex-champion would even appear: over the years he had pulled out of a dozen big fights at the eleventh hour if mayhem happened not to be on his mind at the moment, and once he turned up three days late for a network television show.

To the little ole lady on the front desk, who was turning everybody back because the workout really was only for sports writers and photographers, I claimed in a moment of inspiration to be a staff writer for *Sports Illustrated*. Credentials were demanded. Giving the nice ole lady a big smile and a quick flash of my Gulf Oil travel card, I passed through. Though I had no more connection with *Sports Illustrated* than I did with the Third Reich, this phony-baloney yarn propelled me past a succession of guardian angels until I stood face-to-face in the Presence. For the next three or four days I chummed around with Sugar Ray, his manager, George Gainford, and his wife-to-be, Millie Bruce, until you might have thought we had gone to school together.

The longer I hung around, however, the less solicitous Sugar Ray became. Perhaps my hominy-grits accent didn't help. Maybe he became suspicious when he asked if I knew this New York news-paperman, or that Chicago one, or another boxing writer, and I turned out not to know anybody. Or maybe Robinson had simply been around long enough to know that a national publication wasn't about to do any upbeat story on his fading career. Fortunately, for me at least, love had blinded Millie Bruce. She was as enthusiastic about the Sugar Man's career as if he had just won his first Golden Gloves title and his future was not behind him. What's more, she wanted the world told about her man. I shamelessly exploited the lady's good intentions by putting her in touch with some of her old friends on Capitol Hill, whom I happened to know casually, and by running all her small errands for Cokes, snacks or newspapers. (In defense of this deceit I remind you of the law with respect to child-support payments: you don't pay, the kids go hungry and you go to jail.) Consequently, the lovely Miss Bruce saw to it that I had an easy access to all story sources, and, more importantly, that Sugar Ray didn't follow what I suspected was his natural inclination to bash me in the whiskers.

By the time I had finished my story (less than a week from the time I'd bluffed my way into the inner circle), I had come to believe my own propaganda. Only when it was time to mail my epic did I suddenly realize that neither *Sports Illustrated* nor *Good House-*

keeping had assigned me to the story. Before panic could set in I fired the story to the home of Bud Shrake, an old friend from Texas who really was an *S.I.* staff writer, asking that he pass it on to his superiors. Two weeks later I had not heard a mumbling word.

I telephoned Shrake's New York apartment. His house guest, author Bill Brammer, said that Shrake had been in Europe for two weeks—and would not return for at least ten days more. Yes, my piece had arrived; he had stacked it, unopened, along with Shrake's unpaid bills and what he suspected to be several mash notes from a Hungarian lady shot-putter who had become so enamored of Shrake at the Olympic Games she thereafter insisted on competing in high heels. I conned Brammer into cabbing the piece down to the *Sports Illustrated* offices at Rockefeller Center. Meanwhile, Shrake returned early from Europe and lobbied for my prose.

I had been in New York for three or four days, pounding on editorial doors in vain search of writing assignments, when my wife convinced me that I should telephone to get a verdict on the Robinson piece. I fought her suggestion, largely because the thought of a new rejection might throw my id forever out of joint. A nagging wife can move mountains, however. I asked only for "the boxing editor," not being any better equipped with knowledge about how things literary were handled. Soon a well-modulated voice said, "Mr. Cave's office." As soon as I could think of my name I told the lady what it was.

"Oh, Mr. King! Mr. Cave has been trying to reach you in Washington for three days! Hold on!"

Well, I thought, *the caper's over. They've found out I posed falsely as a* Sports Illustrated *staff writer.* I wondered if the criminal penalty might be about the same as for posing as an FBI agent.

Ray Cave did not eat me alive. He seemed, in fact, a nice man. Almost immediately he asked if I would take $1,000 for my article on Sugar Ray Robinson. I bit blood out of my tongue to keep from admitting that I would have accepted a dollar twenty-five. (All this was before I signed with an agent, and grew wise. I now know the Nice Man paid me about half the going rate.) Let those who cherish trivia record that the Sugar Ray article came out as my first magazine cover story on September 6, 1965. It caught me up in child-support payments, and, equally important, preserved what's left of my tattered integrity by turning all my deceptive lies into premature truths.

WALTZ ME AROUND AGAIN, SUGAR . . .

Millie Bruce perched on a high stool munching cheese crackers and sipping a soft drink, maybe ignoring and maybe savoring the smell of liniment and sweat that pervaded the undersized gym of Washington's Jewish Community Center. She said, "I die inside when he fights. It's hard to see a person you love in that ring. He's a wonderful fighter, a wonderful human being. I've never known a man like him. He's something else."

"He" is Sugar Ray Robinson—once welterweight king, five times middleweight champion. Robinson is forty-five now, and there were those listening to Miss Bruce who believed that time has passed him by, along with Harold Stassen and shaving mugs. But Robinson was to fight the next night. Why? Was he broke? "Nobody," Robinson had told a reporter, "has ever been champion six times."

Nobody has ever been champion even once by losing back-to-back fights to unranked Stan Harrington and Memo Ayon—a double sin committed by Sugar Ray in the month before this fight. Yet he was preparing to meet another somebody of widespread obscurity, a chap from Bridgeton, N.J. named Young Joe Walcott (but no relation to Jersey Joe), in Washington's raunchy Coliseum. You knew that if he knocked Walcott from here to Casper, Wyo. it would not be big news anywhere except in Casper. You knew, too, that the once-fearsome Robinson had taken to beating fellows named Clarence Riley and Rocky Randell in places like Pittsfield, Mass. and Norfolk, Va., and that in Rome last year he earned no better than a draw pounding the soft underbelly of one Fabio Bettini. But, waiting for her fiancé to work out, Miss Bruce was all dimples and unshakable faith.

"Of course, Ray's in shape!" she gasped to a question, her dark eyes indignant. "He runs every morning in New York. Twice around the reservoir. I know, because I go with him. I don't run, but I go." Miss Bruce, a trim model who looks as though she could run with Sugar, was quiet for a moment, then apologized for their late arrival in Washington. "Ray's mother was operated on. He just wouldn't leave New York until he knew she was all right. She's a strong and wonderful woman. She's got needles and tubes in her neck, but this morning at the hospital she said, 'Don't forget, Mama told you how to win this fight. Jab him. Jab him, and follow through.' "

Upstairs a friendly little lady bustled about the center's main lobby in distress. Forty or fifty curious people milled about in low humor. Some had waited more than two hours for the workout promised by Promoter J. Edward Weaver, more to ballyhoo the fight with Walcott than to tone the ex-champ's muscles.

"Papers say the public invited," intoned a husky man in workman's clothes.

"We don't have any place to put you," the lady said. "Can't you see the newspapers had it all wrong?"

The lady went downstairs to tell Weaver. Weaver, in turn, edged up to George Gainford, Robinson's crusty trainer-manager, who, with proper solemnity, solved the problem: the public would be admitted to an adjacent basketball court for a few minutes of rope-skipping.

Millie Bruce said, "We didn't know this was to be a public workout. In fact, Ray hadn't planned on *any* workout. He ran this morning. You won't believe him! He looks—why, he's much more handsome than his pictures. He looks so young! A man said to him the other day, 'You can't be Ray Robinson!' And Ray said, 'I better be. I've thought I was for forty-five years.' Forty-five and he's still walkin' and wantin'.."

At the moment Sugar Ray was walkin' circles in a dressing room the size of a small closet, wantin' to know when in hell the show got under way. In his good days Ray Robinson invaded Paris with special troops even Hitler hadn't thought to provide for himself: hair stylists, court jesters, manicurists, handgrips, favored cronies, golf pros and secretaries. His temperamental outbursts rivaled Maria Callas', and he was as independent as Charles de Gaulle. This was the Ray Robinson of the near-Kennedy pompadour, the long purple Cadillac and the $50 tips. He was a merry, mercurial king, who could laugh one minute and bless out the faithful Gainford the next. But when the time came and Robinson fought he was a thing of beauty, jabbing, crossing, dancing, a dangerous cobra striking, a mongoose skirting danger until time for the kill.

"He's a kind man," his Miss Bruce was saying. "In Jamaica, the Dominican Republic, Stockholm—he goes to visit hospitals, shut-ins, all kinds of handicapped people. And he asks no credit for it. He does it even when he's not promoting a fight. He tells me, 'Gump, my luck's been good. I got enough to share.' "

The kind man appeared at the door. There was a stir as the invited and uninvited recognized him, the man who had chopped down Steve Belloise, Randy Turpin, Bobo Olsen, Carmen Basilio, Gene Fullmer, Kid Gavilan. Robinson hit them and their eyes crossed.

Robinson drifted into the gym, wrapped in a white terry-cloth robe. He had a bemused grin on his face that said he knew the joke, and the joke was not on him. He did not, you noticed, walk on his heels. "Honey," Miss Bruce called, stretching her hand toward Robinson. But he was gone, carrying his cockeyed smile to the heavy bag a dozen paces to her left. When Robinson shucked the robe with one shrug of his shoulders he revealed a body even a young man would trade a dozen years for. On smooth, brown legs he shuffled in on the bag, his face carefully deadpan. There was a quick flash of fistic history before your eyes: left, left, left, right uppercut, left hook, jab.

"Punch it out to all cameras," Gainford called. "Right into the lens, Ray. That's it, baby. Both hands." Robinson's fleet grin beat his next tattoo of punches by a split second.

Happily, Promoter Weaver said, "Don't he boss that bag?"

"Yeah," said a newsman. "The bag can't punch back."

Gainford was saying, "Over to the light bag, Ray." Millie Bruce smiled. "I want you to see this. He can *really* do this." Sugar Ray really did it, all right. He made the small gym vibrate with rat-a-tats, now a blurred left, now a matching right, now a crescendo of moving fists and now a raised eyebrow at his manager, as if to inquire why all the overtime. Gainford said, "O.K. Let the crowd in. He'll skip rope. Wait a minute. Somebody cut those bandages off his hands."

Softly, Robinson said, *"You* cut 'em, George." Gainford produced a knife, and he cut 'em.

Pushing toward the basketball court, men with overgrown bicepses talked the fight game. One was Holly Mims, a so-so middleweight who still feels he could have been champion, if only he had gotten the breaks. He fought Robinson in 1951, thought he had won (" 'Man,' he say to me after the fight, 'where they been keepin' *you?'* ") and this week he was to be on the same card with Robinson, but not against him. "I could hit him with a right. I could hit him—but I couldn't put him down," Mims said. He yelled something indistinguishable to Gainford, only to be grandly ignored. The fans who had

waited so long now milled in to stand on a balcony looking down on
the court. They were still, serious, staring at the master.

Millie Bruce again was enthusiastic. "Wait till you see that man
skip rope. They asked him to do it on television. Just come on
television and skip rope." She beckoned Robinson over. The ex-
champ was affable, smiling and extremely brief. His quick handshake
and mumbled acknowledgment of the niceties smacked of old rituals.
Though he looked tired, the only mark on him was a healing cut
above the right eye. He seemed shy and withdrawn, but you realized
his was artful shyness. Like a practiced politician, he gave a tidbit
and with it the illusion of feast. The rule book said, "Smile and keep
moving," and Sugar moved quickly to center court, smiling ever so
slightly.

Millie's enthusiasm grew. *"Look* at this. See, music goes with this.
Only they don't have any." Sugar Ray's rope made its own music on
the hardwood floor: tappa, tappa, tappa, tappa. Abruptly, he
stopped: "That's all." He rewarded the silent spectators with a
lackadaisical wave, and for a moment he threatened to smile.

Promoter Weaver frowned his way over to Millie Bruce. "God, he
looks tired."

"Sure, he's tired. He ran this morning. Two times around the
reservoir.

Weaver looked doubtful. A tall man who once boxed lightweight in
the intramural program at West Point, his chest has slipped and his
hair thinned. He asked, "How far is that?"

"A long way," Miss Bruce said vaguely. "You know, Ray's been
up four straight nights because of his mother's operation."

"That mother thing worries me," Weaver said. "That can mess him
up." The promoter tapped his head. "Up here."

"Don't worry about Sugar. He just needs a good night's sleep."

The boxing crowd clustered around Robinson, their professional
eyes inspecting him for flaws. They thrust out hands, still wanting to
shake with the "champ." Robinson endured their advances, then in
response to some private signal he suddenly broke away, jig-danced
over and pecked Millie on the cheek and followed this with a mock
left uppercut to her chin. Robinson was acting. He is not talkative as
he once was, and one gets the feeling around him that he would love
to shuck the burdens of being a celebrity. But he is still not ready for
the last hurrah.

Gainford spoke to the crowd. He said how Sugar Ray appreciated their coming by and would be grateful should they come out to back him Thursday night. Then he told how Ray's ol' mama was bad sick, and how Ray needed rest because he'd kept a faithful four-day vigil at her bedside. Everybody clapped, but Robinson wasn't around to hear. He had vanished to the private world of his dressing room, where no hands awaited the fraternal grip and you did not need to grin, even slightly, unless you felt like it.

George Gainford started in the amateurs with Ray Robinson back when hamburgers cost a nickel and only Wall Street lawyers had heard of Wendell Willkie. He was in his corner twenty-five years ago when Robinson launched his pro career by knocking out Joe Echeverria. This night he sat in his shirtsleeves in his small room at the Mayflower Hotel, mopping his brow and complaining about Washington's awful heat. He said, "I can't tell you one thing about that boy we fight tomorrow. I don't know his record, his manager—I don't even know how many arms he's got."

Can Sugar Ray Robinson win the title a sixth time?

"Feeling he can win is fifty percent of it for a fighter, you know? And Ray's convinced the champ can't beat him."

Maybe so. But the record book says Joey Giardello *has* beaten him.

Gainford nodded. "Sure," he said, "Ray lost to Giardello. But for the first time in his life Ray went in the ring *thinking* he'd lose. And maybe that was my fault. I told him not to take the match. But after it was over Ray said, 'Hey, that guy can't beat me! I go six rounds waiting for him to drop something on me. Time I woke up I could take him outa there, it was too late.'"

If and when the bell tolls again for Sugar Ray, how does he take the champion outa there?

"By wanting to. By thinking he can. By keeping mentally ready and in good physical shape. These fights I'm getting Ray—they help keep him ready."

Of late, it was pointed out, they also help keep him in the losers' column.

George Gainford waved a huge paw, as if to slap down an irritating gnat. "Aw, Ray dropped a couple. That Harrington in Honolulu bangs Ray's head with *his* head in the sixth. Ray's no bleeder, but an artery breaks. Only way I can stop it is by using a solution that— well, one drop in the man's eyes and he's blind. Hell, we don't need to win bad enough to go *blind*. Last four rounds my man sees so much blood he thinks the Red Cross is pumping it. But he goes into the tenth ahead—then the blood got him."

The way Gainford tells it, blood got in the way down in Mexico, too—Mexican blood in the veins of jingoist judges. "Ray beats this Memo Ayon person down in Tijuana like the United States whipped ol' Hitler. Even the Mexican newspapers say we win eight rounds." (The less generous judges said Robinson won only four.) Gainford is trying hard. Uncomfortably, one realizes this is the first time he has heard a person dredge up alibis for Robinson.

Though Giardello expressed doubts about Sugar Ray's worth as a challenger ("he's on a losing streak and is not rated among the contenders"), Gainford, like Robinson, still had hopes on this night. "Figure it out," he said. "Giardello fights anybody else, he's scuffling to pick up thirty, forty thousand dollars. He fights Ray, he's *got* to make a hundred thou—and don't expect to have a tough time of it." (Giardello figured it out a little differently later. He signed to fight Dick Tiger instead.)

Outside, in the muggy afternoon just turning to dusk, a ragged band of conventioneers stood on the sidewalk hoo-hawing. Somewhere inside the hotel Robinson slept. He had spent this day before the fight visiting television stations, hospitals and a children's home. Twice he had called New York to check on his mother. Assured she was doing fine, he had eaten a broiled steak, green salad and iced tea before retiring early. Robinson's telephone calls went to Gainford, a querulous sentry all evening turning away newsmen, strange voices who claimed old ties with Robinson and the frankly curious.

"Naw," he said into the telephone, "no way you can see him tonight. Her, either. Them people's asleep. Ray's tired. Maybe tomorrow. . . ."

He hung up, shaking his head. "I spend half my time on that thing," he said. "But it proves people don't forget what Ray's *been*. They still want to see him, talk to him—just reach out and touch him.

"He's lost some leg—speed—stamina. Even some punch. No use kidding ourselves. He's lost some of all of it. But he won't get hurt in the ring, because I'm pretty choosy about who I put Ray in there with. I match him with what he's equal to today, not what he could have handled a few years ago. This boy Walcott—why, ten years ago the commission wouldn't have permitted the match. Ray would have beat him on his lunch hour." Gainford grinned: "I don't know much about Kid Walcott. But I know he can't hurt Ray Robinson."

Rocky Randell couldn't hurt Ray Robinson either. A few months before, in Norfolk, Randell swooned quickly in Sugar's presence, so fast, in fact, that when Weaver, who made that match, offered to give Randell another shot at Robinson in Washington, D.C., the boxing commission refused to license the bout.

"We figure to fight the champ in September," Gainford went on. "Whether we get him or not—I'm gonna give you a little scoop—this is Ray's last year in the ring. He wins the title, fine—he goes out on top. He loses it, or don't get a shot at it—well, Ray's gonna put a show troupe together and tour the Orient and Europe. Those cats *crazy* about Ray. So, either way, we fight this kid tomorrow and then we tune up maybe three, four more times before Giardello. And that's all, brother. That's all."

The refrain was familiar: just one more, and then one too many and an obscure end. Would Ray Robinson spend his last days grubbing nickels?

"Shoot, man! You better wish you had *some* of what Ray's got. After we fight Basilio in '57 the government holds up $352,140 for back taxes. Two months ago we finally win a court decision. Ray's gonna get a lot of long green back with compounded interest and all that jazz. And he's got show-biz money coming down the road. He's also gonna invest in closed-circuit television fight promotions. Man, that's where the bread is today—capital gains and everything."

Fight day brought a slow, weeping rain. Robinson stayed in bed while Gainford battled with the telephone. One man invited the former champion to visit a nightclub in which he owned, expected to own or only dreamed of owning a minority interest.

"You offering him money?" Gainford asked.

Well, not exactly . . .

"Don't do us no favors," Gainford said, hanging up.

Another man volunteered to permit Robinson to loan him $300 to finance his son's hernia operation. Sugar Ray snored on, blissfully unaware of the twin opportunities.

At 10:40 A.M., barefoot and in a white robe, Robinson sat down to a breakfast of steak, dry toast and hot tea. Millie Bruce, who had lunched the previous day on Capitol Hill with old friend Pegga Hawkins, wife of a California Congressman, gave him a report on her sightseeing expedition. She regretted not having visited John F.

Kennedy's grave on this first Washington trip. Sugar Ray listened, chewing methodically. "We'll be back, Gump," he consoled her.

Finishing breakfast, Robinson thumbed through a deck of cards while giving stock answers to reporters who had come in. How does it feel to be forty-five? "I hadn't thought about it until you asked me." (He had given the same answer a week earlier on TV.) Did he think he still had enough stuff to win the championship? "Yes, I truly do. If I didn't I would quit." Somebody commented on an expensively woven linen coat he had worn the previous day. It was "a little somethin' I had made up on the Riviera." Once, talking of his loss to Ayon in Mexico, he permitted himself an open grin: "In Tijuana you got to read the last rites over 'em to win." Then he went back into his shell. He appeared relieved when time came to excuse himself to dress for the weigh-in.

Shortly before noon three men got out of a taxi and scuttled under the marquee of the Washington Coliseum to avoid the rain. One of them was Young Joe Walcott, who did not carry about him the fine flush of youth. With a ducktail haircut, dark glasses, padded-shoulder sports coat and tight, black pants, Young Joe might have been an aging rock 'n' roll singer. He chewed on a toothpick, turning his lumpy face up to sneak a look at the blue-letter marquee. If he expected to see his name he was disappointed. TONIGHT, it read, giving him no hint of fame, SUGAR RAY ROBINSON. HOLLY MIMS IN CO-FEATURE.

Walcott's advisers, a fat man in a gold coat and a fatter one whose suit looked fresh from an ashcan, trooped into the office to inquire about the weigh-in. A myopic lady in a print dress knew nothing. At the arena's main gate a lone ticket attendant told them to go around to the stage door at the rear of the building. They walked rapidly through the rain, the man in the gold coat holding a protective newspaper over his head. Rain dripped down Young Joe's seamed face, but he did not mind. Just one more indignity to bear in a life of cheeseburgers and long bus rides. After much door-banging a crotchety old man with a red face appeared to disclaim knowledge of any fight, whereupon he slammed the door. The trio made the long trek back to the front of the arena, Young Joe volunteering his only spontaneous remark of the day: "Man, I'm gonna walk *all* my weight off."

This time the entourage was admitted, after more confusion, to a gloomy, battleship-gray room in the depths of the Coliseum. A young, officious man took Walcott's pulse, poked him in the ribs and asked an embarrassing question: "The papers say you have a 6-10-2 record. That right?"

The pugilist looked uncertainly at his two handlers. The gold coat shrugged in the manner of a lawyer whose client is caught with hot goods. With a laconic "uh-huh" Walcott pleaded guilty. He was guided into an adjoining room to be fingerprinted. They are not very trusting in Washington. Half a dozen prelim fighters were going through the same ritual. None of them bothered to look up at Walcott.

Sugar Ray arrived a good half hour late. He walked in easily, wearing dark slacks and a paisley-print sport shirt, his eyes harboring the cloudy look of a man just aroused from deep slumber. Gainford bellied a path through forty-odd gawkers clogging up the narrow hall. Everybody hi-Sugared and howdy-Rayed as Robinson sidestepped an old-fashioned set of scales on rollers, shucked his shirt and dropped onto a straight-back chair.

Young Walcott either fell or was pushed from the fingerprint room. Little rivers of sweat ran down his body, and you wondered if maybe the fingerprint expert had overexercised his thumbs. He seemed uncertain whether he should speak to Robinson or ignore him, as Sugar was ignoring *him.* Young Walcott weighed 156 but looked smaller. When the ex-champ mounted the scales—in shorts, under-shirt and sneakers—there was a moment of consternation. Sugar Ray muttered under his breath, stripped to the skin and still came in ten ounces over the agreed 160-pound limit. More mumbles. Gainford said, "Lemme see, Ray." His thumb performed a certain magic on the scales. "Hunnert and sixty on the nose," he proclaimed. Nobody disputed him.

Standing at ringside in the empty arena, Ed Weaver said, "This is my first promotion here, but I've promoted five cards down in Virginia. Tell you anything you want to know."

All right, what was he guaranteeing Robinson for the fight?

Weaver's eyes flicked around the empty seats. "Around five thousand. If I take in ten I can break even. No way to know on a fight like this. But all I want to do is bring good, clean boxing attractions to Washington. I think the game's worth saving. Good, clean, honest cards will bring the public back in droves."

Why didn't this good, clean, honest card match Holly Mims against Robinson?

"Off the record?" Weaver asked.

No.

Weaver hesitated. "Come on, pal. Don't put me on the spot."

It was suggested that Gainford didn't want Mims for his aging tiger.

"Don't quote *me* saying that," Weaver protested. "All I know is Sugar Ray Robinson has been a real gentleman. He's done everything he said he would do."

Had Gainford picked Young Joe Walcott for Sugar Ray?

"No. I did."

How young was Young Joe?

"Uh—twenty-six, twenty-seven, maybe." A young man assisting Weaver said, "Twenty-nine. He's twenty-nine." The promoter glared at his buddy.

What was Walcott's won-lost record?

Weaver hesitated before he said, "Eight wins, ten losses, one draw." Then he made West Point mathematics suspect for all time, adding, "Walcott's batting .500."

Walcott, he was told, had admitted to a 6–10–2 record and to being thirty. The promoter looked abashed. "Well," he said, "you can't ever tell what one of these young punks will do in that ring. It just takes one punch . . ."

They hadn't been in action two minutes before you knew Walcott did not have the one punch. Sugar Ray could have beaten him in snowshoes.

The surprisingly good crowd—nearly 4,000 paying from $2 to $7 per seat—had rocked the arena when Robinson appeared fifteen minutes late following Mims's easy win over a half-bald Baltimore fireman. Robinson, bobbing and dancing in the white robe with "Sugar Ray" etched on it in apricot hues, ignored the cheers. By contrast, Walcott had paused on the ring apron to stare in disbelief at a tiny knot of fans applauding him. His next act was to misstep into the rosin box, turning it over.

At the bell Walcott seemed confused. Before he could get himself untracked Sugar Ray had hammered several quick lefts on his nose. Robinson rocked Walcott with a right uppercut and a moment later nailed him with a straight right that had Young Joe retreating. Robinson returned to his corner untouched by human hands.

In the second and third rounds Robinson jabbed and followed through, just as his mother had told him to do. The crowd applauded

Robinson's showmanship, and it was easy to feel you were watching the Sugar Ray of old.

Round four brought Walcott a painful lesson in the art of in-fighting. Sugar's hands worked at his opponent's torso and under the chin. At ringside, in a white sequined dress, Millie Bruce came out of her chair, yelling: "Come on, baby. Come on, love." When Robinson paused to pull up his trunks Young Joe thought he saw his chance. He tried a long, looping right and immediately got tangled in his own shoelaces. Exposed, vulnerable, he struggled frantically for balance. Sugar Ray feinted a punch that could have sent everybody home to early supper, but he did not throw it. He dropped his arms, laughed aloud and tugged again at his shorts.

It was more of the same in the fifth. Robinson boxed Walcott off-balance three times and reprieved him three times. Once, when Walcott moved forward, Robinson chortled aloud, embraced him in the middle of the ring, then wheeled and mashed poor Walcott's sore nose with a stinging left.

But maybe Sugar hadn't been all that sweet. The exertion was taking something out of him. Suddenly, between the fifth and sixth rounds, he looked old.

At first the crowd thought he was resting for the final big push. There were cries of "O.K., Ray, now's the time," "Put 'im away, Sugar Boy." But the old combination one-two-three now misfired. So did some long right hands. Punches that earlier rocked against Young Joe's chin now slipped harmlessly over his shoulders. Fanning herself with a copy of the official program, Millie Bruce grimaced.

It was hot under the ring lights. Sugar Ray gasped through the seventh, sweating buckets. Walcott hit him in the face a number of times, his first meaningful blows of the fight. In the eighth he did it again, and now Young Joe was looking tough. Robinson wasn't grinning anymore. There were scattered boos at the bell.

In the ninth Walcott pounded Robinson in the body, and though Sugar had chopped home a few blows of his own they lacked power. When the two pawed and clutched a moment later in the center of the ring a voice from the $2 seats yelled, "Waltz me around again, Sugar," and too many people laughed.

Many in the crowd were already heading for the exits before the end of the tenth, in which nothing happened except that Young Joe sent in a few more futile body blows. At the finish there was a roll of boos. In Robinson's corner, awaiting the decision, Gainford reproachfully eyed the crowd. Sugar Ray, tarnished but the obvious winner, accepted the victory calmly. All three judges favored him heavily. But the cheers were mostly for Walcott as he swaggered from the ring, proud, apparently, that he had not been knocked out.

Sucking a soft-drink bottle in his dressing room, Robinson thanked the writers who came by to see him. The old conceit, the old lip, the old arrogance were there, if his reflexes and the punch were not. No, he hadn't been hurt—but that boy was tough, no doubt about it. No, the heat hadn't bothered him too much. No, he hadn't really been looking for a knockout. He would be sharper for Giardello if he went the distance a few more times. Nobody was counting, but Robinson had gone the distance three of his last four times out.

Gainford was saying, "I tol' Ray after the third it was too hot up there to go for a KO. I tol' him box easy."

Somebody questioned Gainford's logic. How was it better to pant through ten rounds than end it early?

Gainford looked pained. "Aw, man." He walked away.

Promoter Weaver bobbed around, flushed in the face, talking of getting Giardello in the same ring come September. He had made $3,000. No telling what a title fight would do.

Soft-voiced, Robinson chased the dream. "I'd like it here in Washington. Outdoors in that big ball park, maybe. It ain't too cold here in September, is it?"

Gainford was ecstatic over young Herbie Lee, an AAU champion on the card, who had just made his pro debut with a three-knock-down TKO. "He's got good moves. And he's still in high school. The right man handling that boy—shu, he could go all the way! He could be another . . ."

The newsmen rushed off to meet their deadlines. The last curious fans faded away in the halls. Houselights dimmed over the empty arena. Gainford gathered up Robinson's fight paraphernalia, methodically stuffing a small bag.

From the shower, standing under a sting of spray, Sugar Ray called, "Hey, George! What was that cat's name I fought tonight?"

Presumably, Sugar Ray learned "that cat's" name. He should have, at least, for the Washington bout was but one of five matches he fought Walcott at widely separated points—winning them all, of course, because Young Joe couldn't lick a stamp if it cost more than a nickel. Three of these "fights" occurred between the time I wrote the story and its appearance in print some ten or twelve weeks later. After it appeared, the Robinson-Walcott series suddenly got harder to book than the Nasser Sisters in the Catskills. Robinson is an old pro; no doubt he suspected this would be the case. At any rate, he stormily refused to pose for cover pictures for *Sports Illustrated* photographers when he fought his return bout with Stan Harrington in Hawaii. The photographers took one of the ring action for their purpose, however, and there was nothing Robinson could do about that. There was nothing he could do about Harrington, either. Poor Sugar got the be-jesus beat out of him.

Sugar Ray never got another shot at the title, of course. He continued to fight nobodys in Endsville. A few weeks after the Walcott series limped to a halt the ex-champ fought for gas money up in Johnstown, Pennsylvania, where he decisioned one Peter Schmidt, a part-time milkman from Toronto billed as "former lightweight champion of Canada"—an honor about as meaningful as being an ex-notary public. Willie Pep, another ex-champ who once had more class than an unmortgaged Rolls Royce, beat another nonentity that same night in Johnstown. Of all sad words of ring and pen the saddest are these: the doubleheader card lost money.

Robinson's last fight of record was with Joey Archer. At twenty-seven, Archer was certainly old enough to shave but he looked like a kid against Ole Sugar. It wasn't even close, and after he'd mopped the blood up Robinson said he'd learned his lesson for good. He hung up the gloves again. But hold on, there—he was soon back, boxing "exhibitions" in whistle-stop arenas where the lights tempted cat burglars to come out of retirement. His opponents were worn-out old foes Robinson had once fought when all the marbles were at stake and while the world looked on. One of these has-beens was ancient Bobo Olsen, balding and stiff-gaited now, trying another of his own interminable comebacks. I am saddened by the mental picture of those two old ghosts stumbling around the ring and panting like fat twins who had just missed the bus, poking at each other ineffectually while wondering, maybe, where time had flown.

For a while Robinson was a campaign aide to John Lindsay during the mayorality race in New York. You'd get a glimpse of the Sugar Man on TV now and then, walking to work with the mayor, when Lindsay tried to set a cheerful example during the subway strike.

Somebody gave lip service to the idea of Robinson becoming a Big Man in the Lindsay Administration, working on special problems vaguely having to do with physical fitness or race relations or maybe doing some fuzzy something for the poor. Nothing much came of it. When last heard from, Robinson had put a song and dance act together and was working small nightclubs in New Jersey, the critics hinting that he was to be confused with neither Frank Sinatra nor Fred Astaire.

That big wad of dough Robinson was allegedly to receive from the Federal Government as a tax rebate? Well, by the time enough legal mumbo-jumbo had been mumbled to satisfy the law and papers shuffled and interest penalties affixed and various bills and fees paid, Robinson took home a fraction of the booty: around $30,000. That kind of bread never did go far where Sugar Ray Robinson was concerned. It wasn't enough to get back the three apartment buildings he'd once owned in Harlem, or his string of dry-cleaning shops, or the fancy lingerie shop, or the barbershop, or the glittering café with his name spelled out in lights.

I suppose we shouldn't spill too many tears over Robinson's plight. He ran through what he says was three million dollars, cool. He shook hands with de Gaulle and had whole continents crazy about him, and bought fine wine for his share of the swinging chicks. He fed his ego as well as he did his stomach, and there was a time when Sugar Ray wouldn't touch a plank of steak unless he knew it had cost $15 rock bottom. Back there in 1950 he was up against a pretty tough middleweight one night, a muscular fellow who billed himself as George (Sugar) Costner. The referee had hardly given the boys their mid-ring elocution lesson (shake hans now 'n come out fightin' 'n may uh bess man win) until Sugar Ray made sure everybody knew who the best man was. Robinson said, "Listen, Costner, there's only *one* Sugar. And that's me. So let's touch the gloves now, man, because this is your last round." It was. The real Sugar hit the bogus one with a straight right. Costner stopped like he'd seen a snake, got this terribly dumb look on his face and tumbled down in a way that would have been instructional to the walls of Jericho.

Time changed all that. But then time, some other smart man said long before I did, changes everything. Shortly after Rocky Marciano so brutally knocked a paunchy, over-the-hill Joe Louis upside down, in 1951, I visited my father in Texas and mentioned that fight. My father, like Sugar Ray, Joe Louis and even Shirley Temple, had grown older and maybe he had mellowed. "Yeah," he said in his serious monotone. "I sure hated to see that happen. Time was, Ole Joe would of tore him up. Ole Joe was one tough nigger."

It might not have been enough to satisfy Stokely Carmichael, but knowing my old man it was just about his finest hour.

CHAPTER 5

God, Man,
and William F. Buckley

There's not a lot I can add to the following piece about William F. Buckley, Jr., the aging *enfant terrible* of rightward-listing politics in our fiefdom.

I felt such self-satisfaction on completing the work that I entitled it "The Last Word on Buckley," simply because I thought that it was. Willie Morris telephoned from *Harper's* to exercise his editorial prerogative: he wanted to call the piece "God, Man, and William F. Buckley." Willie had the notion that my title was "too full of your own ego." Editors rarely lose arguments whether right or wrong, and Willie Morris did not lose this one.

Throughout my talks with Mr. Buckley I felt that we were in some sort of uneasy competition; that we each wanted the invisible trophy more than either of us would have admitted. Perhaps I was again wrong: maybe the paranoids have been after me so long that I figure everybody is. On the other hand, I admit to a certain zest for competition, and there can be no doubt that Mr. Buckley is no more prone to turn his back on a contest than is the Green Bay football team. Since we represent opposite political dicta as surely as Senator Eastland has differences with the Twentieth Century, it is probably natural that we would not be entirely at ease with one another. We had our moments, but I always harbored this feeling that perhaps I should sit with my back to the wall, and I did note that Mr. Buckley had a tendency to glance over his own shoulder on occasion.

To Bill Buckley's credit, let it be said that he seemed more at ease than I. That is no small victory for him, considering that my hand held the pen. If you are scoring points in the contest, mark one up for his side for that bit of gamesmanship. He is, in every sense of the word, a tough man and I surely would not want to work as a millhand if he owned the mill.

GOD, MAN, AND WILLIAM F. BUCKLEY

He is an advantaged Ivy Leaguer who "would rather be governed by the first 2,000 people in the Boston phone book than by the faculty of Harvard," an international globe-hopper strong for States' Rights, a Hondo 50 hot-rock who plays the clavichord; in one moment a mixer-and-mingler with a Rotary Club grip and in the next a Grand Duke icily looking down his nose to accept the peasant's birthday bows. He is an author who sometimes sides with censors, and a celebrated intellectual who has spoken of "the hoax of academic freedom" —a swinging Old Fogey who has become a legend in his time.

In case you just got off the Greyhound, the William F. Buckley, Jr., herein described is the same one who publishes *National Review*, ran a noisy third for mayor of New York City in 1965 on the Conservative Party ticket, attacked his alma mater in *God and Man at Yale* hardly before the ink dried on his parchment, and who as a six-year-old boy wrote the King of England that England had damn well better pony up her war debts. A devout Catholic, he assayed the encyclical of Pope John XXIII as "a venture in triviality"; a failed politician, he thinks he was "hit by grace when political intelligence was distributed." He is an East Side swell, by way of rural Connecticut, who excites support for his aristocratic polemics even in the *lumpen* wastelands of Queens. He can publicly describe a debate opponent, Gore Vidal, as "a philosophical degenerate" only moments before privately offering to stand him to drinks. His enemies, laid end to end, would reach from here to Southern Purgatory, to which they variously damn him for inciting racial hatred, dividing the Republican party, defaming Democracy, and betraying the John Birch Society.

New York's literati in their posh watering holes often speak of Buckley in terms of "charm," "verve," "style" and "wit"—the same hosannahs they sang in the name of John F. Kennedy. Yet his hard ideological precepts are as far removed from Kennedy's as sourdough biscuits are from caviar.

He would justify U.S. bombing of Red China "on the grounds the good guys of this earth have got to keep the bad guys from getting nuclear bombs." When will the Africans be ready for self-government? "When they stop eating each other." "Segregation is not intrinsically immoral," and the Freedom March on Washington was "a mob deployment." Buckley would abolish the graduated income tax, farm subsidies (but not the oil depletion allowance), unemployment compensation, collective bargaining, most welfare programs, Sin in the aggregate, and, for all I know, Christmas seals. *National Review* ("My number one love") is committed "to standing athwart history yelling 'Stop!' "

One of the reasons why Bill Buckley (consort of the late Senator Joe McCarthy, Goldwater and Young Americans for Freedom, to throw in a little guilt-by-association) is the social darling of so many Establishment liberals belongs to Irving Howe, editor of *Dissent* magazine and author of works bitingly critical of Pop Culture politics. Howe's theory harks back to the 1920's and 30's when every cocktail party had its adopted Parlor Pink as surely as it had flappers, bathtub gin, Sweet Caporals, or a florid Mr. Money Bags or two dedicated to cussing the NRA's Blue Eagle. He sees Buckley as the reigning Red-White-and-Blue Boy of the smart set—something fashionable to have around, like an expensive bauble from Tiffany's, the more useless the better, to give the place a little glitter and shine. Howe has speculated why "this elegant jackanapes took in certain people" thus:

"Perhaps one reason is that we have no tradition in the U.S. of right-wing intellectuals. Think of the archetypal American revolutionary and you summon an image of a stumbling primitive who wants the U.S. to quit the U.N., drop the bomb, bust the unions, clean up the reds, abolish the income tax. But that someone wanting a good many of these same things could also write a paragraph of lucid prose and make a clever wisecrack was not really within the bounds of our experience . . . In the last two decades American intellectuals have tended increasingly to substitute judgements of taste for judgements of belief; they have responded to candidates more and more in terms of personal style, rather than in political content. He [Buckley] could become a fearful, snapping pet, whose neatly-structured sentences gave weary liberals and worn radicals a tremor of *Schadenfreude*—with the tacit assumption that it didn't really matter what he or anyone said, since things would go along on their usual course."

Mr. Howe obviously is shocked that anyone who can tell Renoir from Warhol without eyeglasses, or whose grasp of history goes beyond a vague suspicion that the Greeks invented track meets, would rub elbows with Bill Buckley at the bar. His is an antiquated notion in bright circles where one cannot beat one's path to the booze without stepping on the polished toes of Jules Feiffer, Murray Kempton or Arthur Miller. Indeed, weekend guests at Buckley's Connecticut acres have included such old ideological foes of the host as Richard Rovere, George Plimpton and Steve Allen.

Norman Mailer seems to find in Buckley the greatest show on earth. "No other actor"—Mailer has written—"can project simultaneous hints that he is in the act of playing Commodore of the Yacht Club, Joseph Geobbels, Robert Mitchum, Maverick, Savonarola, the nice prep-school kid next door, and the snows of yesteryear." John Kenneth Galbraith calls him "the only reactionary I ever met with a sense of humor." Publisher Tom Guinzberg (Viking), Buckley's old roomie from Yale, thinks "many liberals find Bill—well, bearable, because they sense he feels pain." Murray Kempton finds in Buckley an admirable mixture of naiveté, sentiment and geniality to go with his gingerier qualities. "There are occasions," Kempton wrote, "when Buckley tempts you to remember Macaulay's grudging compliment to Burke, which was that he generally chose his side like a fanatic and defended it like a philosopher." Even Michael Harrington, who once described Buckley as "an urbane front man for the most primitive and vicious emotions in the land," speaks approvingly of his inner sense of irony, and of how "remarkably relaxed" he is in private.

Some months ago I resolved to inspect William F. Buckley, Jr., in a clinical sense. Not that I merely wanted to see the jumping eyebrows in action, catch a breathing glimpse of the Barrymore profile, or even gain absolution from my liberal sins. Though these prospects intrigued, my higher aim was to take a personal look at Buckley's fatal charm under glass, and, having looked, to judge arbitrarily whether he has "mellowed" and "doesn't honestly believe all that jazz"—as some friendly liberals contend—or whether he really skins and eats babies alive. I knew that our more obvious dissimilarities (Yale vs. Texas Tech, Skull & Bones vs. West Texas Boosters, oilman-financier father vs. dirt-farming daddy) might preclude an immediate appreciation of Mr. Buckley's subtler charms, but I was willing for him to take that risk.

I now report that Mr. Buckley can, indeed, charm the socks off a rooster; that his wit is not mere illusion; that he is an instinctive aristocrat who even while accepting the tribute of a Park Avenue doorman can look down his nose as if sniffing something slightly malodorous; that he drives in Manhattan's snarled traffic as if Lin Piao and the Red Guards are in hot pursuit, and that he is a refined, polished gentleman who, sitting among artifacts of culture in his own home, can call a guest a son-of-a-bitch in an Oxford accent and with the cold eyes of a lynch-mob leader.

Bill Buckley's *National Review* offices lack the luxury of his Connecticut estate or his elegant pad in New York's East 70's where a marble staircase carries blood-red carpeting up beyond range of the naked eye. The offices sprawl over three floors of a decrepit building on East 35th Street between 3rd and Lexington Avenues, a neighborhood of modest circumstances with shops doing commerce in pizza by the slice, tap beer, artificial flowers, and the tabloid New York *Daily News*. You get the impression that the trash wagon does not always come around on schedule and that nobody raises a lot of cain with City Hall about it. A jukebox wails away in a corner pizza parlor while pompadoured young men and their green eye-shadowed auxiliaries snap their fingers to what sounds to the unskilled ear like a chorus of ex-truckdrivers wailing and grunting some primitive, pre-Hoffa lament of the road while beating on dishpans with tire tools.

The elevator at 150 East 35th sneaked up on the third floor to make its deposit in a hall littered by cardboard boxes. A middle-aged lady with dark hair cut in a severe dutch bob greeted me in Mr. Buckley's office: he had been unavoidably detained but do please have a seat. I sat at a long table. The lady came bearing the latest issue of *National Review* like a beacon, along with a bound volume of Buckley's syndicated newspaper columns. "To get the current topics first," she instructed, "read from back to front." I said perhaps that was as good a way to read Buckley as any, smiling to show that I was really one of this earth's Good Guys and could therefore be trusted with nuclear bombs. The secretary disappeared, wordlessly, to adjoining quarters and I turned to inspect the battleground from which Bill Buckley fights against the world, the liberal flesh, and the Devil.

Buckley's desk was a jumbled profusion of books, papers, memos and manuscripts unflaggingly marking it as an editor's place. From it he directs a staff of twenty-odd, including several reformed old leftists whose dreams have turned to clabber, in getting the weekly word out to 97,000 of the faithful. Photographs and paintings of sailing sloops brightened an otherwise cheerless room that has walls the exact color of Gulden's spicy brown mustard. Buckley's maps pull down from the wall; one assumes that if they were all pulled down in tandem one would have a perfect view of a flat world.

The bulletin board displays Buckley's sense of humor. (He once posted a picture of Karl Marx wearing a Goldwater button.) A telegram, curled, aging, and with a dateline from somewhere out there on the wrong side of the Hudson, warned: S-747 AND H.R. 1932 TO DESTROY WALTER-McCARREN IMMIGRATION LAWS, THEREBY FLOODING AMERICA WITH 750,000 TRAINED REVOLUTIONARIES NOW WAITING TO LEAD NATIONWIDE REVOLT. GET BUSY. URGENT. A clipping from *National Review:* "Conservatives are organizing a Paean for Earl Warren. They're going to gather at the Supreme Court and Pae on him." Dear John letters from Birch Society sympathizers told of their cooled ardor following Buckley's excommunication of Robert Welch from the high priesthood of conservatism: *"You utter rat!!!"* . . . "Traitor!" . . . ". . . finks like you who turn their peashooters on the John Birch Society." A Halloween card, signed "A Bircher," contained the singular greeting "BOO!"

Buckley has more brass than seventy-six trombones come marching by, and no suspicion that he could possibly be wrong about anything—a combination that sometimes makes him the most obnoxious meddler since Carry Nation. It is on the record that as a small boy Buckley (1) two days after arriving at a private school proceeded to explain the deficiencies of the institution to its startled president; (2) dictated exactly how short his sisters should be permitted to wear their skirts; (3) crashed a faculty meeting at Millbrook School to accuse a teacher of robbing him of the right to express his political views in class, then "proceeded to expound to the stunned faculty on the virtues of isolationism, the dignity of the Catholic Church, and the political ignorance of the school staff"; (4) arrived late to dinner and after not listening "to more than two sentences" from a girl who was his sister's guest exclaimed, "Look here (what's her name?) Cecily, you are entirely too young to have such positive convictions, and besides I am going to tell you something that will surprise you— you are mistaken in every statement you have made." Buckley's late father, who told the story, added: "He then turned to me in an aside, which everybody could hear, and said, 'I took a dislike to her as I came in the door.' "

On the scene at a San Antonio Army base for less than forty-eight hours, Lieutenant William F. Buckley, Jr., wrote the commanding general, "telling him that he had found a great waste of manpower, that his staff was inadequate, and expressed surprise that such things could be." Buckley was snatched from the brink of military class warfare by an intermediary who counseled him in desperate terms against mailing the letter.

Buckley's father (a native Texan who came up from scratch to leave a $110 million oil fortune) was no shrinking violet, either. He was kicked out of Mexico after taking the wrong side of one too many revolutions, rained interfamily memos on his children advising them on everything from politics to the healthful benefits of walking, and in general exhorted them—in the words of a daughter—to become "absolutely perfect." He insisted that no one speak during the fifteen-minute newscasts of Henry J. Taylor, the only commentator he felt worthy of his attention. "What this country needs," he advised his namesake son in 1953, "is a politician who has an education and I don't know of one. There hasn't been an educated man in the Senate or House of Representatives since Sumners of Texas quit in disgust three or four years ago." Even one of such strong sentiments felt constrained to write Junior that he must "learn to be more moderate in the expression of your views and try to express them in a way that would give as little offense as possible."

That must have been the most wasted advice since the Prime Minister counseled Edward VIII against hanging out with divorcees. Buckley once told a crowd to Norman Mailer's face that as a political analyst Mailer "comes close to being the most ignorant man I have ever met." During the mayorality race he took note of Democratic Abraham Beame's prideful boast that "I was educated by the City of New York" with the withering snobbism, "which fact should be obvious." Buckley saw Republican John Lindsay as "Destiny's tot." Of Arthur Schlesinger, Jr., he has said, "No one believes anything he says, anyway." And the barb that caused thunder on the Right: "For all I know, Robert Welch thinks *I'm* a Communist plot." His passion for verbal hip-shots, combined with the imperial demeanor, inspired Buckley's siblings early on to tag him "the young Mastah," and, years later, prompted James Wechsler of the New York *Post* to say, "You allow yourself to become mellow and amiable, then suddenly you discover he is practically calling you a traitor . . . I just won't allow myself to get amiable."

I was almost to the point of reading Buckley's column when he burst into his office in a great clomping of heels. He grabbed my hand to give it a healthy wring, making a two-syllable word of "Hi!", beaming as if I had at long last come with the rent money or to spring him on bail. He apologized for tardiness occasioned by a luncheon engagement in some distant cavern of the city, then called for office-perked coffee and proferred cigars. Immediately, he began to interview me: what was my background, what had I written, what sort of article did I propose to write about him, where did I live, was I married, what was Lyndon Johnson *really* like? (A technique I had often seen LBJ himself use when I knew him before either of us became as important as we are now.)

We sized each other up like two fighters in mid-ring, Buckley hooking me with a couple of jokes and scoring with an anecdotal right-cross: "When I sent Norman Mailer a copy of my latest book I turned over to the index in the back and wrote 'Hi!' by his name. Knowing Mailer, he'll *immediately* go to the index to evaluate his own role, and that 'Hi!' will just kill him!" We sipped our coffee and laughed at Norman Mailer. Buckley chuckled at a couple of my stories, didn't counterpunch when I jabbed him lightly with a couple of my leftist wisdoms, and was altogether such an eager host that he plopped two ersatz sweet pills into my coffee over protests that I never use sugar. He used all his equipment: the deep, rolling voice; flourishing, theatrical gestures with the cigar; the leaping eyebrows, popping eyes, and the smile that burst suddenly to display a great sea of teeth. He was winning on points easily. Then James Wechsler's ghost warned against allowing one's self to get amiable.

"Your more enthusiastic opponents," I said, "have warned me of your charm. Will you please turn it off anytime I give the hand signal?" Buckley murmured that he would remain alert for my signs of distress. I said I wanted to ask more specific definitions of certain cloudy proposals in his book, *The Unmaking of a Mayor,* and to quiz him on a number of points raised in earlier articles about him that I had secured from the Library of Congress. "How many articles did they send you?" he asked. Oh, maybe sixty-five or seventy. "My God!" Buckley said, "there must have been *thousands!*" Obviously, the Federal bureaucracy had bungled again.

In *The Unmaking of a Mayor,* Buckley frets over being misquoted in the press, or habitually misunderstood by his critics. He makes the valid point that reporters sometimes do not permit the facts to botch up an otherwise excellent story (as he several times proved by producing taped recordings of his campaign press conferences and then comparing his utterances with stories purporting to report them) and he grieves that so few took his third-party candidacy for mayor seriously. There was that nasty accusation that he'd said Harlem residents throw garbage out their windows and then wallow in it (he recalled), the charge that he encouraged cheers for Alabama peace officers who walloped Civil Rights marchers at the Selma bridge, and that he'd advocated "concentration camps" for nonproductive New Yorkers said to sap the city purse through welfare programs—lies, or distortions, or misquotations all.

Buckley had gone on at length in his book about *The New York Times* attacking him for using the term "epicene resentments" in alluding to demonstrators against the war in Vietnam. The *Times* and all politicians smart enough to know what "epicene" means up-braided him for charging the demonstrators with a certain tutti-fruittiness, Buckley answering that "epicene" means sexless (Webster's says it means "one having characteristics of both sexes") and besides, he didn't mean the demonstrators: he meant their *resentments*. Couldn't everybody see that was an insinuation of a different color? Buckley replowed this old ground with me. I then quoted him on the same subject: "I wonder how these self-conscious *boulevardiers* of protest would have fared if a platoon of American soldiers who have seen the gore in South Vietnam had parachuted down into their mincing ranks?" Had he said that? Yes, he had. Well, was not "mincing" a far more suggestive word—and didn't it clearly designate the demonstrators themselves rather than some "resentments" they might harbor?

"I see what you mean," Buckley said, frowning. "Your point is that 'mincing' is a much stronger word than epicene. I tend to agree."

No, I said, my point was that he had called the demonstrators fags.

Buckley's smile was cool; he said they certainly could use me over at *The New York Times*. No, he didn't concede that he'd impugned anyone's manhood: "If one takes metaphor away from the language—God, what have we left? Isn't political rhetoric dull enough already?" He felt that sexual terms are perfectly proper in the political dialogue; one could remark that So-and-So was philosophically sterile without bringing So-and-So's virility into question.

The telephone rang. It was a family conversation, having to do with weekend plans, and I got this insane image of the wife saying to the husband, "Honey, will you stop by the store and pick up a bucket of caviar?" Suddenly, Buckley clapped his hand over the receiver and called to me, "You could, perhaps, crucify me for the use of 'mincing' by seeking its most narrow, personalized definition or application. But then *you* would be squarer than *I* for having suggested a censure of sexual terms. So who's to judge which of us is right? Who's to establish the standard? It's really a matter of . . . sophistication." Buckley dipped back to the telephone as if to signify that he claimed the point.

Michael Harrington's *The Other America* is often credited with inspiring Congress to war on poverty. After debating Buckley, he concluded that his opponent "knows absolutely nothing of poverty." Harrington said he'd been loaded with facts, figures and examples to prove his debating points, but that Buckley rebutted with "rhetoric, or jokes; he simply slid by the questions." Buckley has been shielded from poverty, and the sight of its horrors. He therefore could not, Harrington implied, be a competent judge of welfare programs or pass verdict on how much help society owes the chronically poor. Did Buckley agree? I asked. No, he did not. Well, *had* he seen poverty at first hand: visited a ghetto, known the indescribable odors of a flophouse, seen the desolate camps of migratory workers, or shantytowns abandoned when the coal vein played out?

Buckley stared at me for long moments. I had the notion he was slightly embarrassed; also, that perhaps he'd never before considered whether a personal adventure among the have-nots, to see how the other half lives, might benefit him. "No," he said, "I have not. That's one of my shortcomings." He paused. "I really mean that. It *is* a shortcoming. I'm not the type to have been of any use to Associated Press, say, if I'd been in Dealy Plaza on November 22, 1963. I learn by reading. After all, you must remember that the people who write the best books on the Civil War were not at Gettysburg." Another pause, then: "So while it's true I haven't actually been *around* poverty, I think Mr. Harrington has little or no reason for judging me ignorant of the subject." He seemed nettled and, I thought, for the first time a bit unsure of his ground.

Buckley had written, "The purpose of education is to educate, not to promise a synthetic integration by numerically balancing ethnic groups in the classroom." Isn't there education in children learning to live with, observe, or get to know as individuals children of other races? Buckley nodded, "Sure." Well, then? In tones you might use to a backward child, Mr. Buckley said, "But that's merely a *by-product!* If it happens, well and good. Education, you see, is an *intellectual* rather than a *sociological* process." He sighed. "Sometimes I get so fatigued just explaining over and over what I *mean* when if people would only read or listen . . ."

All right, I had read and listened to his announcement for mayor, and many of his pronouncements during the campaign. Very funny stuff. But how could he complain of not being taken seriously enough when—asked how many votes he expected to get "conservatively speaking"—he'd answered, "Conservatively speaking, one." Or, when queried on what he'd do if elected, had variously answered "Demand a recount," "I hadn't thought about it," and "Put a net under the window of the editor of *The New York Times.*"

Buckley said that well, dammit, political dialogue was so gawddahm *dull,* so bereft of humor, so spiritless; one hoped to bring a touch of life to the game. And one knew, too, that one's serious proposals would hardly get the slightest mention in the press, so one bid for attention by making remarks which one knew would at least get one in the newspapers. After all, he'd had far less campaign funds than the Democrat or Republican candidates; it was necessary to compensate by breaking into the news columns.

He added, "I made many serious proposals during the campaign, dealing with *specific* problems of this city. The newspapers chopped them down to a few sentences, or lost them on the back pages. For instance, my transportation paper contained some *dahm* good ideas—we've a terrible, messy, almost hopeless traffic problem in New York. Among my recommendations was the now infamous, if I may call it that, crosstown bikeway. The newspapers singled the bikeway proposal out, to the exclusion of all others, making it sound extremely frivolous. It isn't frivolous at all." He brooded a moment. "From the standpoint of strategy my timing was bad. I released the transportation paper in the last tremors of the campaign, and there was never any opportunity to counter the impression that the bikeway proposal was a joke. Someone told me it cost me 100,000 votes." He grew a giant smile: "The magic 100,000 votes. Any time my supporters detected some imagined act of madness, some tactical blunder, or thought they did, they were *supremely* confident it had cost me *precisely* 100,000 votes."

There had been much breast-beating, if not many cerebral strokes,

over Buckley's campaign proposal to encourage "nonproductive"
citizens to quit New York. Resolved: that welfare recipients not in-
firm or tied down by small children be required to perform labors for
the City,* and, should they balk, that they be encouraged to seek
climes where Opportunity might knock louder. If they refused to go
—well, their welfare grants would be discontinued. Might this not—I
asked—constitute a rather unfeeling eviction of people from their
chosen ground through a form of glorified blackmail? My God,
Buckley said, his eyes opening wide, didn't people *want* opportunity?
Besides, there probably wouldn't be all that many people involved. I
objected: he'd find thousands who opposed the idea on principle, or
for other reasons of their right, and who, opposing, would not go.
Buckley countered that liberals were such pessimists: maybe he had
more faith in people than I did. Would he propose to enforce his
decree by moving welfare-staters out at bayonet-point? Ah, he said,
the old "concentration camp" concept again! No, he would not want
anyone to have that power, including himself. However, the law gave
the City a wide latitude in establishing welfare qualification standards,
he said, and the right set of standards might motivate more people to
go Question: but some *wouldn't* be motivated and if he should arbitrarily cut off welfare benefits wouldn't there be chaos: hungry families, evictions, more school dropouts, more crime, more festering of
the wound?

Perhaps so, Buckley said. Certainly there would be many problems. How would you administer such a law? Where would you draw
the line? Candidly, he answered his own questions: "I don't know.
Perhaps my idealism convinced me that God and the Conservative
Party would find a way." He'd hoped, however, that the mere introduction of the subject would inspire new thinking on the welfare
problem; sadly, it had not. "All it did was prompt everyone to scream
that Buckley lived to ship the masses off to 'concentration camps'—
an obvious absurdity." On that point, he added, he'd merely suggested a pilot program of retraining settlements for the unskilled or
unemployable. (Ironic, I thought, that the closest thing Buckley has
offered to a paternalist governmental scheme should cause one of the
biggest Liberal uproars.)

Had Buckley "mellowed" as friendly liberals claim? "I suppose,"
he said, "there's a situation in which the Hungarian Freedom Fighter

* A proposal which has long existed on the books, though never enforced.

could be said to have 'mellowed,' isn't there?" The dazzling grin: "No, I don't think I've mellowed. My God, I should *hope* not. No, I think the liberals are finding it increasingly difficult to rebut the charges we make in *National Review*. They just can't meet them head-on anymore. There simply can't be anything wrong with the *liberal* truths, you see, so there must be something wrong with *mine*. Therefore, I can't mean half of what I say—it's merely an affectation, a pose, or I have somehow mellowed like a ripe old pear. So convenient for them, isn't it?" He leaned back in his chair, waving the cigar like a baton, vastly pleased.

Buckley founded *National Review* in 1955. Though circulation has grown from the initial 8,000 to almost 100,000 the magazine continues to lose money. (So do most political magazines with one-eyed views of the issues, whether left or right.) The editor's lecture fees, royalties from writing, and similar undertakings are largely plowed back into the magazine. Buckley led me to the bulletin board and pointed to a scroll attesting that the American Institute of Management deemed William F. Buckley, Jr., worthy of recognition for "his individual executive managerial abilities." Beaming, the honoree pointed to a connecting line he has drawn from the scroll to the document posted next to it: a financial statement showing *National Review* $2,181,222.23 in the red.

Does Buckley feel pain or disappointment in seeing his pet causes repeatedly rejected by the electorate? "Individuals sometimes hurt me," he said, "but not events. I have almost lost the capacity to feel pain in the sense that I expect any sudden reversal of the old trends. I do wish the opportunity to get *across* to more people without having to fight past their taboos, or preconceptions. I get awfully tired"— and here he slumped in his chair as if suddenly blackjacked—"simply saying 'I didn't say that,' or 'What I said was this.' I suppose it's all part of the hot pursuit after publishable copy."

I asked Mr. Buckley about a story involving columnist Rowland Evans. It had to do with their respective Yale educations, and a word that I not only couldn't remember but probably couldn't pronounce on a crooked quiz show.

"Oh, yes," Buckley said, with evident relish. "Evans came on my television show. In introducing him I credited him with having graduated from Yale. He corrected me by saying he had left Yale after only one year, for the military service. Later, I asked a question using the word 'tergiversator.' Mr. Evans said that before he could answer he would require a definition of that particular word. I then said, 'Mr. Evans, you get that *second* year at Yale.' "

"How do you spell"—I asked—"ah . . . that particular word?"

"T-e-r-g-i-v-e-r-s-a-t-o-r."

As I took the spelling down, Buckley said: "It means fink."

We had talked for almost three hours. It was getting dark, now, and throughout the stone jungle little ole ladies with parasols would be fighting or racing former All-Pro linebackers for a cab, and the Pros would not always win. We had a final go at coffee while horns beeped outside, and the blue language of truckdrivers purified the polluted air. Buckley noted in his appointments book that we would meet for drinks following his television show the next week.

Our talk was low-key until I remarked on charges that have been made against Buckley as a racist—one which he emphatically denies, and cites as the blackest of all smears against him. ("If I lived in South Carolina," he once said to explain his position, "I would vote for segregated schools in my community; in Stamford, where I live, I'd vote for integrated schools. I hope that if I lived in South Carolina I would take a position aimed at doing what I could to increase the opportunity of Negroes to the point where I no longer felt segregation was necessary. Maybe it would take a hundred years or ten years.") Sitting in his office, Buckley said he held no brief for militant segregationists like Lester Maddox,* who chased Negroes from his Atlanta restaurant with guns and axe-handles rather than serve them in compliance with Civil Rights laws. "If Maddox had promised to use the axe-handle, should they come into the restaurant, on LBJ, who sponsored the bill, or on Earl Warren, who ratified it," Buckley said, "it would have been easier to understand."

Into the room burst a cadre of revelers: a half-dozen members of the *National Review* staff, returning from the four-hour celebration of lunch, Buckley explaining to me something about a special occasion. He introduced his sister, Priscilla, art director Jim O'Bryan, a jolly man whose name was lost in the joyful noise (and who hugged against his breastbone the bronze bust of some hero unknown to me), and several young ladies whose high spirits might have been equally charged to the natural exuberance of clean-living Conservative youth and generous applications of strong waters. "Had I gone to lunch

* Since elected governor of Georgia.

with them," Buckley said, cheerfully, "the interview would not be over—merely starting."

In my Texas twang I said, "Ah thank ah'll mosey over to the *New Republic* and tell 'em you got some real swangers over hyar."

One of the young ladies reached out as if to tweak my beard. "With that accent," she said, "you wouldn't dare!"

Preparing to leave his office Buckley struggled with an attaché case so stuffed with paper work it would close only after he pressed the top down with one knee. Even then, it played jack-in-the-box with him. "A nice . . . lazy . . . weekend . . . in the country," Buckley said, fighting the locks.

He asked which way I might be going; I said I was to meet a friend at Toots Shor's. "That's about 54th Street or so," he said. "Would you like to ride partway with me?" I accepted.

While Buckley and I talked inside his office, the Devil had invented a machine, christened it "Hondo 50," and parked it in front of the elevator outside the door. "Where the hell," I asked, "did *that* thing come from?" Buckley grinned: "My staff . . . Here will you hold this? And catch the elevator door for me?" Taking his attaché case, I said that I had now carried Lyndon B. Johnson's bags and William F. Buckley's bags in the same lifetime, and believed I would call it a career. Half-lifting, half-shoving the Hondo 50 into the elevator, Buckley laughed that obviously I had little left to live for.

On the street, he reclaimed the attaché case to lash it to the back of the motorbike.

"Ah . . . is *this* what you offered me a ride on?"

Buckley broke out in a great sea of teeth. "Chicken?"

"Well . . ." I shifted from foot to foot, more than faintly agonized.

"Do you want to back out?"

"Yes," I said. "I'd love to. Only, I sure hate to miss the experience . . ."

Curiosity overcame cowardice after a brief but spirited battle; my person was sandwiched between Mr. Buckley and his attaché case. "What happens," I mumbled, "if we fall?"

"We'll discuss that contingency when we come to it. Now, don't try to balance. That's my department."

"Is there anything I can hold on to?"

"Grip the seat," Buckley instructed. I gripped that seat like nobody has before or since, fingers curved under in the manner of someone in the last throes of arthritis. We weaved and bobbed up 35th Street, charting the uncertain course of two dawn revelers. "No, no!" Buckley admonished. "Don't try to balance yourself. It's not as if one's liberalism could balance another's conservatism. The *driver* keeps it in balance." A block away, after I'd climbed up his back a few times and had three or four dizzy spells, Buckley said, "If you insist on trying to balance we may come to grief. Just sit like a *blob*. You can be a blob, can't you?"

So I sat there trying to be a blob, very much feeling the part, cotton-mouthed and feeling vulnerable and exposed, like those nightmares in which you find yourself at the bus stop wearing only your under-shorts, as we nakedly headed up Park Avenue. What would happen to the Conservative Party—I wondered—should one of the True Believers suddenly catch a glimpse of William F. Buckley, Jr., tooling up Park Avenue on a souped-up kiddy-kar in the company of a pop-eyed, pale radical whose beard was flowing wildly in the wind; who, furthermore, believed in majority rule, and who in periodically strengthening his grip on the Hondo seat inadvertently squeezed the living constitutional flesh? No doubt the Stock Market would fall and new cracks might appear on the Liberty Bell.

We hit an intersection where rush-hour cars and cabs had snarled beyond the natural genius of city planners. Buckley said, "Here's where this thing really pays off." Then we scooted between the lines of cars and cabs at an indecently reckless rate. My knees pressed the sides of the Hondo in an effort to protect my navy-blue serge from picking up traces of Yellow Cab.

"How are you?" Buckley yelled.

"Terrified."

"Do you have Medicare?" We caromed around a sharp corner separating the Commodore Hotel from the Heliport in the Pan Am Building, going if not at Mach Two speed then certainly faster than the fifteen-miles-per-hour pace recommended by Mayor Lindsay's traffic signs. We brightened a dark tunnel, gaining two car lengths, when Buckley artfully cut a cab off from its intended path, and emerged just in time to make a screeching halt at a traffic light. A young man in an old car looked us over as if trying to decide whether to call the cops. Ultimately, he said: "Say, buddy, is that a Hondo Fifty or Ninety?"

Though he knew very well, Buckley made a production of it. The brow wrinkled, as he turned in profile; the eyebrow on my side chinned itself on his hairline, and Buckley gazed at the stars as if pondering what to do about God. "I *think,*" he said, "it's a Fifty."

"What'll she do?"

"Three thousand two hundred and twenty-seven," I said, "on the curves."

Buckley's estimate was lower: "Oh, I should think it would cruise at . . . uummmm . . . thirty-five miles."

On we sailed, Buckley trick-driving by looking over his left shoulder to bellow some comment about John Lindsay or pop questions about Lyndon Johnson, all lost on the wind. I bawled did he know a certain New York newspaperman? "He screwed me a couple of times," Buckley shouted (and an old lady in an ankle-length skirt stopped to stare), "but he's a nice fellow. He sent me a copy of his new book."

In front of a Park Avenue apartment house a traffic tangle beyond even the Hondo folks' imagination blocked us. Wretched souls waiting under a canopy for taxis smiled on us. The uniformed doorman stepped into the street. "Do you think you could of straightened this out"—he gestured toward the snarl—"if they'd let you build your bikeway?" He moved closer, leaned in, and confided quickly, "I done all *I* could." Buckley beamed at him down a great expanse of Roman nose. At the next intersection a pedestrian yelled, "Hey, Mister B, what would John Lindsay say?" My chauffeur tossed his head, laughing. "Did you hear that?" he asked.

Eons later Buckley pulled over to the curb. I climbed gratefully off the motorbike while passersby who stopped to stare made a mockery of the old saw that New Yorkers wouldn't pause to see a free earthquake. Buckley disappeared down a narrow lane between two endless rows of honking automobiles.

Columnist-author Robert Novak was the guest on Buckley's television program, "Firing Line." I joined thirty or forty other witnesses to the taping session at WOR studios, situated along a garish slash of Broadway. Buckley communicated with technicians and cameramen by hand signals, smiles and eyebrows. When the floor director said, "Quiet, please!" Buckley turned to give the camera the ole thousand-mile stare, at once reminiscent of Barrymore in the terminal stages of drama and a Biblical prophet. He introduced his guest in a bass role:

". . . author . . . a former newsman in Omaha, Nebraska, and Washington, D.C. . . . married to the former secretary of Lyndon B. Johnson—a *most* convenient arrangement all around." The studio audience laughed, Buckley rewarded us with a display of his teeth, and Novak, looking a bit chubby around the chin muscles, managed what I assumed to be a slight tremor of mirth. The two discussed "Politics, 1968" without agreeing on a nominee for either party. Perhaps because Novak adopted a low-key approach, quoting statistics and historians, rather than entering into the emotional exchange of rhetoric and invective that have, in the end, unsettled so many Buckley debate opponents, the show was without real spark.

Later, I waited in the hall with Buckley, two young ladies from Novak's publishing house, Neal Smith (former campaign aide to Buckley) and a young woman who made a point of saying she'd voted for John Lindsay, and was glad, for Novak to join us. Ultimately, it became apparent that Novak had been detained by admirers in the studio audience. "Would you mind very much going for him?" Buckley asked me. "If *I* go they'll grab me, too."

At Buckley's East 70th Street home I warily skirted the Hondo mocking me from the entrance foyer, and trailed the entourage through a large anteroom where red carpeting marched up the staircase. As we entered a well-appointed study, Buckley gestured toward a painting of his own creation and cracked, "Did you see my latest Warhol?" He spoke Spanish on the telephone before pointing the way to drinks. Somebody said we needed ice. "No," Buckley said, "I just ordered some on the telephone." Presto, a maid appeared with ice.

After a round of drinks and chitchat (would it be Romney or Reagan in '68?; how much would the Great Society backtrack in the 90th Congress?; Buckley told the back-of-Norman-Mailer's-book story again) we moved into a living room no bigger than the Carlsbad Caverns, with antiqued pieces, smartly set off by off-white and red, that did not come from Discount Gene's. It was there, over bite-sized sandwiches and wine, that I encountered a small gale. Novak remarked that "the most dissimilar campaigns" he'd known were those of two men presumed to be at least ideological first cousins: Ronald Reagan and Buckley.

"They're both fine actors," I said, "but then again—perhaps where Mr. Reagan talked issues, Mr. Buckley cracked jokes."

I assumed this to be a witticism, it being clear to all Americans old enough to qualify for Operation Head Start funds that Mr. Reagan's campaign, being one of imagery, was by design almost as void of gripping issues as a bathing beauty contest. The humor was overlooked by Mr. Buckley.

"You son-of-a-bitch," he snapped. "You haven't read my book!"

Where I was raised, the code instructed that if somebody called you an S.O.B. without prefacing it with a mitigating smile, you hit him in Memory of Mother. Mr. Buckley was as far from smiling at the moment as I am in this one from being named in a codicil to his will. I felt the heat of blood while wondering whether to hoot and dance in the tradition of the Old West, meanwhile probably making a pluperfect ass of myself, or whether to pass the whole thing off with the kind of sophisticated drawing-room worldliness they do not teach at Texas Tech. Perhaps because it crossed my mind that anyone who would upbraid the King of England at age six might, at age forty, be inclined to hit back, I decided on a policy of nonviolence.

Cleverly, I said, "No, I've read your book." Mr. Buckley's eyes might have frosted his wine goblet.

Ten minutes later he took Novak to a crosstown party, leaving me alone with the wine, the maid, and my memories.

My personal observations of William F. Buckley, Jr., are limited to those instances cited here and to one earlier encounter at a Washington party touting his latest book—hardly enough to pose as expert. They are, however, enough to permit the formulation of certain indelible impressions by one who has read all his books, many of his articles, speeches, debates and columns, interviewed many of his friends and foes, and for more than a decade observed him at work.

Well, how about it—does Buckley "believe all that jazz"? Yes. He believes all that jazz because, for one thing, he was taught from childhood to believe it as surely as he was taught to believe the dogma of the Catholic Church. He believes it because (as examples from childhood up to day-before-yesterday have shown) he is congenitally incapable of presuming himself without Solutions. He believes outside the popular political pale because of ancestral precedents: a family history boasts that four generations of Buckleys were "all prone to unpopular beliefs"; the Buckleys' reverence for ancestors is rivaled only by the Japanese.

Most of all, however, he believes it because of his limited experience with The World; he knows nothing of life in the streets. ("He has," ex-roomie Tom Guinzberg said, "a rather childlike naiveté about many things. There are whole areas outside his experience.") When Buckley inspires his followers to rail against public assistance to unwed mothers and their illegitimate offspring, you must remember that he has never known (1) a girl "in trouble" who wouldn't have the money to buy an abortion even if the law permitted, (2) a home without all-providing, all-counseling parents, or (3) a hungry child. He can call for an end to unemployment compensation because he's never drunk twenty-cent beer with an out-of-work stiff drowning the pain of not having the rent or money for the milk bill; he does not, therefore, realize that to end unemployment compensation would (1) strip the last thin ribbon of hope from that man, and (2) relegate him to the ultimate humility—the welfare rolls, which, in time, Mr. Buckley also would purge.

When Buckley says that if he were a South Carolinian he would vote for segregated schools, one must remember that he *is,* in truth, at least a part-time South Carolinian: a family retreat at Camden, S.C., was always full of grinning servants to welcome "the young Mastah" home from Yale or the San Antonio military base wars. No doubt, like countless Negro cooks and butlers in the South that I have often been told of over drinks at the country club, they didn't want integration "forced" on them. Perhaps that is why Buckley can advocate that South Carolina's problems be settled by South Carolinians, or Mississippi's by Mississippians, without recognizing the wart-obvious fact that he is leaving the solutions to Strom Thurmond and James O. Eastland. Buckley can write, "In today's all-white neighborhoods it is reasonable that the schools should be overwhelmingly white. In today's Negro neighborhoods, it is reasonable that they should be overwhelmingly black. "Not a word"—noted Laurence Stern in the Washington *Post*—"about improving the tired physical plants or tragically undermanned staffs in the slum schools, which Buckley would preserve in the full purity of their deprivation."

Likewise, when Buckley speaks of his "distrust of public education," one must remember that Buckley was not educated in tax-supported schools. It hardly seems necessary to add that man fears the unknown. In short, Mr. Buckley has had but fleeting contact with The World as most of us know it: full of old debts, breadcrumbs and social terrors.

Admittedly, Buckley is a man of great energies and impressive personal accomplishments: author, lecturer, debator, editor, television personality, columnist, public figure, international ski-bug, world traveler, expert sailor. When I remarked on this to a close friend of Buckley's, however, I was reminded, "Well, if you had the advantages, money and help he has, then you could be pretty productive, too. Taking nothing away from Bill, and he has a hell of a lot on the ball, he's got research people to look up his facts, staffers to make appointments he wants, or to be buffers between himself and bores or pests." When Buckley drives up to his house he can abandon the scooter at the curb, and somebody will spring out to park it. He doesn't have to grocery shop, drive the kids to school in a car pool, or stand in line at the tax office while an IRS employee counts on his fingers what he owes Uncle Sam thirty minutes before the filing deadline. Buckley will never fret over whether Social Security will see him through to the grave, whether his children will be equipped to face the world or accepted in it, or wonder whether he can rescue his wife's gift from Lay Away by Christmas. He is fortunate in one sense, almost tragically unfortunate in another. Knowing how difficult it is for me to conceive of how it must be to be rich, I think of how impossible it is for Buckley to conceive of being poor.

For some—a John F. Kennedy who could have his eyes opened by a glimpse of the wretches in Appalachia, a Nelson Rockefeller raised to ways of philanthropy, a Franklin D. Roosevelt who was pushed by personal ambitions and the accident of illness to growth beyond the bounds of *noblesse oblige,* an Averell Harriman atoning for the industrial sins of his forefathers—there is always the prospect of being smitten by humane grace; of achieving some degree of understanding, and, in turn, the empathy that leads to the inner-gnawing doubts that sire compassion, and, in time, points the path to social reform. For a William F. Buckley, Jr., born to absolutes, nurtured on dogma, possessed of an ego that would shame de Gaulle, and the self-certainty that precludes even the thought of Doubt, there is less hope of stumbling upon New Truths, or even of seeing life through the other fellow's eyes, however myopic or temporary the view.

CHAPTER 6

The Battle
of Popcorn Bay

Maybe Jack Valenti and I don't sleep better at nights for the same reason, but that doesn't mean we disagree in all things. "I have never seen a bad movie," the ex-White House aide confided in the ear of the world the very day he signed on as chief goose-greaser for the flicks. The suspicious will deduce that Valenti's $175,000 annual wage may have made some old clinkers he has seen look a lot better in retrospect. I am reluctant to question the purity of his motives, however, for if Mr. Valenti is willing to have me as co-sponsor of his sentiments then I will hire the hall.

The reason I have never seen a bad movie is because *I believe!* Everything! Charlton Heston as Moses? *Yes!* I know that Doris Day is the sweetest virgin in her age group regardless of race, creed or color, and that somewhere over the rainbow Judy Garland happily skips through the Land of Oz with no thought of suicide. When the silver screen tells me that the State is about to orphan Susan Hayward's baby through Mommy's electrocution, you'll find me out in the neighborhood drumming up money for the Save Susan Hayward For Motherhood Fund until the bunko squad convinces me I'm wrong. If Hollywood asks me to conceive of Napoleon as Marlon Brando in tight breeches and a trick hat, or Prince Valiant as Tony Curtis with Bronx overtones ("Yon-dah lies my fodder's cast-tle") or to accept a hair-pieced, double-chinned Gene Autry as the terror of barroom baddies—well, I am happy to oblige and will stare down all those popcorn-chomping wiseacres with pomaded hair who laugh in all the wrong places and yell "Good-bye, Mr. Massey" when Lincoln puffs off on the train following his farewell to friends in Springfield. As a movie critic I would last about as long as the Hope Diamond at a convention of gypsies, because one just doesn't criticize Miracles.

The Sandpiper? Loved it. *The Outlaw?* Went wild. *The Ten Commandments?* Found God.

I was addicted to what we called "the picture show" at an early age. Give me enough time and I would hoard pennies until I had nine. Somehow—riding or walking—I would get across the eight miles that separated the Old Home Place from the Palace Theater in Cisco. The Palace was the most sophisticated place I have ever been where everybody wore Big Mac overalls.

Tarzan was very large in those days. He represented everything a boy could aspire to grow to. He was free, swinging through life on jungle vines, complete master of every ape in his society, unfettered by school, neckties or Fundamentalist parsons. He lived on coconuts, bananas and watermelon; the only way you could beat that diet would be to add a dab of peanut butter or an occasional box of Crackerjacks. The sole fault we found with Tarzan was his disturbing tendency to be Soft On Girls. We finally decided that he hung around with that ole Jane person because he felt sorry for her, her being so poor she hardly had enough clothes to cover her feminine works.

As much as we admired Tarzan when he wasn't mooning around Jane, we reserved our primary accolades for Western heroes. Where else could you get for nine cents runaway stagecoaches, bloodbaths, barroom brawls, cavalry charges, Redmen gone off their skulls on firewater, Good booting Evil in the tail—and suffer a modicum of ole mushy love? Life's noblemen were named Buck Jones, Tom Mix, Ken Maynard, Bob Steel.

Shirley Temple movies we greeted with scorn, and this was long before we suspected her of Republicanism. Shirley was for sissies and the birds. Once, however, I arrived at the Palace and was faced with the choice of seeing Shirley Temple or walking the eight miles back home with my nine cents unspent. Shirley Temple won. She also won me. It was not a thing I have confessed to this minute, but Shirley Temple was my First Love. I doubt whether even Clark Gable could have kept his head and heart had curly Shirley crooned "The Good Ship Lollipop" to him the way she did to me. Ultimately, slipping around so my contemporaries would not learn of my shame, I saw six or eight Shirley Temple movies and would have seen more had my pennies held out. Once I plopped down in a seat in the Palace and when my eyes had adjusted to the gloom found myself sitting next to my cousin Kenneth. Kenneth in a *Shirley Temple* movie? "Lissen," he told me, screwing up his face in anger and doubling his fists, "I didn't wanta come to this ole sissy picture show. Mama *made* me come see it." I said my Mama had, too. Periodically we confided that this scene was "dumb" or that one "makes me wanta puke" or "I just can't stand her." We had contempt enough for that particular movie to last through all three of the day's screenings.

On a Sunday afternoon in my twelfth year I walked to Cisco with a neighboring farm boy to view what many folks might have thought an inferior Hollywood product. The title of that Western epic escapes me, but the star's name lives on: John Kimbrough. Kimbrough was an All-America fullback for Texas A&M in 1939 and 1940. As soon as he'd played his last game he got beckoned to Hollywood. The kindest thing that can be said about John Kimbrough as an actor is that he was tall and dogged and quit after one picture. He read lines like somebody with weak eyes trying to decipher a medical prescription, and his delivery—well, his delivery was straight out of Haskell, Texas, just like John was. Kimbrough had, however, all the right instincts. He walloped up on crooks, removed his hat in the presence of ladies, and rode off into the sunset after having brought a little more justice to a cruel world. Certainly this was enough to satisfy me and my farm-boy companion on that Sunday afternoon so long ago. Indeed, we were so caught up in discussing our hero both as football player and actor that when we reached my friend's house we paid scant attention to news on the radio having to do with some sort of excitement at a place called Pearl Harbor. After a cup of hot chocolate I walked on to my own home, spent an uneventful night and left for school the next morning in a routine way. Our entire student body assembled in the auditorium to hear President Franklin D. Roosevelt's "day of infamy" speech on December 8th. That night I did not go home but by prearrangement spent the night with a friend. Thus it was after school on Tuesday, December 9th, that I returned to our farmhouse.

Mother met me at the gate and she was fit to be tied. We had no radio then and took no newspapers. She had learned of Pearl Harbor and our declaration of war only a half hour earlier when a neighbor chanced by and mentioned it in passing. "Did you hear about war breaking out when you went to town Sunday?" she demanded. Well, yes, I said, it seemed like there was some mention of it. "Then why in thunder didn't you tell us about it when you came in Sunday night?" I mumbled that it had sort of slipped my mind. "Good Lord," Mother exploded. "Pearl Harbor slipped your mind—but you remembered to tell us about that ole cowboy picture show right down to the last gunfight!"

Perhaps I would have been more impressed with Pearl Harbor had I realized that Hollywood's wartime products would thrill, inspire and educate me more than anything before or since. Those World War II message epics were the most satisfying of all movies I would ever see. I wouldn't have missed one anymore than Douglas MacArthur would have considered going AWOL. I became, indeed, a hardened veteran of . . .

THE BATTLE OF POPCORN BAY

The dust of twenty-five years has settled over Pearl Harbor. Now and then a history book reference or a visit from some balding old Army buddy recalls my generation's war in millions of households. Then children all over America, like my own teen-aged daughter, ask the old question, "Daddy, what did *you* do in the War?"

Presumably this innocent query holds no terror for Audie Murphy, Dwight D. Eisenhower, or most of their 15,000,000 World War II comrades-in-arms. But for others (war profiteers, Lord Haw Haw, myself) it is a dubious proposition. With Van Johnson and other MGM-based Doolittle Raiders, I spent *Thirty Seconds Over Tokyo*. I parachuted into Occupied France with O.S.S. Captain Alan Ladd and hit a dozen Pacific beaches behind Sergeant John Wayne. ("Come on, you Devildogs! Do you want to live forever?") I suffered the perils of the Merchant Marine with Humphrey Bogart in *Action in the North Atlantic*. In Italy I took *A Walk in the Sun* with Dana Andrews, Richard Conti and Lloyd Bridges. In Europe I was menaced by the cold, monocled presence of Nazis Eric von Stroheim and Otto Kruger, who listened to Wagner above the screams of their torture victims. In the Pacific I confronted evil, slit-eyed fanatical Japanese officers such as Richard Loo, Benson Fong, or Phillip Ahn, all graduates of UCLA.

We hit our objectives each Saturday afternoon at exactly 1300 hours, when the box office opened in the shabby movie house in Jal, New Mexico. Ahead lay darkness, danger and a gory glory; to the rear was only the ominous crackling of the popcorn machine. Outside, our air raid warden fathers kept their sand buckets handy while searching the skies for enemy aircraft. Jal, perhaps because it was in close proximity to the county seat, only 39 miles from Hobbs Army Air Field and 5,260 miles from Tokyo, was among top Axis targets.

Cynics might have you believe that Hollywood cranked out its tank-burners for mere money: six motion picture companies simultaneously sought to establish title priority on *Remember Pearl Harbor;* among Hollywood's sacrifices in the mobilization effort was abandonment of the annual Santa Anita Handicap. Studios sent out press releases bravely telling how Movieland was making-do with second-hand lumber and nails in constructing sets. Others might recall that MGM's Louis B. Mayer was so upset by Hirohito's sneak attack he only earned $949,765 in 1942 salaries.

Such cynics argue that in the dull prewar years movie attendance had dropped from 85,000,000 to 55,000,000 despite gimmicks like Bank Nite, Bingo, and Free Dishes. Movie moguls, they claim, were quick to discern how promptly war epics turned a homefront buck. I would not have believed these slanders any more than I would have believed Captain Robert Mitchum smoked reefers. It *is* true that picture making, like gestation, normally required nine months from conception to delivery—but that war-time quickies hit the screen in forty-five to ninety days. One actually made the trip from idea to film can in nine days.*

But for us the emotional involvement was total. When houselights came up following the gathering of the last dastardly Nip to his ancestors, or after Dana Andrews had avenged resistance fighters who burst into patriotic songs in front of Nazi firing squads, I was ready for anything. Nor was I the only Homefront Commando magically transported to distant battles. Once, giving Popcorn Bay support to Duke Wayne in hand-to-hand combat against several dozen Japanese infantrymen, Bood Reed swung an early-day karate chop that fractured Ode Joiner's nose. When Bonita Granville refused to romance a whole squad of Storm Troopers and provide future warriors for the Fatherland, wicked Nazis chained her to a

---

* Later on, a film distributor would say of war-time movies, "Every night was Saturday night. You could open up a can of sardines and there would be a waiting line to get in. Only sardines wouldn't have smelled as bad."

post and flogged the poor girl until her blouse ripped. The chief emotion stirred among us desert youth by Nazi maltreatment of Miss Granville's cleavage was burning patriotism.

Typical American superiority was exhibited in a film called *The Fighting Seabees,* in which GI's manning cumbersome bulldozers routed a company of mobile Japanese tanks before dismounting to out-bayonet surviving Nips by a ratio approximating 6 to 1. In *Bataan* a mere dozen Occidental heroes withstood repeated assaults of what had to be a brigade of bowlegged, bucktoothed sadists. *Sahara* saw Humphrey Bogart and a ragtag band of tank soldiers, stranded at an oasis, fight a world's champion sandstorm and a whole Nazi battalion. Perhaps the high point of American superiority was reached by Errol Flynn in *Desperate Journey.* Errol outwitted Gestapo Colonel Raymond Massey to the extent that he blew up a lion's share of Germany right under Massey's nose, then escaped in a commandeered Nazi plane while saying to himself: "Now for Australia—and a crack at those Japs." (Music up and out; the sun shines on Flynn's smile.) Dennis Morgan as a Flying Tiger hero in *God Is My Co-Pilot* confessed to Priest Alan Hale that he had killed a hundred men. Father Hale said substantially what Joe Louis (possibly with coaching from Public Information Officers) had said earlier, and more briefly: "We'll win 'cause we're on God's side." By this logic, one must assume that God was with Hitler up to a point, but switched sides during the siege of Stalingrad.

The Greasepaint War gave the screen some of its most despicable villains. There was nothing a ratfink Jap or bullying Kraut wouldn't do to the clean-cut kid next door. Richard Jaeckel as the sixteen-year-old Marine, "Chicken," in *Guadalcanal Diary,* coughed while learning to smoke. His pithier expletives were suited to Robin the Boy Wonder, and he died a hero's clean death only after speaking well of Country, God and Mother; his corpse was blond and smiling. In *So Proudly We Hail,* the enemy indiscriminately strafed our hospitals, walking wounded including Sonny Tufts, Red Cross doughnut trucks, unarmed medics, wretched refugees who looked like the Hundred Neediest Cases, and Paulette Goddard. Our bombers, on the other hand, spared all civilians, cathedrals, and Works of Art.

German spies and Gestapo agents may have fooled the Allied High Command through the opening reels, but our intelligence forces at Popcorn Bay spotted them on sight. Peter Lorre was sneakily sinister as he crept around in the shadows of waterfront cafés; Sydney

Greenstreet was so openly and arrogantly evil you felt he might write J. Edgar Hoover a catch-me-if-you-can letter. George Sanders tried to trick us with polished charm, but his clipped hair and a dueling scar from the University of Heidelberg gave him away at Popcorn Bay. Walter Slezak's double-dealing was masked behind a catlike purr and the manner of a clown, though in the end he was revealed as just another blubbering tub of rancid Gestapo cowardice.

But Hollywood saved its choice haymakers for the Japs. Even before that day of infamy, Hollywood saw special horrors in the "yellow monsters"—as Scotland Yard inspectors called them in *The Mask of Fu Manchu*. Boris Karloff, as Fu himself, pledged to "wipe the whole accursed white race from the face of the earth"; his followers were urged to "kill the white men and mate with their women." In *Cry Havoc* the primary goal of Japanese invaders on Bataan seemed to be the charms of a detachment of Army nurses that included Ann Sothern, Joan Blondell, Margaret Sullavan, and Ella Raines.

My friend Bobby Dyer came unglued the afternoon we saw *The Sullivans,* a story of five Boston brothers who went down on the same battleship early in the war. At final fade-out the tagalong kid of the family could be seen running Heavenward ("Hey, wait for me!") toward his four brothers, who were grinning at him from the fleeciest cloud that special effects could create. It was more than Bobby could take; personally, I doubt if even Adolf Eichmann could have stood it. Bobby, two years older than the rest of us, gave his parents no peace until they signed permissive papers. Within ten days San Diego Naval Training Station had gained a new Boot, and the Jal Panthers had lost a 127-pound wingback.

Sometimes Hollywood seemed to get its moral preachments tangled. In one epic, a kindly priest took a rock in hand and crushed a Nazi's skull. A short "documentary," *Conquer by the Clock,* gave us a munitions factory girl who, through sneaking time for a cigarette in the ladies' room, sends a dead cartridge to a soldier and the soldier to his death. This failed to suggest—as James Agee wrote in *The Nation*—"that the same thing might have happened if her visit to the toilet had been sincere." In *Passage to Marseilles,* Humphrey Bogart was permitted to methodically slaughter the helpless survivors of a crashed Nazi plane though the crew had done him no particular dirt. Errol Flynn, in *Objective Burma,* had his troops surround a garrison of off-duty Japs (shown eating, sleeping and relaxing) before luring them into the open on a ruse, there to slaughter them with wild cries, oceans of blood and enthusiasm unmatched until the 1964 Republican convention. This violated Hollywood's concept of the code of the American Fighting Man: the Japs, by rights, should have committed an atrocity or two before getting what they deserved, and Flynn should have been more pious in his killing.

The beginning of the Cold War caused Hollywood some blushes. As our wartime ally, Russia had been glorified in *Song of Russia, Days of Glory, Stalingrad* and *North Star.* Most of these films were hastily removed from circulation. *North Star,* however, was subjected to new editing. Russian peasants, originally shown as Nazi victims, emerged as the victims of Communist oppressors; Russian soldiers, who in the first version were depicted as mighty defenders of their homeland, were with a few artful snips of the scissors turned into aggressors. Losing all its cool in *Red Planet Mars* (which had *all* nations seeking peace except for Russia), Hollywood had no less than God preserve Liberty, Mom's apple pie and Free Enterprise at the climax, by bringing about a worldwide religious revival and by causing well-arranged disasters behind the Iron Curtain.

Though Bobby Dyer, Lucky Strike Green and even Mickey Rooney had gone to war, I stayed stuck in Jal. At a time when the world shook with history and bombs I had acne. I think it was *Confessions of a Nazi Spy* (G-man Edward G. Robinson unmasks George Sanders) that inspired me to become an undercover agent so secret it was known only to me. Secret Agent 00–I hung around the pool hall, alert for any rumors of enemy troop movements, inspected the city waterworks for signs of espionage, and tried to catch Deputy Sheriff Elmer Turner contacting Berlin on his police car radio. I never fully trusted Deputy Turner after his investigation of the truckload of Italian spies I caught when they stopped for gas at Houston Wink's service station. Elmer claimed they were itinerant Mexican cotton pickers from Clovis.

To a man, Jal approved of civilian Minutemen, training under police department auspices in Connecticut and California, to meet potential Axis invaders on the beach with .22 rifles and pitchforks. We cheered when the Government herded Japanese-Americans into "detention camps" on the West Coast. We understood that Harry Wismer, broadcasting the Army-Navy football game, couldn't tell us it was raining in West Point, New York, because somebody might flash the word from Jal to Tokyo, Berlin or Rome. Our mothers rolled bandages for the Red Cross and our fathers gamely worked overtime at their desks or lathes. We ostracized the hoarder of sugar or tinned goods, and kept a suspicious eye on the Schultz and Venitti families.

Still, I felt like Crillon chastised by the French King Henry IV: "Hang yourself, brave Crillon. We fought at Arques, and you were not there." Knowing that my family had produced a real, live hero kept me going from Saturday to Saturday until I could return in triumph to Popcorn Bay. Cousin Lanvil Gilbert was pushing across France, Belgium and Germany as an infantry rifleman. I confess that I was momentarily ecstatic when news that he had been wounded at the Battle of the Bulge reached us. Had Lanvil wiped out a Nazi machine gun nest, or captured a Kraut tank company before . . . ?

"No," my mother said, reading from Aunt Clara's letter. "His socks got wet and his feet froze."

Even Hollywood was soon to disappoint me. By 1944, the Rex Theater offered so-called musicals, although no self-respecting Homefront Commando would suffer through the first eight bars of "Don't Sit under the Apple Tree with Anyone Else But Me." James Cagney prancing through tap dances in *Yankee Doodle Dandy,* Katharine Cornell and Aline MacMahon serving Pepsi and cheese tidbits to stateside Johnnys in *Stage Door Canteen,* all the flag-waving and bugle-blowing that was *This Is the Army* (with seventeen songs by Irving Berlin)—these left Popcorn Bay dissatisfied. Nor were we mollified by Hollywood's attempts at wartime humor: Bob Hope and Eddie Bracken peeling potatoes when *Caught in the Draft;* Abbott and Costello zigging when they should have zagged in *Buck Privates;* Charles Coburn and Joel McCrea suffering the hazards of wartime Washington in *The More the Merrier.* We wanted our comedy only to relieve tension just before the battle. When the paratroopers were only two minutes away from their combat-zone drop, they played the scene this way:

First Trooper: "What's the first thing you're gonna do when you get back home, Joe?"

Joe: "I'm gonna kiss my gal like she's never been kissed before!"

First Trooper: "And what's the *second* thing you're gonna do, Joe?"

"*Joe:* "Take off my parachute!"

Spasms of tension-breaking laughter would rock Popcorn Bay. So intent did we become in our missions that only rarely were we disconcerted by technical blunders in the Actors' Guild War: scouting patrols walking in single file, so that a lone well-placed bullet would have passed through nine men marching like ducks in a row; Alan Ladd throwing a heavy hand grenade with an easy, overhand Bob Feller motion so that it carried more than a hundred yards and blew up half an advancing tank column; Errol Flynn blowing up a Japanese aircraft carrier with a single grenade, then swimming with a knife in his teeth to attack a submarine. Until James Agee would point it out years later, I would not notice that after our GI's captured a farmhouse in *A Walk in the Sun* they set about "chomping an apple, notching a rifle stock, and so on—while, so far as the camera lets you know, their wounded comrades are still writhing unattended in the dooryard." Such undetected goofs now appear frequently on my television set. It's like seeing Cecil B. DeMille putting Christ on the Cross wearing a 21-jewel Bulova wristwatch.

As our front-line troops smashed to victory, Hollywood gave us fewer blood-and-thunder pictures like *Fighting Devildogs, Betrayal from the East* and *Destination, Tokyo* in favor of such fluff as *Two Girls and a Sailor, Seven Days Ashore* and *Here Come the Waves.* Driven out of the Rex Theater in search of adventure, I boosted servicemen's morale by waving to troop trains from the Jal depot, but my father stopped this after certain spiteful rumors, probably inspired by Axis counterspies, got out about my hormones. When my mother complained because I had donated some of her favorite pots and pans to the scrap metal drive, I knew the war was coming to an end.

But there was a peace to keep, so early in 1946 I enlisted in the U.S. Army Signal Corps. In my bunk at Fort Dix, New Jersey, I was certain that Hitler was alive and hiding in Argentina. On some Pacific atoll there no doubt remained a company of fanatical Japs it would be my mission to dig out of rock with M-1 rifle, flamethrower and tricks remembered from Popcorn Bay.

First, however, I was assigned to the Army Pictorial Center in Astoria, Long Island. Paramount once made some of its earliest smashes there. When I arrived the old barnlike studios were used to shoot Army training films—"message" epics designed to show new recruits all the glory and horror of military service.

Though my seventy-eight dollar monthly salary was less than Clark

Gable's, I had roles in a number of productions. Perhaps you remember me. If you saw *Nomenclature and Operation of Field Weapons,* you caught me in my first speaking role: I was the battery sergeant who yelled "Fire" to the gunners. My hand held the pointer in *Map Orientation and Characteristics of Coastal Topography.* That was my shovel you saw in *Digging of the Slit Trench,* and I don't have to tell you who fashioned the title object in *Rolling of the Horseshoe Field Pack.* In *Proper Wearing of the Military Uniform,* I was the Times Square Commando who upon delivering his best line to a bar-stool cutie ("Let me tell you about my war experiences, baby") is hauled off by a grim-jawed MP for unauthorized wearing of a fifty-mission crush hat, a sharpshooter's medal, and white socks.

But the role for which generations of fighting men will remember me is that of the Sick GI in *The American Soldier and Personal Hygiene.** In that historic film, so graphic that recruits exposed to it were later known to wear rubber gloves when shaking hands with their sisters, the camera panned to a hospital ward clearly marked by the twenty-second and fourth letters of the alphabet, respectively, then dollied in on the Sick GI.

Bashfully twisting the tail of his hospital robe, he says to a hard-eyed colonel: "But, sir—she *looked* clean!"

And that, children, is what Daddy did in the War.

* I want it clearly understood that my stand-in was the object of the gamier closeups.

CHAPTER 7

Bob Jones University:
The Buckle on the Bible Belt

Anybody who runs around yelling "God is Dead" knows nothing of Fundamentalism. Out there on the wrong side of the George Washington Bridge—in the great, wheated midlands and in the Bible Belt of Dixie as well as in certain frantic parishes of Southern California —God is very much alive. I do not mean merely that He is alive in a mild, Episcopal, anemic sort of way. I mean He is robustly alive and kicking without so much as a headache or heartburn.

This is the same God I knew as a child, though He apparently has changed a bit with age. He was then a paternal figure, reluctant to spare the rod if it would spoil the child, full of Old Testament vengeance, ready to take an eye for an eye if backed into a corner. He was a sort of John Wayne kind of a God who took no guff. He detested whiskey drinking, dance bands, risqué jokes, women who wore lip rouge, tobacco addicts, and working on the Sabbath. Adultery, topless swimsuits, analysts, Pop art or discothèques would have thrown Him into the kind of rage that fathers thunderstorms.

The God I knew through many a long, hot Sunday and in my bed at night was not, in the Texas of the 1930's and 1940's, one who would have involved Himself in a Civil Rights march. He seemed to prefer people to issues. He was pretty well occupied keeping Eastland and Callahan counties in line, there being so many boys there tempted to smoke cedar bark or slip off to the picture show on Sunday. Apparently He belonged to whatever political party happened to be praying at the moment. Or maybe He was an Independent who shifted with the winds, for I remember that His presence was invariably reported by officials of both the Republican and Democratic parties at their respective national conventions.

Of late, however, I note a distinct shifting on His part toward the far right. The Ku Klux Klan, American Nazi Party, Christian National Crusade, Americans for Constitutional Action, Daughters of the American Revolution, the Minutemen, and the John Birch Society—to name a few—have in their turns hinted that if He is not exactly a dues-paying member on their roles, He is, at least, very much in sympathy with their schemes. I have been assured that He opposes the minimum wage, Medicare, recognition of Red China, Catholics in the White House, beatniks, Daylight Saving Time, bussing students, Outside Agitators, and, of course, Earl Warren. That He is strong for States Rights, the Taft-Hartley Act, Free Enterprise, and the American soldier at war. In the days when I knew God, He was much more inclined toward the separation of Church and State. It saddens me to know that Heaven is now just another precinct in the clouds.

Fundamentalism and right-wing causes are very much intertwined in this nation today. Church-State activities reached a peak when the True Believers tried to save America from John F. Kennedy in 1960, and hand it over on a silver collection plate to Barry Goldwater four years later. I was a field man in the Kennedy campaign, assigned for a while to my native Texas. One of my first chores was to debate a Nixonite in front of a delegation of Protestant church ladies. Much on my mind was the fact that most of the ladies were Fundamentalists very skittish over John F. Kennedy's Papist connections. I took pains to consult with a Kennedy staff man on how to alleviate their fears. We composed a little speech designed to assure the ladies in my most soothing voice that (1) JFK was under no contractual obligation to Rome, (2) some of his very best friends were Protestant, (3) Catholics had fought and died for Texas' cause at the Alamo, (4) we are all looked on by the same Deity and, (5) the Pope would not be delivered bag and baggage to 1600 Pennsylvania Avenue by the first available Greyhound following John F. Kennedy's election. I stressed my own Protestant upbringing, my father's years as a part-time country preacher; spoke with nostalgia of brush arbor revivals by lantern light and of Wednesday night prayer meetings. When I had finished, wringing wet in my own juices and trembling in the joints, I awaited questions from the stoniest sea of faces this side of Mount Rushmore. Finally one woman with her hair done up in the severest possible bun and without even so much as a touch of color in her cheeks fired a salvo. "Did you know"—she asked—"that John Wilkes Booth was Catholic?" This being information outside my limited educational opportunities I stammered that no, I didn't know that. "Well," she said, "he certainly was. And you know what *he* did to the Presidency!" The good ladies beamed at her sagacity, nodding their agreement, while the Nixon man innocently cast a bemused gaze toward the Heavens. "M'am," I stammered, "I can't see much logic in what you're saying. Let me assure you that, if elected, John F. Kennedy has no plans to shoot himself." The ladies gave me mingled looks of pity, contempt and exasperation before leaving the hall to have coffee with the Nixon man. The next day, of course, I found that Booth was no more Catholic than, say, Lurleen Wallace.

A few days later a friend called to ask that I drop by his business house (a restaurant) "on a matter of extreme urgency." Because I was already in danger of missing an appointment I tried to put him off. Failing, I begged some inkling of the problem requiring my immediate presence. No dice—but I just *had* to come. This minute. Uttering language the church ladies might not have approved, I dropped everything to rush over to the restaurant. My friend introduced me to a young, handsome man identified as a Church of Christ minister. He had talked with my friend (the minister said) and they agreed it would benefit my soul to listen to what he had to say: they wanted to snatch me back from the jaws of a gigantic mistake. Which particular mistake? "Why," the preacher said, "campaigning for Kennedy!" Then he launched into a long, impassioned, and not overly coherent diatribe against the Catholic Church, all its tenets and fixtures, leaning heavily on "maintaining our historic separation of Church and State."

I broke in to ask if he intended to preach "such crap" from his pulpit—an injudicious choice of words, perhaps, though they perfectly reflected my temper. Yessir, he said, it was his Christian duty to preach it, and he would preach it day in and day out, at night services, on the Sabbath morn, at midweek prayer calls and with his best lung-power. I then pointed out the obvious inconsistency: how could he inveigh for separation of Church and State when—merely by bringing the issue to his pulpit—he would be guilty of violating his basic preachment?

The minister has not responded to that question to this sweet moment. Indeed, I am not at all certain he ever came to see any validity in the question. Ultimately we both lost our cool. Once he'd threatened me with brimstone I called him a pompous ass and a Heinz variety of fool. The next thing you know my friend got grabbed by a burst of Christian charity which prompted him to invite me the hell off his property as an unwelcome trespasser!

Weeks later, after Kennedy had defeated Nixon, I could not put temptation behind me and thus sent my friend the following post-election telegram (with the stipulation that it be telephoned to him sharply at five o'clock the following morning): GREETINGS FROM ROME. CAN YOU ARRANGE LOCAL HOTEL ACCOMMODATIONS FOR POPE, ENTOURAGE, ARRIVING NOON THURSDAY? NEED ROOMS TWENTY-SIX CARDINALS, FORTY NUNS, ONE HUNDRED ALTAR BOYS. CAN GET YOU CONTRACT FOR MANDATORY FRIDAY FISH FRIES SUBSIDIZED BY U.S. GOVERNMENT PROVIDED YOU HANDLE ROSARY CONCESSION IN HAT CHECK ROOM ON PERCENTAGE BASIS. HAIL MARY FULL OF GRACE. SIGNED, LARRY CARDINAL KING. Perhaps I need not add that my friend has not responded, either.

In that same campaign there was circulated in Fundamentalist circles a bogus "Knights of Columbus Oath" which Kennedy was alleged to have sworn. One of these despicable documents fell into my hands, and I can attest that no more bloodcurdling fantasy has been dreamed up even by Alfred Hitchcock going to bed on a stomach full of pickles. It "swore" to kill all Protestants (including infants) with all deliberate speed, so to speak, and to know—in a biblical sense—the Protestant woman wherever she might be found. Though thoroughly discredited, this spurious document was very much in use to show evidence of "the underground Catholic conspiracy" right up until the polls closed.

These experiences are recited not to smear indiscriminately all Fundamentalists with the tar of bigotry (though there *is* evidence that instances of tolerance among many Fundamentalist sects are almost as rare as Republican folk singers) but to stress that they possess the fanatic's zeal whatever their cause: this is black and that is white and never the twain shall meet to form even the slightest puddle of gray. Though I confess difficulty remembering when I last judged a Fundamentalist right on a given issue, I do not argue that Fundamentalists are congenitally incapable of being right. They, however, will argue you to a frazzle that they are *always* right; not only that, but that they have a monopoly on it.

Such bellicosity bugs me. For while I do not mind the Campbellite thinking that Heaven will be disturbed should he play music with his hymns, or that his infant will burn in Hell if he should baptize it, I draw the line at his telling the rest of us that church music and baby sprinklings point the surest road to the great roast awaiting us in the eternal pit. Neither do I begrudge the Baptist his belief that total submersion goes hand in hand with Salvation, or the Methodist his converse Talmud that sprinkling on a few drops of water is enough to cleanse the blackest soul. When they each insist, however, that their way with water is the *only* way—well, my smile grows thin. To be honest, I am irritated only in the mildest way by quarrels over use of the Single Cup, versions of the Virgin Birth, and so on. Such dialogues simply rock me to sleep quicker than Seconal. I don't even mind a little harmless missionary work among the unwashed, being willing to grant that this may even be a legitimate Christian duty, though personally I will slam the door on a Salvation salesman as quickly as on the Fuller Brush man should I not at the moment feel a need for his wares.

One cannot go halfway with these people. If one does not sign on for the round trip then he is pressured, condemned, and prayed over in public until he either surrenders unconditionally to the conformity that is demanded, or he must shuck Fundamentalist contacts altogether. The latter penalty is no great price to pay, in my personal view, but there *are* those who quit their father's church only after the most gut-wrenching agony. Unable to cope with the trauma, they often take to drink and to keeping late hours with widow women. In whole sections of our society where Fundamentalism has the same kind of grip as the legendary company store, people who fail to walk the chalk line according to reigning theological and/or political standards suffer economic privation and social ostracism.

I envy the Fundamentalist one talent: his certainty that there is only one side to everything. It would really be comforting to know that Somebody is preparing a comfort-place for your retirement to Eternity, one that is even grander than those Senior Citizen Villages advertised by Florida real estate men in northern newspapers. It would probably be even more comforting to rest assured that your natural enemies are doomed to fire everlasting. So taken by that notion am I that—if they'd just let me think and vote like I want to and drink an occasional beer—I would be in the front ranks of Fundamentalism tomorrow morning with my list of enemies sworn to by a notary public.

Any movement, whatever its nature, must have an incubator in which to hatch its special breed of chicks. The Fundamentalist has found his incubator in sectarian schools that often are of dubious worth in terms of the larger meaning of education. Some are better than others, offering a smattering of at least half-scholarly courses— or pretending to. Obviously, however, even if you signed up for the same faculty Albert Einstein, Pablo Casals, John Kenneth Galbraith and Clarence Darrow, you would not turn out very many first-rate scientists, cellists, economists or lawyers so long as students were told that they must confine their thought processes to a single book and their verbal exercises to repeating after their dorm's prayer captain.

Many so-called Bible Schools don't even play at education in its broader sense, confining their efforts to bolting down the iron Absolutes beyond the slightest slippage or bestowing their higher honors on the man who can pulpit-pound until he cracks the stoutest oak. The woods are full of them in Arkansas and Georgia and East Texas, for example, and you can find the same in Kansas or Ohio. If one attending such an institution finds too much inquiry in his soul, he is asked to move along before he contaminates Holy ground—and has no choice but to pack his bag. The Supreme Court in *Hamilton v. University of California* (293 U.S. Stat. 245) has held, in effect, that the administrators of private institutions have the right to teach that the moon is made of Silly Putty or that God is a Volga boatman if they wish—a decision far more tolerant, incidentally, than anything its benefactor institutions will permit within their grand duchys.

One of the more "liberal" Fundamentalist institutions is Wheaton College, in Illinois, often billed as "The West Point of Christianity." The arbitrary designation "liberal," however, is based upon small concessions. Wheaton students are allowed to play cards without threat of expulsion as long as the game isn't more exotic than Rook (called "Wheaton poker" by Fundamentalist schools where even to own a deck of cards is to be harshly dealt with) and sons of Wheaton are actually told they may "grapple with the issues"—although some of the zing goes out of that slogan when you realize it ends "but don't lose your Truth."

To be sure, Wheaton has its periodic Inquisitions. A couple of years ago its trustees, suddenly suspicious of the beliefs of a professor of philosophy, called him to account. One crusty judge demanded to know whether the professor agreed with a statement in the college catalogue lauding the Bible's role in the learning processes. "Do I *agree* with it?" the professor asked. "Gentlemen, I *wrote* it." End of Inquisition. Though Weaton has twice banned the campus literary magazine and once permanently expelled a nonorthodox school newspaper editor, it does have moments of giddy individualism. School authorities actually permitted a dissident student to run mockingly for student body president by wearing a military uniform, spouting his campaign promises in a thick German accent, combing his hair in a downward slash across the forehead, and urging votes for "Der Fuhrer."

This boys-will-be-boys attitude would not long be tolerated at most Fundamentalist schools. Certainly the mockery would not have been permitted at . . .

BOB JONES UNIVERSTY: THE BUCKLE ON THE BIBLE BELT

There are approximately five hundred families of Joneses to keep up with in and around Greenville, South Carolina, which calls itself the "Textile Center of the World." It is an old, flawed city of 66,188 set among rolling, red-clay hills reaching into neighboring Georgia. People named Jones attend their looms in dozens of mills, till the soil, and over at the Jones Funeral Home they have for fifty-three years buried the dead with "Dignity, Quietude, and Beauty."

But in circles where the Holy Writ is taken undiluted by Modernism, and political potions taste sweetest when untainted by anything of lesser vintage than McKinley, the only Jones Boys who count are the Bob Joneses: Senior, Junior, and III. They are, respectively, the Founder, President, and Vice-President of what they proclaim "The World's Most Unusual University." Any list of what makes Bob Jones University unusual must begin with the Jones Boys themselves, a trio as inseparable as the Holy Trinity.

Who else owns—free of debt, sorority-house panty raids, and sullen alumni bent on hanging the coach—an educational institution valued at more than thirty million dollars? Who else imports a small-college professor from Virginia (vaguely but officially presented as "a leading scientist") to teach that the world's creation processes "terminated at the end of six days" and that "the world could not possibly be more than 10,000 years old"—yet, on the other hand, claims to be nowhere excelled "in the thoroughness of scholastic, cultural, and artistic work"? Who else forbids students to see Hollywood movies—yet produces films good enough to win plaudits at the International Film Festival in Cannes *and* an award from Screen Producers Guild of Hollywood? Who else toured the Bible Belt during the 1964 Presidential campaign in a bus equally bannered for God and Goldwater—yet insists they do not run a partisan institution?

Nobody else. But then nobody else has a university that is so nearly family-held. The Jones family—father, son, and grandson—control the 185-acre campus sprawled along U.S. 29 on Greenville's outskirts, and they control everything on it. Whether you buy a $4 copy of Dr. Bob Jones, Jr.'s novel, *Wine of Morning,* at the Book Stall or study your Sunday School lesson over ten-cent coffee at Little Moby's, probably the only campus hangout in America pushing Crucifixion Art, every nickel put in the till goes to the glory of God and the Joneses.

There is eighty-two-year-old Robert Reynolds Jones, Sr., called by all—including himself—simply The Founder. Thirty-eight years ago in Florida he founded the forerunner of the present "Fortress of Faith" that is BJU. On his good days, bundled against the chill of his years in a black coat, cape, and hat, he strolls the campus to exchange Scriptural quotations with BJU students: an ancient, Old Testament Zorro, flaying the Devil, Modernism, and liberalism at any opportunity.

There is The Founder's son, balding, fifty-four-year-old Bob Jones, Jr., President of BJU, whose artistic taste runs to Shakespeare, Van Dyck, Sebastiano del Piombo, opera arias, and his own best-selling evangelistic novels. The third member of the triumvirate, twenty-seven-year-old Bob Jones, III, is the school's administrative Pooh-Bah. Bob-the-Third is a lanky, handsome youth who likes to wear tailored pinstripes with narrow English lapels, slant pockets, and pointed-toe shoes; he enjoys tooling around in his red Mercedes-Benz. But despite these eccentricities in son and grandson, they are firmly with The Founder in their exhortations against dancing, watered-down Scripture, and repeal of right-to-work laws, and in upholding total immersion, racial segregation, and eternal damnation for all who go a few degrees wrong.

They like to tell you at BJU of their cultural triumphs: how the Bob Jones Opera Association has produced *Faust, The Barber of Seville,* and the difficult *Ernani* ("last seen in 1928 until *we* did it"), bringing in operatic luminaries to sing lead roles—Cesare Valletti, a leading tenor of the Metropolitan Opera Company and La Scala, Milan; Jarmila Novotna, and Marjorie Lawrence. Or they recall the annual Artist Series' presentations of actor Sir Cedric Hardwicke, violinist Henryk Szeryng and pianist Maria Tipo. They point to trophies won by the school's Unusual Films, or to plaudits bestowed on BJU's Classic Players by Shakespearean scholars. They tell you that even varsity football was unceremoniously scrapped years ago when the Fighting Swamp Angels turned out to have littered the dorms with cigarette butts, beer cans, and other symbols of earthly distractions. And they pridefully say that more students study Greek at BJU than at any undergraduate school in America. All this is true.

But Bob Jones University primarily exists, according to a warning sign in Mack Library, "to exalt the Lord Jesus Christ. The teaching of mathematics, science, literature, music, speech, art, and all other subjects are incidental to this." BJU has supplied more ministers for Fundamentalist pulpits than any school on earth; 5,000 of them attend the spiritual needs of about one million Americans each Sunday. The 612 students in the School of Religion ("Our Preacher Boys," as they are called) must serve off-campus pulpits every weekend. They carry The Word by bus, car, and even horse to hamlets like Reform, Alabama; Brushy Creek, South Carolina; and Fair Play, Georgia. Last year the Preacher Boys distributed a quarter-million Bible tracts, held more than 35,000 services in South Carolina churches alone, and conducted "personal visitations" with almost 100,000 citizens through door-to-door house calls or simply by ambushing unwary sidewalk loafers.

Not for these hearty proselytizers an elastic creed which might include drinks at the country club, or square-dancing at one of the Saturday night stomps in thickets along the creek forks. They endorse a fiery Hell wtih white-hot pitchforks and acrid brimstone, a Heaven where Saint Peter is as real as the armed student guards on BJU's main gates. The Founder sees to that. "If you will trim Jesus down to suit the Modernists," he says, "they will like it. I've never trimmed Jesus down."

He has cut some others down to size, though, and foremost among these is the Devil. The Founder denounced Satan to the mules he plowed as a seven-year-old Alabama farm boy back in 1890. He broadened his audience to include human souls as a teen-age minister who "got the Call" at a backwoods revival in his eleventh year. By the time he was forty, Robert Reynolds Jones, Sr., who thrived in the era of Billy Sunday and John Culpepper, had "led a million souls to Christ."

The Founder has not confined his attacks to Satan. He has, variously, assaulted Billy Graham, the Pope, anti-God scientists, loose women, the National Council of Churches, hillbilly music, whiskey merchants, pie-eating politicians, and lukewarm Christians who eschew orthodoxy. In The Founder's view, "Orthodoxy says the Bible *is* the word of God; Modernism says the Bible merely *contains* the word of God." The "pie-eaters" are politicians who gobble up the false riches of liberalism at the cost of becoming fat in the head, soul, and heart.

In 1928, The Founder made five hundred speeches for Fundamentalism and Herbert Hoover against Al Smith. ("I'd rather see a nigger President.") He and his heirs have expressed hostility toward every Democratic Presidential nominee since. Campus-speaking favorites include homegrown Senator Strom Thurmond, 1948 Dixiecrat candidate for President, who recently converted to Republicanism; Governor George Wallace of Alabama; General Edwin A. Walker; Southern Methodist University Professor John Beaty, author of *Iron Curtain Over America;* radio rightists Dr. Carl McIntyre and the Reverend Billy James Hargis, who, between them, broadcast five hours each week over BJU radio station WMUU*; and *The National Review's* Bill Buckley.

Last Thanksgiving Sunday, preaching to 3,300 in overflowing Rodeheaver Auditorium, BJU's Dean of Men got in pulpit licks against the United Nations, Medicare, the Federal Communications Commission, and labor unions. ("Noah, building the Ark in accordance with God's command, didn't have to worry about unions or time-and-a-half for overtime.") On the bus tour for Barry Goldwater, banners warned: "Turn Back America! Only a Divine Miracle Can Save Us Now!" Still the Joneses get their dander up if you say they run a political institution.

One thing they assuredly do not run at Bob Jones University is a democracy. "If you don't like it here," The Founder has reminded students and faculty alike, "you can pack your dirty duds and hit the four-lane highway." Some of the 3,500 students do exactly that each year. Nobody will say how many, least of all the students themselves.

---

* Standing for "World's Most Unusual University," one of the most powerful FM stations in the area.

They are forbidden to talk to newsmen, writers, or to any stranger whose business is unknown. But in 1953 the registrar, three deans, and a dozen teachers resigned after charging The Founder with insisting that "the tiniest facet of his thought" be considered red-letter Gospel—an act which inspired The Founder to speak on Judas.

Though in theory faculty members are hired for life, they can by contract be fired on ten-day notice. Dr. Bob Jr., who in his role as President spends most of his time traveling to raise funds and recruit students, puts it bluntly: "We do not believe it is a just use of the term 'academic freedom' for a man to be able to say, 'I'm gonna teach evolution or free love in this school.' Academic freedom here boils down to the ability to say or do anything you want to do—so long as it doesn't offend the Bible."

By Jones guidelines, however, the Bible is easier to offend than Maria Callas. You can offend it by listening to, singing, or playing jazz, by picking up a deck of cards; or by becoming inquisitive over the specific biological details of the Virgin Birth. Indeed, your wife can offend the Book for you by wearing slacks or merely by "griping."

Wives are considered under contract to serve BJU in their best capacities the moment their husbands join the faculty. Room and board are computed in salary scales, and salaries are based on "need." Thus an instructor with five mouths to feed is paid more than a childless full professor. Dr. R. K. Johnson, BJU business manager and an orphan boy who came as a student in 1928 and has never left, claims that "fringe benefits of our group far exceed any I've ever heard of. Our faculty members are better off [than] they would be in any other system in the world."*

But BJU is not popular with the American Association of University Professors. There is, academically speaking, a heavily incestuous air about the faculty. All but twenty-six of its 160 teachers got at least part of their education at BJU. Four of ten doctorates (including that of Vice-President Bob Jones III) were awarded on the home campus. "Dr." Bob Sr. and "Dr." Bob Jr. have honorary Doctor of Divinity degrees. The Founder's was granted by Muskingum College, New Concord, Ohio; the President's is courtesy of Northwestern Schools, Minneapolis.

For every Shalt Not binding the faculty, students are restricted by at least a half-dozen. They shall not use the gymnasium, swimming

* One must, however, balance this observation with the notation that Dr. Johnson has favorably compared The Founder with Saint Paul.

pool, or tennis courts in sexually mixed groups; nor borrow anything from townspeople; nor release any information to newspapers. Nor shall they patronize any store (drug, restaurant, or grocery included) that sells liquor, wine, or beer; nor become addicts of "hillbilly screechers, swing bands, or syncopated hop-skip-and-jump music"; nor leave the campus after 10:30 P.M. One violation can mean expulsion. Any student knowing of a violation by any other, but who fails to report it, is considered as guilty as the original sinner.

The Founder, though he has lived long past the three score and ten years allotted by the Bible, has not forgotten the warm-blooded folly of youth. "It is a little dangerous," he warns, "to make love on a moonlight night." Fat chance of that. Off-campus dating is taboo unless special permission is granted; even then, dates must be chaperoned. On-campus dates are limited to two hours; boys and girls must keep a six-inch space between their bodies whether sitting or standing. To be found with a blanket anywhere on campus, except in one's own room, is as final as Doomsday.

"Bob Jones students," says young Dr. Bob III, "do not swallow goldfish. They don't care how many people can pack a telephone booth, and they don't waste their time with checkers, chess, or puzzles." They don't smoke or gripe, either. The college catalogue warns that "no griping will be tolerated"; students must fill out forms each year attesting that tobacco and liquor have not touched their lips since last they signed the pledge.

Most BJU students were raised in hard-shell Baptist churches, though by no means all. Many are from such Holy Roller sects as the Church of God or Assembly of God. Others are low-church Presbyterians, Methodists, and Campbellites. When Preacher Boys go forth to spread the Word, they generally migrate to Baptist pulpits. The school is officially nonsectarian, however. (The Founder quit the Methodist Church of his father in 1939, blasting it as "a honeycomb of Modernism.")

"Our kids are the cream of the crop," Dr. Bob III says. "They've really got to be zealots to make it here. A lot of them come here over the objections of parents who've been softened up by the Modernists." But there is a history of "going to Daddy's Old School," too. In America's small towns and on its farms are fathers who rush their heirs off to Greenville the way Philadelphia Main Line lawyers or fathers holding seats on the Stock Exchange point their sons toward Harvard or Yale. BJU graduates tend to marry each other; rarely do the offspring of such unions escape to other campuses. The school rightfully claims students from all fifty states and thirty foreign countries. But the student body is predominantly Southern, though California, Pennsylvania, and Indiana have sizable delegations.

Most BJU students prepare for careers in the ministry or in teaching. But the School of Business is growing rapidly, and talent scouts for management are increasingly attracted to Greenville. Bob Jones graduates are neat, orderly, and take to corporate discipline. "You don't get any boat-rockers or deadbeats hanging around the water cooler or loafers betting on office football pools," a Bendix Company recruiter says.

It is not difficult to see why the managerial scouts like BJU students. They are courteous to a fault when not rattling about God or Goldwater, and they radiate determined cheer even before breakfast. By edict boys wear ties at all times, and coats to meals. Girls are never without hose; they are permitted just enough facial makeup to prevent possible mutiny arising from the inborn vanity of their sex.

There is more spit-'n'-polish than at West Point. Bells sound for reveille and lights out; attendance at all chapels and meals is mandatory; all classes or discussion groups must be prayed open and prayed closed. All this is "heavenly manna" to The Founder, after which, he says, "garlic and onions can never taste good anymore." To partake of such manna, the BJU student pays $1,000 annual tuition.

If other Fundamentalist schools had done their jobs the way The Founder and God wanted them to, Bob Jones University would not be a going concern today. But other schools would not remain loyal to orthodoxy. They began to harbor a professor or two who "taught evolution as a fact," they surrendered to "the atheistic drift in education," and they came to see symbolism in the Garden of Eden's talking serpent instead of simply recognizing him as a real old snake in the grass.

All this had happened by 1927. Bob Jones, Sr., by then deserved (and sometimes got) equal billing in the evangelistic big leagues with the flamboyant "praying baseball player," Billy Sunday. On one memorable occasion when more than 6,000 erring sinners walked the aisle to give themselves to Deity, Dr. Jones was there to receive them.

Though feeling he was blessed in his ministry, Dr. Jones had nagging thoughts that something was wrong. One day he figured out what it was. "I am tired," he told his wife, "of leading boys and girls to Jesus Christ and then seeing them attend institutions which shake their faith. Honey, I am going to build a school."

They called it Bob Jones College when doors opened in September 1927, among five hundred acres of sandy-land pines nine miles outside Panama City, Florida. Following the Depression crash of 1929, Dr. Jones moved the school to "more centrally located Cleveland, Tennessee." There it remained until 1946, when the city of Greenville offered free the present 185-acre campus.

"Some of the money was mine and some of the money was a gift of God," is about as specific as The Founder gets about financing five buildings of Spanish architecture on the original Florida site. The Founding Class of 125 tilled twenty acres to produce campus food, milked a twelve-cow dairy herd, and operated a canning factory. Governor Bibb Graves of Alabama came to dedicate a school pledged by charter "to combat all atheistic, agnostic, pagan, and so-called scientific adulteration of the Gospel." But Dr. Jones did not want to found "just another Bible College." Though giving "special emphasis to the Christian religion and the ethics revealed in the Holy Scripture," he would "conduct an institution of learning for the general education of youth in the essentials of culture, the arts, and sciences."

One must wonder, though BJU's official family does not, whether these scholastic expectations have been realized. Only a few deep Dixie and prairie-state schools enthusiastically welcome BJU products for graduate work. The school is not a member of the Southern Association of Colleges and Secondary Schools, nor is it affiliated with national education organizations. The Joneses claim this has nothing to do with poor academic ratings. Long ago The Founder got on record that "we can render better services spiritually and even educationally without holding organic membership in an association." BJU has also refused federal grants rather than sign "the so-called Act of Compliance and be at the mercy of federal control." The official line out of Greenville is that BJU would be cheerfully admitted to almost any academic circle it wished to join, but is choosy about whom it circles up with.

This contention is judged closer to pure truth on the BJU campus than in more detached quarters. One can imagine academic heavyweights wondering about any institution where an anthropology course is described in the school catalogue as "a Christian interpretation of the problems of evolution and human origins," or where the clinical psychology course bears down on "the application of Biblical principles to the diagnosis and treatment of mental problems." Nor does it help when a BJU lecturer, asked about radioactive dating methods that show the world to be several million years old, responds that "scientists mistakenly assume that God has never accelerated radioactive decay rates."

Sometimes even the Joneses can't seem to make up their minds exactly where their school belongs on academic charts. One moment Dr. Bob III will tell you, "We're unusual in our objective to teach the student what he already believes. We don't throw out a bunch of theories about the religions of the world or philosophy and that sort of thing." In the next, he tosses off the names of BJU graduates who are "recognized masters in the world of arts and letters." He cites Clifford Lewis, a member of the Founding Class, as the author of *233 Precious Poems* and *Japan Needs Jesus.* And the "Christian novels, books of inspirational sermons, and volumes of devotional verse" by BJU's own Dr. Bob Jr. "have been critically acclaimed in *Bible Banner* and *The Christian Herald.*" The same Dr. Bob (author, president, actor), you are given to understand, is skilled enough on the boards to have "turned down offers of Hollywood screen tests."

Junior Jones is not, in fact, a bad actor, nor an inexperienced one. In University dramas, his roles have included Shylock, Macbeth, Lear, and Pontius Pilate in the screen dramatization of his own novel, *Wine of Morning.**

Wine of Morning, a two-hour color production, won not only the National Evangelical Film Foundation's four top "Oscars," but high praise from the French Institute of Cinematography, the Canadian Kodak Company, the Italian Motion Picture Institute, and critics at the International Film Festival in Cannes. It has been shown on TV in Switzerland, enjoyed a Paris run under sponsorship of the American Embassy, was praised by a Russian official for its "breathtaking photography" (though not its Christian message), and has gladdened BJU coffers as the all-time box-office smash of evangelical filmdom. A twelve-minute full-color production, *The Flying Angel,* a trailer on how movies are made at BJU, was voted the Intercollegiate Film Award for Short Subjects by the Screen Producers Guild.

* Dr. Jones does not need screen tests at BJU. He is casting director.

BJU ranks, in fact, with UCLA, Boston University, and the University of Southern California as a king of collegiate cinema-making. It is not likely, however, to send its graduates to Hollywood tasks. Signs posted in the block-long shooting studio warn against vanity, and remind one that talent is God-given. "When we first started the movie thing here," says Dr. Bob Jr., "some people were afraid we might be going Modernist. But that wasn't it. We just decided the Devil had been granted a monopoly on drama long enough."

In Christian lore, Christianity and persecution are synonyms. Holy wars . . . raw meat for the lions . . . plagues of locust and famine. Evil kings: Herod and Pharaoh and the king of Moab. Bondage and dungeons and crucifixion. You understand how deeply ingrained all this is when you hear The Founder growl, "We took on all the enemies of Jesus Christ when we founded this school." The theme is everywhere. In Melton Wright's *Fortress of Faith,* the official BJU story, we are told: "There have been well-organized, well-financed schemes to smear Dr. Jones' name and to ruin his influence, ruin Bob Jones University, and cripple the whole Fundamentalist movement through Dr. Jones." And The Founder himself is fond of saying, "The door to opportunity swings on the hinges of opposition." Sometimes the Jones clan seems to give the door a push.

Take the Billy Graham case. Billy Graham, the biggest mover and shaker on the revival circuit for the past fifteen years, was a BJU student briefly in 1936. He left, by his version, because the school proved something of a disappointment. "He couldn't stand the discipline," says young Bob III, quoting lessons learned at his granddaddy's feet. "To be an evangelist," The Founder says he once told Reverend Dr. Graham to his face, "the Lord wants a man to have brains in his head, grace in his heart, and guts in his belly—and you, Billy, don't have any of them."

At BJU they think Dr. Graham has "trimmed Jesus down." He has welcomed to his platform Catholic Cardinals, pie-eating politicians, and representatives of the National Council of Churches. He has prayed over Lyndon B. Johnson's inauguration, and insists on preaching only to racially integrated audiences. He has kind words for the United Nations, and he attended an Inaugural Gala where—in the words of an ex-Preacher Boy now filling a Georgia pulpit—"had been gathered three hundred bartenders to pour whiskey and one preacher to pray." President Jones has listed Satan's "three forces in his war against God" as "Modernism, Neo-Orthodoxy, and the New Evangelicalism. Of these three, the last group is the most dangerous." You know where that puts Dr. Graham, don't you?

"Why, I tried every way in the world to help Billy," The Founder says. "He asked to be considered one of my Preacher Boys, even though he quit us here before his shirttail had time to come out, and he asked to return here and speak to our students." Dr. Jones welcomed the Prodigal Son with an honorary Doctor of Divinity degree. But those were the days when Billy Graham scolded labor unions and warned that "over 1,100 social-sounding organizations are communist or communist-operated in this country." Times changed, and so did Billy. He got to running with "those who proclaimed only the humanistic virtues of Christ," says The Founder. He put down extremism, broke bread with the New Nixon, and played golf with Jack Paar. In 1957 The Founder refused to permit a campus Prayer Day asking blessings on Dr. Graham's Madison Square Garden crusade, saying he wanted no part in "the great compromise." In flat-earth Fundamentalist circles, it was the shot heard across the world.

Greenville, South Carolina, goes with Bob Jones University like cornbread goes with sweet milk. When Dial-A-Prayer service first came to Greenville, so many people called they overloaded the phone circuits. The city has 126 churches: 119 Protestant, 61 of them Baptist. The biggest thing on local TV is Billy Grammer and his Gospel Guitar. The program is sponsored by a roach powder and a stomach tonic; Billy always twangs out a Sacred Number dedicated to "all you shut-ins out there in television-land." Greenville is the kind of town where everybody calls the noon meal "dinner," and supper is on the edge of bedtime.

Guests may drink a little whiskey in the "private clubs" up on new Highway 29, but downtown in the old, gone-to-seed section, BJU Preacher Boys shout their warnings of hellfire next to red-paint reminders that "Jesus Died For Your Sins." On the wide, sloped streets where the middle class lives there is an aura of faint decay and gentle Southern decadence. Down in the city's bottoms, the yards of shack-dwelling textile mill "lint-heads" are grotesquely beautified by sprays of flowers growing from the centers of whitewashed auto tires anchored in the ground.

Greenville is the Old South, and the Old South is of the Fundamentalism to which the Jones Boys owe their allegiance. This faith fed on the region's inbred clannishness and historic reluctance to change its stubborn clinging to old values. You see this stubbornness there today in die-hard segregationists, village cops who fear One World Government, working men who suspect labor unions; in the Ku Klux Klan's perverted distortions of Lee's Lost Cause, and in ancestry worship to rival the Japanese.

The frontier church often became school and sideshow as well as spiritual pillar. Early-day evangelists were often more acrobat than prophet. Even today's modern "faith healers" (Oral Roberts, for example) tour in tents and employ musical minstrels common to roadshow traditions. This "old-time religion" tempted each act to top the other, just as vaudeville did. It bred cultists who tottered on the brink of religious hysteria: folks who went in for foot-washings, talked in tongues, kept multiple wives, or as the late Governor Earl Long of Louisiana said, "chunked snakes and caught fevers."

This was the Fundamentalism I knew in childhood: a combination gaudy tent show and grim Puritanism. One might with impunity jig-dance in the throes of the Holy Spell, but tap not one foot in response to bows drawn across catgut strings. It was a personalized religion: God was as real as the truant officer or the superintendent of schools. The Founder of Bob Jones University knew this personal faith. He would "lie in bed and talk to God," he "met God in a personal way out in the woods," and he "felt God's tap on the shoulder." It was, really, a form of faith in one's self, an extension of ids and egos.

The first thing you see in the Administration Building is a sign warning: "Visitors Will Not Smoke in BJU Buildings." The second is a door marked "Do Not Enter."

I ran the gauntlet of signs last November. For several days I had prowled the campus unannounced, observing students and teachers (though failing in attempts at meaningful conversation with any of them), attending Thanksgiving services, taking stock of the physical plant. Student patrolmen looked me over but never approached. One patrol car stayed close while I circled among homes in the faculty compound (where the Joneses have the biggest homes), but when I kept going the patrol car did too.

When I called on Dr. Bob Jones III shortly before noon one day, a pretty young receptionist said, "Young Dr. Bob's out to dinner." Waiting, I eyed bigger-than-life oil portraits of the Jones Boys and their wives which dominate the Administration Building lobby. The portraits reminded me of those I had seen over mantels in the homes of Texas oil millionaires, where all nose warts and chin duplications had been carefully painted out.

Young Dr. Jones received me an hour later. He was faintly bathed in the sunlight which streamed through stained-glass windows. He appeared more than six feet tall, slim, and even younger than his years. His dark hair had been neatly clipped in accord with school rules. He had a firm handclasp and a wide mouth that often smiled when his eyes did not. In his narrow-lapel pinstripes and pointed shoes he would have been called a "jellybean" in the brush country of my youth.

The office with its stained glass, paneled walls, deep carpet, and executive desk was altogether attractive. It took a while to decide what was missing: books and ash trays. Bob III's desk held but a single copy of *National Geographic,* two sheets of paper, and a telephone. Several times I tentatively reached for a cigarette. Each time Jones eyed me furtively.

When he learned my mission, Dr. Jones held Christian rejoicing to a minimum. "No," he said, "I'm afraid I can't help you. Not unless you promise you'll write a strictly *factual* story." I said I hoped to, but that in matters of religion and politics folks often had trouble agreeing on facts. Young Dr. Bob scowled. He said, "I will *not* talk about politics or religion. If you want to do a factual piece about our facilities or our accomplishments, fine. But no religion and no politics."

I quoted the sign from Mack Library: "Bob Jones University exists to exalt the Lord Jesus Christ." I read the names of BJU political speakers, and mentioned the Goldwater tour. Didn't that put the school somewhat into religion and politics?

Dr. Jones was vexed. "But this is not a *partisan* institution. I tried to explain that to reporters from *The Nation* and the *New York Times.* It didn't do a bit of good. They wrote the same old stuff the liberal press always writes. Taking quotes out of context . . . poking fun . . . distorting. We can't trust the liberal press! We're nice to 'em, and then they go off and knock us."

I said, "The door to opportunity swings on the hinges of opposition." Young Dr. Jones recognized I was quoting his grandfather, and that is when I realized his eyes do not smile every time his mouth does.

We talked politics and religion for two hours. The exchange began when I mentioned Billy Graham. I had asked where Dr. Graham had "gone wrong." To tell the truth, it was like hunting with a baited trap.

"I just don't *understand* him," Dr. Jones said. "He had everything. God had blessed his work . . ." He shook his head, leaned back in his chair and his eyes got bright. I had seen that look in the eyes of a hundred preachers. It meant singing was over and the sermon would begin.

He said, "God has blessed this school. He raised it up and He has sustained it. This school is worth thirty million dollars and has no debts. We serve a great God. . . . People support this school because they know the Devil won't get one nickel of their money. We haven't compromised.

"The Duke Foundation offered us a grant of two million dollars. We turned it down—they made their money in tobacco. And we've turned down federal grants. We know that with any amount of government money comes a like amount of government controls. No whiskey-drinking bureaucrat is going to draw us a blueprint for preaching the salvation of Jesus Christ the way he'd draw a blueprint for some urban renewal scheme. Why, if we ever compromised Jesus Christ, then by law this school could be closed down. The Founder had that put in the charter.

"We get kids with a lot of character," he said. "They come here because they can't get what we offer at the bohemian colleges. They don't want a campus where they can buy pep pills and tranquilizers or go on alcoholic sprees. We've got a *monopoly* on a certain kind of kid. Other schools handed us that monopoly on a silver platter by stressing materialism and intellectualism—and they're the twin foes of the Gospel."

Didn't liberalism rate high among "foes of the Gospel" at BJU? Young Bob III reluctantly nodded, as if he had a headache and feared sudden motion. "I guess you'll bring in the Goldwater bus and make that *sound* partisan. So I'd better explain. We hold with old-fashioned Christian Americanism. We think it made this country great. We think it serves freedom, and we think it serves God. Now we aren't partisan, but when liberalism crops up we fight it. And if liberalism crops up in one political party more than in another . . . well, that's not *our* fault, is it?"

I knew better than to suggest social responsibility as a Christian virtue. The Jones Boys consider social Gospel worse than no Gospel at all. Young Dr. Jones once said, "Our graduates are not crusaders against social depravity and political injustice. They are warriors against Sin, and the Scripture refers to the Christian life many times as *spiritual warfare*. So our efforts are not primarily for the purpose of making a *better world,* but rather to spread the good news of salvation."

Dr. Jones had been quoted as saying racial segregation is taught by the Bible. I asked for the Scriptural citation. "That always gets quoted out of context," he said. "I don't want to discuss it. If I had confidence you'd print the whole thing . . . well, it's so long and complicated—. No, I don't want to talk about that."

I persisted. Hadn't he said God has decreed the Negro to be "a servant's servant?"; that the Negro "is happier when waiting tables"; when serving mankind in special ways "God intended"?

After a long pause Dr. Jones replied: "Look, I'm not a racist. This isn't a racist institution. I don't want to go beyond that." We observed twenty seconds of silence, then he went beyond it. "I've known some fine Christian Nigras. I'm for the Nigra having his rights; I sure am. But I do feel . . . lots of us feel . . ." Then with a firm resolve, he declared, "That's all I'll say on the subject, sir. I don't see it has anything to do with Bob Jones University."

Was there even one Negro student in BJU? Had there ever been?

"Well, now, that's a matter of record. No, sir. I expect you knew that or you wouldn't have asked the question. But that's no reason to—we're not, and I'll say it again, a *racist* institution. We don't teach hate. We teach love of Jesus and love *by* Jesus for his children.

"Now sir, that's absolutely the last word I'll say on the Nigra subject."

Soon our conversation became desultory. We quarreled mildly over theology, but without much spirit, and when my senses reeled from craving tobacco, I traded final handshakes with him. At the door I asked, "Do you know where I can get a copy of your father's novel, *Wine of Morning?*" Out in the world of carefully curried public images and PR men, two assistant vice-presidents would have materialized carrying freebies. But with Dr. Bob Jones III, charity did not, this day, begin at home. "Yessir," he said. "You can buy it at our bookstore."

And I could be secure in the knowledge that "not one nickel" of

my purchase price would go to the Devil, or to Americans for
Democratic Action.

If you think the purveyors of Heaven
don't know how to give you Hell, then you should see what the mail-
man lugged over as a result of the foregoing opus. Lord, how the letters rolled in!

Among the first to be heard from was Junior Jones, whom you will
remember as actor, casting director, novelist and current BJU president. Dr. Jones advised me, through *Harper's,* that he had read my
"silly and asinine" little story, then went on to rake yellow journalists, liars, and a conspiracy to do him and Jesus in. Indeed, even
before the article appeared he threatened a lawsuit. The good Doctor,
spotting a house ad in *Harper's* which touted my piece in the
upcoming issue, made up his mind from the three or four blurb-lines
that he "knows libel when I see it" and demanded a copy of the
whole works for his lawyers. Somehow he read into my story a charge
that the Jones Boys were living off the fatted calf in a manner illegal
or shameful, though as far as I am concerned that notion is his sole
property and not mine. Two BJU trustees added their voices to the
chorus, one alleging: "This smear attack on BJU appears to be part
of a definite conspiracy shared in by *The New York Times, The
Nation,* so-called *Christian Century* and other far-left periodicals."
He went on to say BJU is a nonprofit organization, the Joneses keeping only such money in salaries as to hold body, soul, and—one presumes—an occasional red Mercedes-Benz together; that a twelve-
member board of trustees guides BJU's destiny, and, further, that the
Truth is nowhere in me. *Harper's* editors responded that they are convinced "the Jones family does in fact exercise effective control of
BJU" (a logical premise: the Jones Boys recommend new trustees
when vacancies occur, run the day-to-day operation, the Board meets
normally but once a year to ratify the direction the school is going,
and the operating charter was, after all, written by The Founder) but
that "this fact does not in any way imply that the Trustees are guilty
of dishonest management or that the Jones family has enriched
itself." I am willing to take the Jones Boys' word that they are up to
nothing foul and to take Congress' word that nonprofit charters aren't
really licenses to steal. (Though I cannot help pointing out they *are*
effective in excusing taxes.)

Numerous loyal old BJU "Preacher Boys," most of whom now run their own Bible colleges if one takes their letterheads at face value, wrote in a way that did not show any predisposition on their parts to turn the other Christian cheek. Several, seizing on my comment relative to suffering nicotine fits while honoring BJU's order not to smoke in its buildings, promised me an early death from cancer; to a man they scribbled some particular biblical passage I should apparently beware. I am not the first cat curiosity killed, so I looked the citations up. They promised me all sorts of trouble in the Afterlife, as I interpreted the Word, and for all I know they may very well be right.

Perhaps the correspondents followed a predictable pattern. Dr. Jones once engaged LBJ's right-hand man, Bill Moyers (himself a Baptist minister), in a spiffy exchange of letters about Sin in High Places. On another occasion he wrote a high government official that not only would his institution refuse to sign the Statement of Compliance necesssary to receive Federal funds, but that "As far as I am concerned, you can take any further communications you want to send me and stick them somewhere; and I don't care where you stick them . . ." Who says the meek shall inherit the earth?

A few folks got mad on the other side of the question, too. SMU messaged me tersely that Professor John Beaty, one-time BJU guest lecturer, was (1) no longer on the SMU faculty, and (2) was a long time dead. One of New York's larger law firms took pains to "deny categorically that the Duke Endowment ever made, or offered, any grant to Bob Jones University." A graduate of Muskingum, while admitting that his alma mater had, indeed, granted The Founder his honorary doctorate some years ago, hastened to assure me that such a thing could never happen again.

Not all the correspondence was angry in tone, though friends of BJU may find comfort in knowing that most laudatory comments came from such sin dens as Yale, Harvard and UCLA. Several ex-BJU students wrote to say that my article had more truth in it than poetry, though, admittedly, they had not stuck around the campus long enough to be granted their degrees. One such fellow particularly impressed me. "Your article," he wrote, "was supremely fair and also engrossing. I chose intellectualism but I believe God still loves me." He seemed a good witness for my side in the controversy until I read his postscript: "Incidentally, occasionally I smoke a pipe. And I want to be a writer."

Score another for the devil.

CHAPTER 8

Hedy, Ecstasy and Me

If anybody ever writes a book called *The Wit and Wisdom of Benito Mussolini,* no doubt a half-dozen literary editors will strain their equipment rushing it to me for review.

I don't know why book-page editors have universally deduced that if an author can't write a lick or if a book's subject matter is such as to curl Orville Prescott's southmost lip into a permanent sneer, then I am perfectly situated to review it. Whatever their reasons, or however accurate their instincts, America's book-page editors have crowned me heavyweight champion reviewer of the Non-Book book. I should not be one whit surprised should it develop that *New York Review of Books* has the Sears-Roebuck Christmas catalogue in the mail to me this minute, it being a matter of record that my last assignment was a cookbook with which the publisher mailed out free wedges of cheese. Just once I wish they would let me criticize something really *good:* works that would stoke your inner fires and cause you to count up life's follies. The latest inspirations of Jacqueline Susann, maybe, or an ancient volume of Nick Kenny's poems.

Among the literary giants whose works have been assigned to me for critical attention are Miss Hedy LaMarr and Lyndon B. Johnson's mother. Miss LaMarr's field of expertise is sex while the late Mrs. Johnson's was the infant LBJ, and though it may cause them to purge me from the rolls over at Democratic National Headquarters I confess a natural preference for the former. This causes me to find that *Ecstasy and Me* has it all over *A Family Album,* though to be fair I should note that the latter was perhaps handicapped by having no nude pictures of its subject. By the fairest standards available, however, I am compelled to report that of all the Non-Books I have officially showered attention upon the greatest was *Ecstasy and Me—* a judgment which will not, I almost hysterically trust, encourage Miss LaMarr to sit soon at the Remington keyboard again.

Among my all-time favorite Non-Books is *Alpalca,* a novel by Texas oil tycoon H. L. Hunt. Mr. Hunt is a work-a-day patriot who lives in Dallas, Texas, in a replica of George Washington's Mount Vernon home, though of course H. L.'s pad is bigger than George's was because George didn't have the oil depletion allowance going for him. Mr. Hunt knows almost as much about the craft of fiction as I do about bringing in gushers. He knows even less about politics, and, I suspect, is not in the same league with Miss LaMarr when it comes to sex, because he had his raven-haired pulp heroine lose her heart to a man whose scheme to save the world from Democracy (by giving each citizen a number of votes in direct ratio to his net financial worth) apparently gave off some overpoweringly heady musk.

Not only do I get all the hot authors, I am fast developing a reputation as a past master of exotic subjects. Who else has been tapped to pass literary judgment on the authorized biography of evangelist Billy Graham ("The number of decisions for Christ, apart from those of telecast viewers, was 61,148.") or on tomes about spelunking, Chinese checkers, or President Johnson's sense of humor?

From all this I have accumulated a grand total of $500, a suspicion that book-page editors consider others better qualified to comment on Sartre or Updike, and the everlasting enmity of numerous prominent folk so sensitive that minor earthquakes occur wherever they step. There also has developed among authors who take themselves seriously a paralyzing fear that one of their books may somehow be assigned to me, an act that would probably (1) start rumors their next book is being published by a vanity house and (2) cause everybody at literary cocktail parties to look at them as if they'd come in wearing brown shoes and had compounded the gaucherie by carrying the latest art of Harold Robbins under their arms.

Were it not for Non-Books, however, I would have precious few reviews to my list of credits. It has reached the point where I actually search *Publisher's Weekly* in keen anticipation of the memoirs of Senator Bourke B. Hickenlooper or How-To books on making rattan furniture, and only last night I had this wonderful dream that Baby Jane Holzer is reducing her experiences to writing. No matter what the Non-Book writers come up with, however, I know that my zenith as a critic was reached when they handed me Miss LaMarr's remembrances of things past in a plain brown wrapper and told me to do my stuff. You should not go through life without knowing something of . . .

HEDY, ECSTASY AND ME

Do you remember when you had acne and a changing voice, and how your palms would sweat on your Buttercup as you sat there in some darkened theater, all popeyed and breathing like a dray horse, while Clark Gable rained kisses on Carol Lombard or Baby told Bogie that if he wanted anything all he had to do was pucker up and blow? Or the terrible dryness that gripped your throat while Hedy LaMarr— perhaps cloaked in scant raiment as the savage beauty Tondelayo of *White Cargo*—undulated her charms in a most disturbing way? And how, later on, you might have a tough time keeping your mind on your upcoming Tenderfoot Scout tests because all these very un-scoutly fantasies kept swimming before your eyes: you and Carol Lombard, you and Baby, you and the savage Tondelayo: all hair and heat and hands . . .

Well, this is America where the shine boy has The Dream and it is the Land of Opportunity where office boys rise to be board chairmen and the tired poor huddled masses yearning to breathe free can jump off the boat and make a quick killing in kumquats, funeral wreaths, or hula hoops. So why *not* you and Hedy LaMarr? "Why not, indeed?" Miss LaMarr seems to ask in her maiden literary romp.

Ole Tondelayo does not go four paragraphs before she hikes up her literary skirts to give us a long look at her libido. Before she gets off the invocational page she has shared confidences about several old flames including "a whip-brandishing sadist," a fellow "with a classic case history of impotence," and a gent "who took his pleasure with a girl in my own bed, while he thought I was asleep in it." The authoress is all the way over on page three before she tells us that the second lady in her bed was her very own maid. On this same page she advises that "sex is personal, and its expression, in whatever form it takes, is private." She warns that she has changed the names of some prominent folk and fuzzed up the setting of certain spicy stories so as to obscure their identities "because"—primly, now, Hedy—"I do not intend to assist any reader's morbid curiosity."

Me neither.

Ecstasy and Me is either the worst piece of trash ever written or a revolving, blue-ribbon, pluperfect put-on. I mean, there is no way that somebody trying to give it to you straight could hit upon such an incongruous mixture of piety and sewer gossip and sustain it for 318 pages so that you are still laughing wildly when you reach the final words. (And they are too, too much, those sign-off words: AUF WIEDERSEHEN! Really, Hedy!) The publisher must have a cheek full of tongue when he has a psychologist preface us that the book "is probably as good for Miss LaMarr's psyche as it will be for many a guilt-ridden reader for whom this gutsy confessional may offer resultful therapy, if not instant emancipation." We have got Vietnam, the white backlash, Red China with nuclear missiles, and grocery prices soaring into the blue, yet the publisher is so confident of mankind's future that he has put 50,000 copies of Miss LaMarr's scatological thesis in print.

I was on Capitol Hill the other day and every secretary up there has got a copy of *Ecstasy and Me* in her hot little hands. They are staying at their desks lunchtimes, bringing in thermos jugs of martinis so as to lubricate their tubes while they pant over this latest in a series of Hollywood confessionals. This book will, no doubt, be bought by types whose last book acquisition was the Gideon Bible they copped from a motel room. The girls are going to whisper about it at coffee klatches in Pocatello, and I would like to draw the minimum wage for all the hours they'll spend speculating as to what famous person it was who did what to Hedy where.

Miss LaMarr is the only woman in the world who got into a house of ill-fame by mistake (she ducked in while running from one of her six suspicious old husbands, who somehow didn't trust the poor girl) and who wound up . . . well, doing a turn on the wheel, you might say, because she didn't want to make a fuss and was reluctant to embarrass the nice young man who came in thinking she was a common . . . you know. There is a particularly lurid passage in which Hedy confesses that she could not keep her eyes off another of flickdom's chicks ("perfectly shaped breasts and semi-erect nipples . . .") and how, eventually, she made out with that chick and a few others of the same gender. Then she allows she "doesn't think anybody could call me a lesbian." Possibly a deaf mute couldn't.

Once in a while Miss LaMarr calls time out to remind the "dear reader" (yes, she actually calls you that!) that she is a lady of good taste. "A good painting to me has always been like a friend. It keeps

me company, comforts, and inspires." "I have usually been fascinated by mental types." "I have never liked beer. It's plebeian. It goes
with dirty undershirts." Wonder what goes with dirty linen?

If there is a sensual experience that Miss LaMarr has not had, then
it belongs to the future. She has made out in cars, dressing rooms, on
the stairs, with girls, and in coeducational bunches. She has peeped
on folks with Errol Flynn, attended funny shows in Mexico, and
estimates her lovers at "hundreds." She drops names of world-
renowned statesmen, both living and dead, in suggestive ways that
will not comfort their wives or widows.

I cannot always believe Miss LaMarr. I cannot, for I conjure up
pictures of Miss LaMarr (or her ghost-writer) cackling over the
typewriter while reading the latest inspirational passage to friends
who are breaking up, actually choking on mirth, and begging the
author to please for God's sake stop it, no more, I just can't stand it.
The author has, in fact, gone to court to prevent publication of her
book. Miss LaMarr told a judge that what the publisher proposed to
print was not what she had written. The judge was not convinced, and
so loosed the work upon the land. May he live in torment forever.

Miss LaMarr goes on at some length of how one rich husband almost went broke trying to buy up all prints of her first film, *Ecstasy,*
in which she swam around in the nude, and tells about that terrible
misunderstanding when she was charged wih shoplifting some months
ago. Mostly, however, she just ruts around in several sets of bed-
clothes.

Those of you who still have an occasional wild fantasy about
ecstasy should know that if you scratch Miss LaMarr on the bottoms
of her feet she becomes "paralyzed." Actually purrs. God, what I
would give to have known that back in my days of innocence and
acne!

CHAPTER 9

Yesterday's Heroes in the Mickey Mouse League

Among the many bronzed works of my likeness that I once anticipated leaving behind in the old hometown square was one with its eyes on far stars, chest out, chin determined; arm cocked in a way at once promising beauty and vengeance and good. In this particular opium nap my monument's bronzed arm was eternally frozen in motion just before releasing the Bomb against Notre Dame, Southern Methodist or even the Chicago Bears. Sometimes time got tangled, for it seemed that I would be throwing the ball to Jim Thorpe or Red Grange, both of whom graduated slightly ahead of my class. But no matter the receiver's name or talent, I would lead him perfectly and hit him right in the hands and on the goal line, so that the only way he could avoid scoring a touchdown was by repealing the law of gravity in mid-stride.

My All-Time Greatest Quarterback monument was, like the living model whose memory it honored, a triple-threat man. Sometimes its great bronzed leg would swing high in the air, booming a coffin-corner quick-kick of 99.9 yards out-of-bounds on the New York Giant $\frac{1}{64}$-inch line,* and then again it would squirm and stiff-arm and beat and thresh its way 101 game-winning yards against Army while bells rang and lights flashed and sirens went off even as American flags burst from its ears. It was a damned fine statue.

Pity that it was never raised, save on the shifting sands of many a time-blown daydream. Making All-America was one of my very best dreams, sustaining me from the cradle to—well, not much over the age of thirty-five, though for a while there last summer in camp with the Philadelphia Eagles new hope flickered like fireflies.

This is no literary X-K-97 quarterback sneak. I had not been bugled

* Denotes record.

141

to the Eagle camp to displace Norman Snead, King Hill or Jack Concannon. George Plimpton is the only pro quarterback I know who writes better than he throws, so be it understood that I was in the Philadelphia camp not as a lordly warrior but as a lowly writer. There was, however, one brief shining moment in which I was a cleated Camelot. I shall eventually tell you about it short of being put under a peace bond. Meanwhile, let us reason together about unreasonable ambition.

Mine was to be an All-America Quarterback. The only seasons in which I actually played quarterback, strangely enough, were those in which I organized and coached my very own teams. One of these teams had the name of King's All-America All-Stars, and on it were such football greats as Billy Royce Sweeney, Alvin Hawk King and Hugh Edgar Schrader. If you have not heard of them perhaps it is because you happened not to be in the rural Texas community of Scranton in 1940, a year in which Frankie Albert and I plied the same trade. Albert quarterbacked Stanford University to the Rose Bowl that year, while I quarterbacked King's All-America All-Stars to six consecutive, luckless defeats. The season convinced me that I was playing with less help than perhaps even a brilliant eleven-year-old quarterback should have. Otherwise it put no blemish on the dream.

Years later, at the Signal Corps Photographic Center in Astoria, Long Island, I followed through on a midnight inspiration by organizing and coaching that military institution's first football team in history. I was a playing coach. No one was able to beat me out for quarterback, a situation that came as no surprise for I well knew my lethal talents and further knew who was head coach. We had what you might call a spotty year, beginning with a 0–21 loss to the A-B-C Rams, a group of Astoria sports who could usually be found recombing their locks in the plate-glass reflection of the neighborhood candy store, but who proved very spirited at rough games on the particular Sunday afternoon when we played them on a vacant lot littered with broken glass and almost directly under the Triborough Bridge. I blush now to recall the circumstance of that game, it having been matched because I saw in the A-B-C Rams a "breather" team to serve as the unfortunate unit against which I would practice to perfection the throwing of touchdown passes. The civilian team's lack of cooperation with Our Boys In Uniform on this given Sunday caused me on Monday to make the smartest of several key decisions in my coaching career: I telephoned West Point to cancel a scheduled midweek scrimmage against the Army Plebe team on the excuse that my troops would be occupied with unforeseen "field maneuvers." We were at that, though the maneuvers were those on our practice field and were for the purpose of trying to determine why a team given perfect quarterbacking had failed to function as masterfully as had been presumed. We never did find out what the trouble was.

There were many problems indigenous to coaching (or quarter-backing) the Signal Corps eleven. Ours was a small and most unmilitary unit, totally unarmed save for the symbolic billy-clubs the guards wore at the front gate, and in contact with soldiering only when Authority herded our whimpering legions into trucks once annually for the drive to Fort Dix, New Jersey, so that we might technically qualify as fighting men by firing on the rifle range. More than half of us routinely failed to qualify. I am not giving in to a natural tendency toward exaggeration in relating that one of our party shot himself in the left wrist and a bystander in the rump at such a spot as to constitute a bull's-eye. It was the first bull's-eye we had seen in a long time, and I am afraid that many of us cheered.

We had barely 200 enlisted men in our ranks, three or four times that many officers with illustrious records as desk commandos, and possibly 1,500 civilian employees, most of whom were women. That may not have been conducive to thinking football. At least half the 200 enlisted men available as potential football recruits were either too old, too dedicated to preserving their facial features, or too fond of training at the next-door Studio Bar to be of any meaningful help in games of force or skill. Of the remaining 100 warriors, some 70 percent apparently presumed themselves too intelligent to play football.

I greeted thirty-odd hopefuls at our opening workout. By Thanksgiving Day when we closed the season with a rare victory against Fort Totten, we numbered a few less than twenty, even counting our walking wounded. Our only practice field was the baked-earth compound fronting the photo unit's three decrepit wooden barracks; it was crisscrossed with so many sidewalks that it resembled an airfield for Toyland Airlines, Inc., a condition that inspired my cleated gladiators to run with unusual care and to seek their physical contacts as far from concrete as possible. Workouts were conducted under the eyes of our less athletic comrades-in-arms who, draped over the second-story balconies at the west end of the barracks, serenaded us with hillbilly songs or ribald couplets while showering the field with beer cans. I learned never to throw a pass when scrimmaging from south to north, out of fear the receiver would dash through the compound gates, across the street, and pop into the Studio Bar for the pause that refreshes.

Neither were we the spiffiest-looking outfit you ever saw. Our uniforms were hand-me-down concoctions begged or stolen from larger military bases, or purchased piecemeal as we could scrape together enough Special Services funds for yet another helmet or one more jersey or two. When we took the field we resembled last year's slightly faded Easter eggs, our helmets, jerseys, and trousers being of varied hues. I think we may have originated psychedelic clothing. No doubt this is a great honor, but it didn't help any in trying to pick out receivers on pass plays.

Rank having its privileges, I was the only player to obtain a brand-new set of gear top-to-bottom: baby blue jersey and trousers artistically trimmed in burnt orange, with burnt-orange helmet, matching socks, and—well, yes, shoelaces. I had chosen jersey number 00 because of the suspicion that it might attract attention, cause admiring comment, and somehow (combined with my Little Theater limp) lend a colorful aura of dash. I came to regret the choice: hardly a game went by without the opposition early singling me out as "Double Nothin'."

Though we missed an undefeated season by what might be conservatively termed a comfortable margin, I was offered a football scholarship by a large Eastern university which I do not intend to embarrass by name until all prospects of blackmail appear to have vanished.* Discharged the following summer, I reported for pre-school workouts. Two days into the grind the coach called me aside during a pass drill to inquire whether I thought I might throw a little better pass *left*-handed. The experiment that followed did not set off any street dances. I was subsequently shifted to fullback and there created immediate terror. How it happened was I ran into my quarterback as he turned to proffer his first handoff, he going down like a poleaxed steer and out stone-cold before he knew the ground. Then a halfback reached for the resulting loose ball, by which time I had disengaged the quarterback and was therefore at liberty to step on the eager halfback's arm, breaking it just below the elbow. Attempting to get my bearings after the second encounter, I somehow

* We're less than $5,000 apart right now.

got turned around in the wrong direction and ran full force into a pulling guard whose playbook had not led him to anticipate two-way traffic. Until then I never fully appreciated the expression "he never knew what hit him." My next recollection is of the coach, speaking to the sky: "I have played in the Rose Bowl," he thundered. "I was six years in the NFL. I defensed Blanchard and tackled Nagurski. I don't drink or smoke and never dogged it a day in my life. Why, why, O why?" He said a few other things, but by then his more thoughtful assistants were leading him out of earshot and, besides, I think he started crying about that time, though I was pretty addled myself.

Yet the coach was understandably reluctant to give up on me. He had seen the damage I could do; no doubt he dreamed of harnessing my raw power for larger purposes just as Franklin Roosevelt dreamed of the TVA. All during my quarterbacking days at the Signal Corps Photo Center he had received packet after packet of clippings from the sports pages of the Long Island *Star-Journal* extolling my special skills. I never got up the nerve to admit that I had a fair idea who had mailed them, nor to brag that I had once been a part-time sports stringer for that same newspaper. Despite a good press, I was given my unconditional release.

A week later I was on the campus at Texas Tech, though I did not stay much longer than it takes to tell it. Coach Dell Morgan had yielded to my pleas for a tryout as a quarterback on his Red Raider squad. He proved not to be a patient man. In less than fifteen minutes he had removed me from my natural position. He briefly tried me at every slot but team physician before calling me in for a bit of fatherly advice along the lines that maybe I should try show business. "You got a real funny approach to the game," Coach Morgan said. "You learn to do a little soft-shoe and crack a few jokes, no telling how far your act might take you." Thereafter I confined my football activities to writing sports for Texas newspapers, and to recalling over grog those days of glory when I had won high school letters on the powerful Jal, New Mexico, and Midland, Texas, aggregations.

There was never a game but that I approached it with the sure knowledge that a hero would be born that day. No number of missed tackles, aborted blocks or public fumbles ever took away the certainty that I was an all-the-way threat on the verge of yet another winning touchdown. I should not have been surprised had the half-time entertainment consisted of my coach riding me piggyback around the field the better that I might acknowledge clamorous acclaim. Alas, in the only game I could be remotely credited with winning, the newspaper accounts gave another lad credit for the punt I had blocked and turned into the safety that constituted the day's only scoring. For days I went around Midland pulling up my shirt as if I had experienced recent Presidential surgery, the better to point out my belly bruises as evidence of a miscarriage of justice.

When I showed up at Hershey, Pennsylvania, in the summer of 1966 to write a *Saturday Evening Post* article on Ollie Matson, I do not recall that I consciously hoped to make the Philadelphia Eagle squad. I did report to the practice field early and in a sweat suit, it is true, so that Coach Joe Kuharich would have the opportunity to observe my spiral passes at his leisure. Kuharich is a preoccupied man, however, and quite possibly would have stalked by Ringling Brothers Circus without noticing their tents.

One morning the workout was being concluded with a passing drill. Sam Baker, the Eagle kicking specialist and clown-in-residence, ran over to where I was hurling passes at thirty-odd little boys on the sidelines, barking that Coach Kuharich wanted me to go in the game for Ron Goodwin at wingback. Next thing you know I had my head in the huddle, while everybody stood around open-mouthed and Baker rolled on the fifty-yard line in spasms of pure joy. After due confusion and red faces all round, some good sport made the decision to let me stay in the lineup. Immediately my hands started sweating.

With the snap of the ball I leaped downfield, head-faking, shoulderfaking, snorting, wheezing, and showing them moves which I guarantee that not even Max McGee knows. Be-damned if Jack Concannon didn't throw me a perfect strike and be-damned if I didn't hang on to it. Nate Ramsey, the defensive back who had come over to pick me up, tagged me down at the point of catch. I swaggered back to the huddle, winded but full of pride, figuring that I had gone about fifty yards on the play until I heard Kuharich call, "Okay, second down and seven." Three straight times I made Old Pro Nate Ramsey look like the rawest rookie, Concannon hanging the ball in the air and my fantastic fakes getting my great hands clear so that I plucked it down with alacrity. For a nagging moment I worried about Nate Ramsey losing his defensive gig. Then I recalled that there's no room for sentiment in the pro game: the other guy's after your bread and butter. I sneered at him, then, whooping all the old fight-talk I could recall from fields dimly remembered, threatening the Washington Redskins and bawling defiance at the New York Giants. Then I looked up to see Ramsey imitating what must have been a blind duck, running all splay-footed and largely in place, jerking all over like St. Vitus inventing the new dance step by the same name, and making chug-chug sounds like a locomotive. At the same time my own teammates were bent over in the huddle, giggling and poking each other in the ribs like Cousin Kenneth and I used to do when we chanced on the ladies underwear advertisements in the Sears-Roebuck catalogue. The crusher came when Concannon asked, "You think you're about ready for me to throw you one *overhanded?*"

Well, maybe I never made All-America but I am a football fanatic from the word blood, and felt a kinship of frustration with a group of athletes encountered while writing for *Harper's Magazine* of . . .

YESTERDAY'S HEROES IN THE MICKEY MOUSE LEAGUE

Saturday night in Burkburnett, Texas, is not much fun even if you have the wind with you. It's even less pleasant after Heaven has sent 3.8 inches of rain, you've been trampled and wallowed until you can't tell where mud ends or bruises begin, and you've been humiliated by a fifth consecutive loss without once knowing the solace or dignity of a touchdown. So the Odessa-Midland Comets of the Texas Professional Football League were throwing no hats in the air following a 0–13 dunking by the Burkburnett Kings. They knew that $2 sports were safe in the stands with blondes by their sides and healing waters in their jugs, sneering at them as "The Comics" or as "The Scoreless Wonders of the Mickey Mouse League."

Before joining the Texas Professional Football League in its maiden season last year the Burkburnett Kings—representing a town of 7,621 in flat, lonesome country near what was once a storied outlaw strip between Oklahoma and Texas—had for four years tormented the Red River Football League, largely composed of Oklahoma oil hamlets and Arkansas cotton villages. They won forty-five games, lost hard in six, and grudgingly accepted two ties. Their guts-and-elbows football put a certain premium on rowdiness. On this night last September the rowdy Kings had stopped just short of drowning the neophyte Odessa-Midland team in rainwater, blood and war whoops. With the official carnage over, the Comets could look forward to a post-game meal of chicken-fried steak or hamburgers, a bus ride home through 400 miles of prairie night, and Monday morning jobs as pipe fitters, schoolteachers, barbers, salesmen, oilfield roughnecks and dental lab technicians.

R. D. Pierce, a twenty-nine-year-old fullback, district manager for Gulfco Wellhead Company, and father of three small children, gingerly removed his soaked red jersey as if afraid of taking hair, hide, and all. Pierce was bone-tired; perhaps his spirits were almost as low as his football wages, which in turn were considerably lower than the $14,000 to $16,000 annual average paid in the National Football League. He had repeatedly hurled his 230 pounds at the Burkburnett line, doing it no particular damage and getting joylessly manhandled in the process. The Comets had made but three first downs—one of them on a penalty. His body throbbing with aches sufficient to last him for about three days, Pierce wondered aloud whether all this dadgummed football playin' was showin' a man much profit.

Bob Windham, young, big as a treetop, and only a month earlier released by the big-time New York Jets of the American Football League, asked Pierce how much he'd been paid for the game.

"Sixteen dollars," Pierce said, managing not to sound boastful.

Windham, the Comet center and co-captain, nodded. "Well, ole buddy," he said, "in a way you're gettin' more money than Donnie Anderson. And the Green Bay Packers paid him $700,000."

Pierce paused in the act of shedding his shoulder pads, intrigued. "How the hell you figger that?"

Windham fingered a cleat burn on his leg. "I figger it," he said, "at about $8 a yard."

It helps to have a sense of humor in the Texas Professional Football League or on any of the minor league pro football teams now doing marginal business. Bush-league pro football is for neither the timid nor the fragile. Everything comes hard: finding a practice field, meeting the payroll, touchdowns. Often you must listen closely for the roar of the crowd. When the Tulsa Oilers defeated the Sherman-Denison Jets, 30–27, for the championship of the Texas Professional Football League last December, only 400 eyewitnesses could attest to the crime. Yet, the TPFL is operating again this season (its second) and has expanded to include new franchises. Nobody seems to really mind the grinding bus trips and lumpy motel beds, the routine fractures, or the constant flirtation with bankruptcy. Players who risk serious injury each time they put cleats on (many of them family men with salaried jobs and little or no financial security) shrug off the possibility of being maimed or brained even though payment of their basic medical bills would constitute their only compensation. The clubs are simply too poor to be successfully sued.

Football's minor leagues are in shaky health. Though the Annapolis Sailors won the Atlantic Coast Football League in 1964 they did such dismal box-office trade that the team shifted last year to Alexandria-Arlington, Virginia. The new Virginia Sailors, sparked by former NFL players past their prime, posted an 11–1 record for a second straight title. Even so, they averaged only 3,900 fans per game—some 1,100 short of what club officials call "the break-even point." The Continental League, also operating in the East, and the Professional Football League of America, in the Midwest, sent a corporal's guard of their best up to the majors for tryouts but sweated out every payroll.

Pro football really pays off only in the big leagues. Last season the NFL drew a record 5,542,508 for an average crowd of 52,786 paid. The rival AFL also had its best year: 2,160,236 paying customers working out to a game average of 34,291. Tickets ran from $6 up. Everybody made money. Not long ago, however, even the big boys were poor. Where the Green Bay Packers picked up winner's checks of $23,600 per man in playoff money last January, the NFL in 1926 voted members of its championship team "eighteen engraved gold footballs, not to cost more than ten dollars each, and a suitable pennant, not to cost more than thirty-seven fifty." In 1937, Sammy Baugh and his Washington Redskin teammates felt rich with their winner's shares of $234.26. As recently as 1950 the Cleveland Browns realized only $1,113 per man from the championship game. A major league franchise went for $100 in the 1920's; for $50,000 by 1940. Today, franchises run from seven million dollars up, provided you can find one for sale.

Minor league officials now predict similar growths. There are enthusiastic declarations by club moguls in all Texas Professional Football League cities that "our crowd potential" is 15,000 or maybe 20,000 or even 25,000 per game. Such happy prognostications ignore last year's attendance figures as well as certain laws of physics. The

Dallas Rockets play in a dime-box stadium that seats only 3,300—and must compete for the football dollar with the Dallas Cowboys, defending NFL Eastern Division champions, and an SMU team good enough last year to host the Cotton Bowl. Burkburnett, with a tiny population and miles from any major city, couldn't stuff more than 6,000 fans into its stadium with a cannon tamp and has never drawn even half that figure for one game. Pasadena must buck the Houston Oilers, Rice Institute, University of Houston, and a dozen junior colleges known more for the ferocity of their football scholars than for general academic excellence. TPFL games are played on Saturday night in competition with the best trombones country club money can buy, "Gunsmoke," neighborhood poker grudges of long standing, square dances, triple-header bills at the Star Lite Drive-In Theater, and the spirited bloodlettings of high school "B" teams.

George Schepps, Commissioner of the TPFL, is an old head who dabbled in baseball as club owner or general manager for fifty years. He envisions working agreements with big-time professional teams much as major league baseball franchises once sponsored or owned dozens of affiliate farm clubs from the Class AAA International League to the Class D Cotton States. As in baseball, the parent club would farm out its young, unseasoned rookies. In exchange for playing experience it would pay all or most of its trainees' salaries. "In a deal like that, *everybody* wins," Schepps says. He is now working toward a union of minor league teams, largely to pressure major league clubs into a paternal relationship. The big league clubs, possibly because they have a costless natural breeding ground for their players in the collegiate system, are not exactly jumping at the opportunity.

Bob Windham, the young Comet center who came within a hair of sticking with the New York Jets last season, thinks his chances for the big time were vastly improved by the recent major league expansion and unification. "No big league team will get over three or four players worth a damn from the college draft," he predicts. "There just won't be enough talent to go around. They've already dipped into their taxi-squadders. They'll have twenty-eight teams up there by 1970, and if you figure it at forty-man squads that's *one thousand one hundred and twenty players* they need! Why, they'll be beating the bushes for guys who can tell a blitz from a quick kick."

Maybe so, but big time football isn't as easy as it looks from an armchair. Writer George Plimpton discovered this a couple of seasons ago playing "last string quarterback" for the Detroit Lions. In his only series of downs under game conditions, in a pre-season scrimmage, Plimpton came within one yard of the ignominy of moving his offensive unit backwards thirty yards to a safety. Even legitimate players sometimes stumble. Tom Kennedy, who played at little Los Angeles State, started last season with Brooklyn in the Continental League. Perhaps he was as surprised as anyone when the New York Giants, desperate for quarterbacks after an injury to Earl Morral, called him up in mid-season. One wonders what fantasies of glory that human package knew in his hotel bed on the eve of his first NFL start against the Washington Redskins. Reality arrived with the 2 P.M. kickoff. The Redskins threw Kennedy for multiple losses, intercepted his passes or batted them down, forced fumbles, and played hob with the green quarterback's person. With seven seconds left, the mediocre Redskins showed an amazing 69 points on the scoreboard. Kennedy, gritty to the end, tried to keep the Giants in business by throwing out of bounds to stop the clock. Unfortunately, Kennedy's clock-stopping throw came on fourth down and thus benefited Washington. Claiming the ball inside the New York thirty, the Redskins proved that nice guys don't win by kicking the world's most superfluous field goal for a club record 72 points. Later, sitting mesmerized in front of his locker, Kennedy appeared to be in deep communion with the dressing room walls. "I didn't think it would be this tough," he mumbled. "I didn't think the transition would be this much."

At twenty-four, Bob Windham—agile, tough, six feet six inches tall and weighing 270 well-kept pounds—might realize his dream. Others in the low minors, however, hopelessly chase rainbows: men whose legs have gone back on them along with their hairlines, 150-pound backs who would be gobbled alive by the swift, brutal Brobdingnagians of the NFL, chubby tackles whose only credentials trace back over four or five years to their local high school teams or to a season or two of service ball with the Fort Desperation Spastics.

Then there are men like Byron Townsend, who doggedly cling to the pigskin periphery and to the past. For them the most terrible of sounds is the bang that ends the game.

Byron Townsend was a legend in a state noted for its vicious and sophisticated football. He was twice All-State at Odessa High School, twice All-Southern and twice Schoolboy All-America. The first time he carried the ball, as a fifteen-year-old sophomore, he ran fifty-two yards for a touchdown. In 1946, when Odessa High defeated San

Antonio Jefferson for the Texas State Championship before a big crowd in the Cotton Bowl, Townsend out-dueled another schoolboy superstar named Kyle Rote. At the University of Texas he led his team in so many departments the statisticians were tempted to record his exploits in a separate set of books—this in an era when the Southwest Conference was blessed with the likes of Doak Walker (Detroit Lions), Bill Howton (Green Bay Packers), and Rote (New York Giants). These fifteen years later Townsend can name the half-dozen records he still holds.

Townsend had it all: his pick of campus cuties, flashy convertibles, a dude's wardrobe, adoring wealthy "sportsmen" eager to toss him the keys to their plush pads along with a $20 bill and a comradely wink. He was named to the *Collier's* All-America team, took a bow on a national TV show or two, played in so many All-Star games he lost count, and had more eager talent scouts panting after him than Miss Maidenform Bra. Only a decade ago a football nut with a flair for larceny, impersonating Townsend, toured the nation buying Cadillacs, booze and diamonds in his name. Before they caught him entering the Sugar Bowl in New Orleans one New Year's Day (wearing a gaudy but expensive drugstore cowboy outfit) the bogus Townsend had cashed $67,000 worth of worthless checks on the real one.

The real Byron Townsend opened the 1952 football season with the Los Angeles Rams of the NFL. He had a fine rookie year until he injured a thigh. The next year Townsend played football for the U.S. military. Lured by money, he jumped to the Canadian League following his military discharge in 1954 and performed like a star until a severe neck injury forced him out of the game in mid-season, 1956.

Townsend came home to nurse his wounds. He worked at a half-dozen jobs in two years, doing best as a salesman because his name opened doors in a country where a football hero outranks movie queens and Presidents. Soon new stars appeared in the football galaxy. Things started going to pot for Byron Townsend. His marriage to a former campus belle cratered. He was broke. A couple of the wealthy sportsmen who had told Townsend in his salad days that they'd back him in the business venture of his choice ("Yew jest name it, boy!") offered hard luck stories. Suddenly, nobody cheered anymore. One night Townsend parked his car on a lonely road and lost a decision to a .22 caliber pistol. His life was saved, he says, when the bullet hit his breastbone and ricocheted out along a path free of vital organs.

Now thirty-seven, Townsend lives with his mother in Odessa and works as a "professional laborer" (pipe fitter) at the H. U. Stone Gasoline Plant. He plays a lot of gin rummy, rarely misses a televised football game, and drinks Lone Star beer at the Sands Lounge just north of Broncho Stadium—the same field where as a schoolboy in the 1940's he brought 20,000 football-crazed Texans to their feet, whooping and ringing cowbells, almost every time he packed the ball. At one stretch Townsend led Odessa High to twenty-six consecutive wins.

Last year Byron Townsend was part-time wingback, emergency quarterback, and full-time head coach for the Odessa-Midland Comets of the Texas Professional Football League—positions for which he received no guaranteed salary. Like his players, Townsend accepted a percentage of the gate, concessions, and program advertising after current bills were paid. One night his cut was only $9—less by a dollar than each participant got for the first pro football game on record.* The biggest check he drew was for $34.

Every time he left his pipe-fitting gig three hours early to conduct football practice it cost Townsend "$15 straight time or $20 overtime." ("I lost so much money trying to coach," he says, "that I quit my professional laborer's job for the rest of the football season.")

Townsend entered coaching as casually as Odessa-Midland entered the TPFL. John Hatley, a much-traveled Old Pro (Chicago Bears, St. Louis Cardinals, Philadelphia Eagles, Denver Bronchos) was savoring a rodeo in Burkburnett last summer when somebody invited him to play football for the Kings. Hatley mulled it over while a Brahma Bull stomped a cowboy or two, then declined, but returned to his job as a beer salesman in San Angelo determined to start his own team. Before he could apply for a franchise his brewery assigned Hatley to Odessa (Pop. 80,338) and Midland (Pop. 62,625), twin cities eighteen arrow-straight miles apart in desertlike oil country. Hatley telephoned Bryon Townsend: was he interested in forming a team to play in the TPFL? "Sure." Would he consent to coach the club? "Sure." Hatley immediately christened himself general manager and president. Within a few weeks he coaxed together a group of young men headed by a twenty-five-year-old lawyer-politician, State Representative Franklin (Ace) Pickens, and a veteran sportscaster, Jay Mehaffey, to serve as directors of the Permian Basin Football Association. The closed corporation offered a limited amount of stock for sale (at $1 per share), secured the Comet franchise, signed a local

* Latrobe, Pennsylvania, vs. Jeanette, Pennsylvania, in 1895.

high school teacher, Jim Daniel, as assistant coach and got together $3,700. They opened for business $3,000 in debt.

Trouble came in quick-step. Coach Townsend, looking over the ninety candidates who had answered a public call for tryouts, noted their peculiar sizes and shapes and that many seemed puzzled by which end of the football to pick up. He proved himself every bit as astute a politician as Barry Goldwater in blurting, "There might be three or four ball players in the whole bunch." Club officials hastened to explain to their coach that such candid expressions, however accurate, did not sell tickets. Some of the Comet hopefuls quit early because they didn't cotton to working out in 100 degree weather,* or when they learned they'd have to furnish their own football shoes. ("Mr. Norman," a husky bartender told one of his favorite customers, "I won't be servin' you no more. I'm gonna play professional football for a livin'." He lasted three days, at the end of which he found that his old job had been filled.) Townsend sweated and called on his Lord as he tried to bring order out of this chaos. Meanwhile, TV-man Jay Mehaffey's daily sportscasts presented the Comets as a cross between Notre Dame and nitroglycerin, even though night often found Coach Townsend sadly shaking his head unbelievingly over a bottle of Lone Star at the Sands Lounge.

Three days before the opening exhibition game in Uvalde (Pop. 10,293) the Comets' football uniforms were seriously overdue. Townsend got on the phone to order them shipped directly to Uvalde; they arrived two hours before game time. Odessa-Midland broke in its new finery in losing by a score variously reported as 0–13, 0–19, and 0–21, there being a certain casual air as to details. A week later, showing all the poise, polish and fight of the Egyptian Tank Corps, the Comets were embarrassed in a second exhibition, 0–26, by Burkburnett. At this point the boo birds tagged the team "The Scoreless Wonders" because "We wonder when they're gonna score." Precisely at this point, too, General Manager–President John Hatley was abruptly transferred 300 miles to Fort Worth in the interest of beer sales. This prompted cynics to speculate over how much trouble he'd had arranging it.†

Lawyer Ace Pickens moved up to the club presidency. "The night

---

* The Temple Baptist Church in Odessa took advantage of the weather to ask, on a front-lawn sign, "You think it's hot *here?*"

† The cynics were wrong. Hatley drove back hundreds of miles each week to play linebacker for the Comets.

of our first League game," he admits, "I didn't expect a crowd of over two or three hundred. People were calling us 'The Comics.' I'd see friends on the street and they'd laugh and yell 'Punt, punt.' " Pickens hired a lone ticket seller; delivered the tickets to him only thirty minutes before kickoff time: "I didn't know he had to count 'em, sort 'em, record their numbers for tax purposes—all sorts of things." He was amazed by the long line of fans waiting at the stadium. Hastily, he telephoned several Jaycee friends who rushed over to help. The kickoff was held up almost an hour to seat the crowd. Counting the $7,000 gate paid by almost 4,000 fans the Comet officials danced and hugged each other in undisguised joy. "We'd have got at least another thousand bucks," Pickens said, "except that we ran out of tickets. We finally opened the gates and let the rest in free." More than 5,000 fans witnessed the tardy kickoff.

The good crowd was a testimonial to Jay Mehaffey's gift of mendacity. Though the weather forecast called for oceans of rain (and black, rumbling clouds were banked up on the horizon) Mehaffey's televised sportscast an hour before game time predicted "a perfect night for football." Doyce Elliott, who followed with the official weathercast, refrained out of community spirit from mentioning the imminent deluge though he may have found it difficult to look the camera in the eye.

The Comets and the Sherman-Denison Jets had been at it five minutes when the storm hit. West Texas is infamous for cycles of flood and drought: this was no drought. The ball floated away unless the referee kept a foot on it between plays. Only near the fifty-yard line could spectators see the turf. Lightning bolts knocked the stadium lights out four times. Witnesses swear that the first time the lights went out Comet linebacker Bill Lisenbee was in the act of making a smashing, head-on tackle. "My God!" Lisenbee cried out from the soggy darkness, "I've gone blind!" Once the lights failed as a pass was launched and an official caught it in the nose. Several unscheduled intermissions were called while electricians struggled with fusestats, wires, and Anglo-Saxon expressions. By game's end only thirty-three fans remained: twenty-six had crowded into the press box while seven sat smugly under protective sheets of polyethylene plastic. The Comets lost, by the curious score of 0–5, on what pool hall comedians in Odessa cracked was "a safety and a field goal scored in the dark."

Whatever its artistic shortcomings, the game was a financial smash. "We'd been about a ten-minute drive from the poorhouse," Ace Pickens recalls. "Our next three games were on the road. It cost us about $1,600 to go to Pasadena, $900 to Burkburnett, and around $1,700 for the Tulsa trip. We couldn't have made it without that first big payday."

They almost didn't make the 660 miles to Pasadena the following week. The team left Odessa at 5 A.M. on Saturday, fifteen hours before the kickoff, in a chartered bus that may have come direct from Dogpatch City Lines. Three hours later the ancient vehicle expired a few miles outside the hamlet of Eden, near which there definitely is no garden. Thirty-four Comets straggled to town, drank coffee, and listened to Weeping Willie Nelson sing cowboy laments on the jukebox, while Coach Townsend tracked down the county's only mechanic. A rest stop at Austin was unexpectedly extended for another hour when the bus evidently turned to stone a second time. Lesser men might have shouted expletives and quit. "We *had* to show up," Pickens says, "or forfeit the $1,500 appearance bond we'd posted. That little ole rule kept us going several times."

The Comets chugged into Pasadena less than one hour ahead of the 8 P.M. kickoff. They dressed for the game at their motel. Fifteen minutes later motorists wondered if those nuts in red and white uniforms, pushing an old bus up the Gulf Freeway, had lost an election bet. Once inside Pasadena Stadium the bus mired to its axles in mud, and in view of 1,500 fans. The Comets slogged to the kickoff afoot, less than five minutes ahead of a bond forfeiture, whereupon the Lord broke his covenant by again sending rain—and a 0–25 defeat. On the return trip home the bus only broke down twice. This led some of the players to sourly predict they'd soon grow soft and fat, being coddled this-a-way. The next week, at Burkburnett, there was that 3.8-inch cloudburst, a fifth scoreless defeat, and R. D. Pierce drawing $8 a yard. Wags now suggested that the Comets give up football and hire out as rainmakers.

Later, at a mid-week practice session, thieves called on the Comet dressing room to pick pockets clean of some $200. A high school stadium where the team practiced was claimed for more urgent uses, the Comets moving to an abandoned baseball park with dressing facilities so small players had to suit out in shifts. The players rebelled because the park had plenty of rats but no shower facilities. Management then begged use of the American Legion park and fieldhouse, but had to quit their lease when the Legion demanded $40 a night to turn on the lights. "We couldn't practice until 5:30 P.M. because the guys had jobs," Townsend explained, "and it got dark an hour later. But we couldn't scrape up that forty bucks even twice a week." Ultimately, the Comets cut workouts to Tuesdays and Thursdays. They were held on a vacant lot; the more fastidious players showered at home.

A small mutiny occurred when the Comets were no longer permitted to sign tickets for their road game meals, but had to eat off the $5 handed them. "Signing tabs didn't work," Ace Pickens admits. "Too many of the boys got tempted by expensive planks of steak. We found if we gave them cash they'd settle for cheeseburgers." The boys clamored for a better bus, and, amazingly, got it through a lease arrangement with a major company. One day quarterback Dwayne Thompson (Ranger Junior College), official player representative, turned up in Pickens' office with several hard-eyed colleagues to demand a financial accounting. The squabble over the books consumed two hours. Tempers flared. "We're not being *paid* for serving as directors, you know," a club official said in a huff. "You ain't down there blockin' or tacklin' nobody, either," he was reminded. Finally the troops grudgingly agreed that there was nothing in the treasury for anyone to steal.

In their fourth league game, against Tulsa, things briefly looked up. A new quarterback, former Little All-America Vince Tesone (Colorado Mines) got the Comets on the scoreboard. They led the unbeaten Oilers, 16–13, with only seconds to play. Then Tulsa kicked a field goal for a tie. The Comets cried foul: host Tulsa had insisted on playing fifteen-minute quarters (contrary to TPFL rules specifying twelve-minute ones) and the Odessa-Midland boys contended that under the twelve-minute rule they had won the game. They might have been awarded it, too, had they followed the edict of another league rule requiring that all protests be filed in writing within twenty-four hours of the alleged violation. Nobody did.

The Tulsa rhubarb and tie brought out 3,000 fans when the Comets returned home to play the Dallas Rockets. Coach Townsend lectured his charges on the opportunity to win new friends and influence people. Whereupon they lost three fumbles, drew eighty yards in penalties, made only four first downs, and experienced their sixth scoreless loss (0–14). "That game killed us at the gate," Pickens says. The evidence supports him. Only 500 paid to see the next home outing against Pasadena's Pistols. Most of them left holding their noses after the Comets, en route to a 13–34 drubbing, fell behind 0–27 at half time. Those old tormentors, the Burkburnett Kings, came to town to thrash the Comets a third time, 27–19, and to end Quarterback Tesone's career with a shoulder injury. The game drew only 250 die-hards and produced one good laugh. Byron Townsend, playing wingback, ran deep on a naked reverse. Spotting four defenders eagerly awaiting him, Townsend wisely chartered a course to carry him safely out of bounds even though it meant a long loss. By the time Townsend reached safety he was running rapidly and he was running almost due north. A fan who presumably knew Townsend's recreational habits convulsed the bench when he yelled, "Catch 'im, boys! He's headed for the Sands!"

Coach Townsend's job was a many-splendored thing. Short a quarterback against Sherman-Denison he played the position himself. His eyesight was temporarily lost to him when a jarring Jet tackle sent one contact lens flying, perhaps into orbit, and drove the other up into an eyebrow. Thereafter, if pass receivers ran their patterns more than ten yards deep the quarterback couldn't see them. The Comets' 40–12 loss didn't surprise the bookies.

Two hundred disaster-lovers showed for the final home game against unbeaten Tulsa. Townsend, emulating Knute Rockne, reminded them of how the Comets had been gypped of victory in the first Tulsa game and called for vengeance in blood. It worked. Though Tulsa outdid the Comets in everything but half-time cigars smoked, Odessa-Midland knew its one taste of success. They scored twice in the second period, and made it stand up for a 14–10 victory—perhaps because Jay Mehaffey had imported a giant professional wrestler, Terry Funk, and a former Canadian League toughie, Bill Ossilinee, to put spine in the Comet defense. (Mehaffey paid the ringers out of his own pocket, all of which was perfectly legal since TPFL eligibility rules provide only that players without a discernible pulse may not participate.)

In the season's last game, at Dallas, the Comets could hardly field a team. In addition to Tesone's injury they had lost Eldon (Rocky) Ford, a thirty-year-old oilfield worker, who suffered a fractured ankle *and* a broken leg on the same play. Tommy Lee (Pockets) Hill, a 162-pound defensive back, went up in the air during a rare scrimmage session and came down with his neck broken. LeRoy Allison, a twenty-year-old machinist who'd never played football until a friend dared him to go out for the Comets, suffered a mangled knee. Minor bumps and bruises were numberless: everybody over twenty-five moved as if they had bursitis. The survivors finished in Dallas before what veteran crowd observers have estimated at sixty-three persons. R. D. Pierce kicked three field goals, but somebody kicked four for the Rockets and that was the ball game. The Comets wrote a final record of eight losses, one tie, a single victory, and a $1,572 dollar deficit. Even so, they got a trophy at season's end. They led the Texas Professional Football League in paid attendance with a total of 8,227 for five home games.

Why do they play for peanuts and broken bones? Ace Pickens: "For the love of the game. Not over three or four played for the money. We play for the love of the sport—the love of contact." *We?* He sits behind his law office desk with diplomas on the walls, a thick carpet on the floor, and with the cool look of a man leading in the game of life 40–0 long before the first half ends. He is well-dressed, manicured, smoking a superior brand of cigar; none of his bones are on the mend. You know the last thing he made contact with was an inner-spring mattress or perhaps an $8 beefsteak, so you look to see if he's pulling your leg. He is not. Pickens looks as determined as the meanest member of the suicide squad roaring downfield to violate the deep safetyman, and you realize that he has achieved total identification with the team.

Tommy Lee (Pockets) Hill comes on the same way. Hill is drinking cheer at the Chat 'Um Lounge, a black-and-tan hangout where beer goes for thirty cents. There is a brown paper sack on the table, and in the sack a pint of bourbon. You cannot buy liquor by the drink in Texas, except in private clubs, but you can buy ice and set-ups. "Soon's I get outta this harness," Pockets Hill says, indicating the brace on his neck, "I'll be out there again. We can get us a good team goin' here. Them boys *hit!* You give us the right trainin' and the right coachin' and we'll beat anybody." Tommy Lee Hill doesn't have much to compare the Texas Professional Football League with, his experience being limited to high school football some six years ago. But a man doesn't develop much identification working around as a hospital orderly, fry cook, or service station hand—or not working at all about 25 percent of the time.

The League gave linebacker Bill Lisenbe, thirty-four, a chance to prove something to himself. "I always wondered if I could play pro ball. I was pretty good at Academy High School—that's near Temple —but couldn't go to college. I went out for the Comets just to satisfy myself I could make it." Lisenbee was wildly happy with his year and hopes to play again. Gene Williams, a tough split end who has never heard a footstep in his life, and the only Comet named to the TPFL All-League squad, had nothing much to prove: he had been All-State at Kermit High School in 1958 and starred at Texas Western College. Williams played for the contact: "I like to hit people." Williams can't go around hitting people in his desk-bound job, so the Comets provided him a healthy outlet.

"We're not eat up with comforts," Byron Townsend concedes. "These ole boys just love football enough that they'd play it in Hell with their backs broke. Only a couple of 'em have any chance to go up. Still, nothing satisfies that ole football bug but playing the game. You just *got* to play." Warren Sheelar, a twenty-four-year-old assistant coach at little Sul Ross College, located in the isolated village of Alpine near the Davis Mountains, had to play so badly he drove to Odessa to serve as middle linebacker at all home games—a round trip of approximately 350 miles. John Hatley, at an age when most men use the country club bar more than the golf course, commuted 600 miles to play. "Hatley said he had more fun than he did in the NFL," Townsend grinned. "I did, too."

Townsend talked as he sipped Scotch and water at the Golden Falcon, where indoor athletes may loosen up at a dollar a shot. This Saturday afternoon in December, two weeks after the Comet season had ended, bar trade was as slow as a TPFL end sweep. Dressed in slacks, a white shirt, tie, and a smart white sweater, Townsend had just witnessed on TV a game in which Johnny Unitas of the Baltimore Colts had made "the million dollar fumble" permitting Green Bay to sew up the NFL Western Division title. "I sure felt sorry for that ole boy," Townsend said of Unitas, who earns about $50,000 annually quarterbacking the Colts. "You see how down-in-the-mouth he looked walking off that field? When a ball player messes up like that *nobody* feels worse than he does."

He was sorry over having missed the Texas Professional Football League's business meeting, then being held in Dallas. "I wanted to go, but Ace Pickens told me there wasn't room. A couple of days later I found out one of the directors wasn't going, so I asked to take his place. Ace and Jay Mehaffey said that well, Jim Daniel (the Comet assistant coach) hadn't got to go anywhere so why not let him go?" Townsend furrowed his brow. "I sure hope they sell the radio rights. We'd get two thousand bucks out of it."

Townsend reminisced about the season. "We started out making junior high mistakes—some guy would be standing around watching to see where a punt was gonna role, and it'd bounce up and hit him on the leg. But we soon corrected those. We got younger players as the season wore on. At the end we only had about nine of the old heads that we started out with." He reeled off the names of a few TPFL players who, however briefly, were once in the big time: Sherman-Denison's Harold "Hayseed" Stevens (New York Titans),* Tulsa's Charley Barnhart (Denver) and Raymond Hayes (Vikings-Rams), Dallas' Jim Faulk (Baltimore Colts), the Comets' Gary Crain (Miami Dolphins), himself, and Hatley. He recalled that Dallas quarterback Doug Tucker "beat Arkansas in the Cotton Bowl a few years ago and threw eight touchdown passes in one game for Lincoln in the Professional Football League of America."

"I'm beating the bushes," Townsend enthused. "Using all my old contacts to turn up some good boys for next year. We'll be better. I told the board if we don't win the title next season, I'll resign." He was desperately hopeful of the future that day. "We've just *got* to keep this league going. I don't know what I'd do without it." Though he speaks of football with love, Townsend harbors ambivalent sentiments about his own career. "I made a lot of mistakes. I wish I'd gone to Oklahoma. Bud Wilkinson coached a style of ball that suited me better. I went to Texas because a bunch of big shots around here—oilmen and money men, you know the type—pressured me into it. They slapped me on the back and promised me the moon and when it was all over they didn't know me." Townsend now regrets that he didn't hit the books as hard as he hit the line: "Making money's not easy. Five o'clock comes early and that's the time I crawl out for work."

"**N**ow it is September"—poet Wallace Stevens wrote—"and the web is woven./The web is woven and you will have to wear it." The web is woven for the Texas Professional Football League's second year, too. Muscles are coming slowly awake after months of hibernation and new dreams are being hung out to air. Last year's bruises, flash floods and fried foods are forgotten—shunted aside like some

* Now defunct.

dimly remembered nightmare on a bright summer day. The Comets, sailing off on a new adventure, are as full of hope as Columbus and certain that they won't again go five games without scoring. Jay Mehaffey is considering new ways to trick TV customers into Broncho Stadium, and Ace Pickens hopefully predicts 10,000 fans per home game. Everything is pretty much the same—except that everybody is a year older, and a new head coach will be in charge.

A few weeks ago Comet officials announced that assistant coach Jim Daniel was being promoted to the top job—a decision, it developed, they had privately reached midway of last season. Well, they had enough precedent. The name of the game is Win—and if you don't win you fire the coach whether in the NFL or "the Mickey Mouse League." Townsend was retained as "director of player personnel," a title perhaps more impressive on paper than within his own heart. The true football warrior knows that the game is on the field, not in somebody's front office. For Byron Townsend, the game may soon be over.

CHAPTER 10

On the Rocks
& with a Twist of Lemon

Now and again a rare and beautiful thing happens to the writer: his typewriter produces exactly what he meant for it to. How this happens is a mystery. Much of what the writer finally blesses as done comes from his typewriter strangely incomplete. Sometimes he knows this: he is simply powerless in the moment to do anything about it. The words won't come, though a deadline has, and so he must move on to the next adventure.

There is a haunted, guilt-ridden feeling about letting-go prose that just isn't equal to its potential. I liken it unto the feeling I had as a boy when I secretly wondered if the place called Heaven, which so occupied the thoughts and plans of most adults around me, really existed as part of the celestial scheme or was merely the career high-point of some obscure, gifted practical joker who had existed no more than terrestrially some centuries before. Yet I suppose that most writers, especially those of us who depend wholly upon the craft for our bread, market some prose that really isn't ripe. There simply isn't enough time to polish and refurbish each word so that, like an off-the-cuff speech by Everett Dirksen or a drill squad marching as one at impossibly oblique angles, it has a unique cadence or special perfection all its own.

At other times the writer may, in the heat of creation, be smugly satisfied with a given bit of prose—so much so that he wakes the wife and kiddies to share it as a pre-dawn gift, or brags about it to bewildered strangers. The discovery some months or weeks or even days later that time has eroded the Art beyond any crying of it is the type of disaster that keeps suicide in the language. Perhaps it will have been tardily found to harbor multiple technical flaws or—even worse—to have failed by several nautical miles to get the author's message across.

The following article is my happy exception to the rule. Not that I expect the Pulitzer advisors to present me a scroll in reward of it on my next birthday, for it is not free of certain faults of form. By the sternest test I can apply, however—that of whether the piece transmitted what I meant to say exactly as I meant to say it—it ranks as my personal favorite.

Naturally, some of you will want to know why this is true. If I could answer the question, I would not be here at the Gateway Motel, near Lackland Army Air Base, Texas, thumping on the typewriter and wondering if the management will take my check. I would be over at Chase Manhattan for my daily inspection of the vaults, and beating Fame off with a stick.

ON THE ROCKS & WITH A TWIST OF LEMON

When I got into the cab I was in no mood to talk.

I had just come from a story conference on a television script for an educational TV channel: mad, hung-up and boiling bitter juices. The reason for my *angst* was this fantastic Hollywood pussel-gut sent in as Executive Producer and who, though he wouldn't have known the Capitol Dome from M-G-M, had been telling me how to write a screen treatment about Congress. And him two hours off the plane.

He was grossly fat, and his belly had bulged lewdly behind a respectable facade of starched stripe shirt. He had duck-waddled over the blue carpet, prowling and poking holes in the air with an unsmoked cigar carried like a prop.

("I wanta show with some zing. I want it full of that ole bathos and pizzaz and Yankee Doodle Dandy, Baby. Ya know, Sweetheart? Take a new Congressman from out in Indiana or Wyoming or one of those Godawful wheat places, dig? He comes to Washington. To the Senate, Baby, and right away faces all this conflict over a certain bill. Maybe a bill the President opposes, ya see? Even the goddamn *President,* Sweetheart! And this neophyte Senator from out in Idaho or where-the-hell-ever they grow wheat—he takes this bill and puts it over even with *The Prez* against it! Passes it . . . you know . . . solo! Solitary! See whatta mean?")

I had leaned back on plush leather cushions, my jawline going slack, and maybe I even pinched myself to verify the nightmare. The fat boy from Goofusland kept pushing a Vicks inhaler in alternate nostrils, shifting the cigar and the inhaler with each change, making mighty sniffles, bouncing around looking like a gob of jello would if jello went to spoil. He was in considerable need of a shave and pants press. The shine had been routed from his shoes by scuff, his fingers were like plump, stained, link sausages. The starched striped shirt was an incongruous monument to grooming in the personal junk-yard of himself. He seemed, I thought, more the type to produce those sexsational movies our American Legion superpatriots drool over on Stag Night than to conjure up films for educational television.

("One man show, Baby! Ya with me? I mean *everybody's* against this bill, ya unnerstand, Sweetheart? Speaker of the Senate . . . the what-ya-may-call-it . . . Chairman? Or Floor Leader like that Everett Dirksen person. But this *one* Senator, he's young. He's . . . a little Rock Hudson in the teeth and some of Duke Wayne in the jaw, ya know? Well *he* changes it all. And with *one speech inna Senate!* This happens maybe his first week in Washington . . . first month, anyhow. Speech you can really pour the ole heart and guts inta, ya know? I mean *Drama,* Baby! Lift the slobs outta their arm chairs! Ya with me? Ya see where I'm going, Baby?")

Yeah," I had said, "and I see where *I'm* going. Out on the street, Sweetheart, and charge a buck a head to tell this story and get rich embalming the poor sons-a-bitches who die laughing at you. Ya dig, Baby?"

And had walked off from six-hundred lovely, much-needed green dollars.

Educational TV! For the love of God!

So I was in no mood to exchange special ignorance with Diamond Cab License No. 345678. Chatty cabbies pain me. All that folklore jazz about how cab drivers are supposed to have the wisdom of the ages right in there along with the ticking meter is a crock of some-thing soft, and the something soft is not custard. Most of them couldn't find wisdom with a road map—and would charge you for the wrong zone if they did.

But it fell my lot to draw a talker.

He was wizened and stooped and wrinkled. Older, even, than his rattle-trap cab, which no doubt he had to fight to keep from the clutches of the Curator over at the Smithsonian. He was black as midnight in Haiti, and his most dark jaws had started moving the instant his foot touched the brake in response to my street corner wigwags.

The car radio was on, throwing my temporary chauffeur into vocal competition with Frank McGee. ". . . *some fifty miles off course,"* McGee was burping into the microphone, *"but well within the footprint perimeter . . ."*

"Git in, git in," the wizened little black man urged, like maybe something hairy was gaining on me. "Yesser, whur to? Well, they down! Yep, sure are! This is a wunnerful country . . ."

"Central Control," McGee burped in his turn, *"will keep us posted in all recovery operation . . ."*

"Whur can I take you? You hear about them as-tro-knots maken it? They down in the water and everything's *good!* Things shaken all *a-round!* Big doens!"

The double burst hit me broadside. I only stared, goggle-eyed, trying to separate the McGee voice from the cabbie's. Trying to sort out the big doens.

"Wunnerful country," my host said, eyes bright, head nodding ratification of his own sagacity. "Yesser, things is changen. Things is *sure* changen! Getten better all time!" He had slipped the car into gear. Two blocks down the street and he slowed his glee long enough to inquire where I wanted to go.

I said, "Capitol Hill. Corner of—"

"We git a few things straightened out this be the best country in the world. And we *getten* there. Sure are! . . . You say the Capitol?"

"Yeah. New Jersey and C streets."

"Sure proud them boys," he said, gesturing with one wrinkled, dark hand toward the radio. "Them as-tro-knots. Weken do anything any country in the *world* can. Yesser, sure can! This a *wunnerful* country . . ."

"Yeah," I said. "For we have got freshman Senators who raise wheat in Idaho and pass bills even The Prez opposes. And in their first week, too. Ya with me, Sweetheart? Ya dig?"

"Yesser," he said, by which he meant he did not. "Sure glad they down safe. Them as-tro-knots . . ."

We passed by the gloomy site of old Griffith Stadium. It is surrounded by slums now, and wrecking balls have ruined it for the rats and weeds. Babe Ruth hit some shots there, and Mickey Mantle.

Once I saw the Yankees get first-inning homers by Mantle and Elston Howard and some slap-hitting infielder who didn't habitually hit home runs, but did that day, and six runs crossed the plate before rules permitted the Senators to touch a bat. Memorial Day double-h .der, 1958? 59? 60? No matter. A long day for Washington fans. They had thrown beer cups and seat-cushions at outfielder Jim Lemon in the second game. Normally he was their idol by virtue of heroics at bat. But on this particular day he couldn't hit his hat size, nor could he have trapped a grizzly bear in a 'phone booth. Now weeds grew on the spot where Jim Lemon had been repeatedly handcuffed by soft pop-ups. The old order passeth . . .

My driver said, "I give that Russian boy credit. He got out and turned flips in space. But what *we* done ain't bad. Is it?"

"Not bad at all," I said.

Nearby, a dingy building with stunted spire. The-Church-Of-God-In-Jesus-Christ-On-Georgia-Avenue. That's how the pulpit-pounding, hymn-singing preacher referred to it on the radio each Sunday morning. ("They'll be no dice-rollin' and whiskey-drinkin' and wimmen-chasin' in Heaven!" he had once thundered. A friend of mine, nursing his Sabbath hangover with a Bloody Mary, had observed morosely: "Be Hell if they ain't.")

The old man clattered on. He said, "You too young to recollect much changes. Me, I recollect lotsa changes. I was born in '86." (His permit, stapled to the backside of the front seat, gave his birthday as 6-16-96. Had he lied to me, or to Commissioners of the District of Columbia?)

"Yesser, I recollect when it wasn't just Nig-grows got kicked around, but the Irish, too. Now we've had us a Irish Pres-i-dent. We even had us a Irish *Kathlick* Pres-i-dent."

We passed a pawn shop. Wispy memories of a smutty joke came to haunt me from the past, like a ghost in tattle-tale gray sheets: *Meet me at the pawn shop, honey, and kiss me under the balls.*

"He was a good man," the hackie was saying, "and they shot him."

On the sidewalk a small girl turned her chocolate face up to her mother. The woman bent to hold a handkerchief to the little nose. Groups of men milled in front of a sleazy gin-mill. Two young boys cavorted among them, bumping shoulders, arms carefully folded and hands tucked under the armpits, laughing. (What had we called it back in Texas, all those eons ago? Rooster-fighting?) Loan company . . . Dixie-Pig stand . . . Ajax Liquors. Perhaps eighty people were in view on the street, only four or five of them white. An unkempt Negro with long sideburns stepped from the curb and hailed someone across the street: "Hey, Mutha . . ."

The prattle again. ". . . she got in my cab back when he was runnen, Kennedy was runnen against that Nixon. And she was huffy and said ta me, 'imagine haven a *Kathlick* Pres-i-dent. This a *Prota*-stant country.' And I said to her, 'A *Prota*-stant country? Why, lady, don't you know it was three or four Kathlicks hepped sign that Constitution we got?' And would you believe she didn't know it? I said, 'This a country for all *kindsa* peepul!' I was mighty tickled when he won. And then they shot him."

On our left, the John F. Kennedy playground. It is in a low-income area almost wholly Negro. Poverty is there, and all that goes with it. Pain and prostitution and hunger and illiteracy. The crime rate is among the highest in the city's precincts, maybe even in the nation, and cops patrol in pairs with dogs trained to kill. The playground had been an instant success. Whooping kids had swarmed by the dozens over colorfully-painted old World War II aircraft and retired locomotive engines and refurbished heavy-armor tanks. Somehow the equipment had turned a barren plot, where winos used to guzzle their Smokey Pete, into a wonderful fantasy land. The John F. Kennedy playground gates were locked, the grounds still: an island of silence in a sea of merry shouts and caustic curses and stick-ball games among whizzing vehicles. Congress had refused, a couple of weeks earlier, to appropriate $89,000 for its maintenance and operation. (In the same week, Congressmen drew $2,500 each as reward for their monthly labors. Multiply times 535.)

A wunnerful country . . .

On the radio Frank McGee explained how impressive were certain maneuvers Gus Grissom and John Young had made with the *Molly Brown.*

"I recollect," the cabbie said, "when President Ruse-a-velt usta ride horseback 'round here. *Thea*door Ruse-a-velt. Back there whur I picked you up at. Wasn't nothen but woods there, then."

Out the window. A gaudy girly-girly movie. Trailways Bus Terminal. A sailor and a girl stood near the entrance, holding hands. (Is there a law somewhere that every bus station must have a sailor and a girl holding hands?) Liquor store. Parking lot. *First hour thirty-five cents.* A jeweler was having a fire sale. Next week it would be a going-out-of-business sale, and the week after that a God-knows-what-sale.

A red-on-yellow sign: *Let Madam Somebody Solve Your Troubles. Palms Read. Spells Ended.*

Frank McGee spoke of space exploration costs. Billions and millions. Sums too vast to comprehend. *Rooms, $1 and Up.* People scurried by a soap-box evangelist without looking at him. At a sidewalk stand two unshaven men in baggy trousers awaited buyers of flowers and potted plants.

"Woods," the driver said. "Wasn't nothen but pure-dee woods. But we maken progress."

I said, "How about Alabama?"

"They walken," he said. Like he'd scored a point. "Yesser, they *walken!* That what I mean. We maken *progress.* Everything gonna be all right . . ."

I said, "You think they'd be walking if the thing hadn't been pushed?"

"Speck so," he said. "In time. Time do *every*thing."

The buildings were taller now, and new. An infinity of windows. Smart dress shops. Apartment house with extended marquee. Three blocks more and the apartment houses would have stiff-spined doormen in front.

"That Governor Wallace. Don't see why *he* can't see it. Change *comen!* Time *roll on!* He oughta know. He can't be *too* dumb. He *Governor!*"

We paused at a red light. A matron wearing a mink stole waited on the corner, her eyes seeking something in darting looks. (Tryst with a lover? Shopping spree with a girl friend?) A vexed frown wrinkled the matron's forehead. She shifted the mink stole and looked at me, somehow angry and contemptuous. I winked, a greatly exaggerated drooping of eye with grotesque distortion of the mouth, tongue lolling out, and she made a big thing of looking away. We left her nibbling at a painted thumbnail.

"Can't have hate," the old citizen philosophized. "Even that Wallace, we can't——. Whites can't afford ta hate Nig-grows and Nig-grows can't afford ta hate whites. *Everybody* gotta git a-long."

I said, "Don't you ever get impatient?"

"Time," he said. "It sets its own pace. You can't make time trot when it wants ta walk." His comment had a practiced, patented sound. How much was I being put on?

"Do you vote?"

"Naw. But not because I'm Nig-grow. It's just I always been here in D.C." My careful search for sour-mash humor, for irony, for a mocking smile, revealed nothing in face or tone. "They letten us vote for Pres-i-dent now." I wanted to ask (but somehow did not) why he hadn't voted when the District of Columbia got the franchise last year.

We tooled past Federal Triangle. To the right were massive, uniform, government buildings possessed of a spit-and-polish look. A grim, antiseptic sameness. *As much alike,* I'd heard somebody say in my youth, *as nigger soldiers.* To the left a neoned, multi-styled clutter of private business firms with a garish, carnival midway atmosphere about them. Ahead, the Capitol was a picture postcard at the far end of the wide avenue. ("Dear Folks: Wish you was here. We seen the wax museum and Congressman Dowdy and Kennedy's Grave. It has a picket fence. Leave here Thursday for God's Country. Ella Mae's had a upset-stommich. Love. . . .")

The driver was nodding *yes yes yes* and mumbling to Frank McGee. A huge fountain spurted in a triangular park where several streets crossed. In the summer small boys, mostly Negro, violate local ordinances by bathing in it. Police routinely run them off on the hour; just as routinely they stream back after satisfying the law by mock shows of terror. (Congressmen and Senators have their own plush swimming pools, courtesy of the taxpayers. President Johnson dedicated a new one the other day at the same time civil rights workers were sitting-in at the White House. The press came, and afterwards there was a whiskey bash during which diversion the White House embarrassment got removed.)

The Washington Monument stood tall and unshakable off to our right. Somewhere, I knew, below my line of vision, fifty U.S. flags snapped, crackled and popped their breakfast-cereal sounds in the wind. I had once talked a Congressman out of displacing the uniform beauty of those flags. He wanted to ring the Monument with standards of the individual states, and he had the power to do it, too. The prospective hodge-podge had revolted me, and so I had talked him out of it. Not with logic, but with the kind of language politicians understand. ("Go ahead and do it. I can hear your opponent now: 'And after votin' for all those socialistic bills, what'd your so-called Congressman do? Why, he passed a law removing Old Glory from the Washington *Mon*-u-mint!'") Maybe, I thought, it was my Finest

Hour in ten years on the Hill: my most important contribution to the experiment of self-government. Well, it seemed little enough. Would I go down in history as The Man Who Saved the Flags At the Washington Monument? Would patriots sing paeans of praise? Would politicians dust off their July 4th speeches and invent me new virtues? Would somebody make an educational TV film about my valor? ("Awright, for this next scene we'll have him running through shot and shell holding the flag over his head . . .")

The driver said, "We getten there. That speech the Pres-i-dent made to Congress. You hear that speech?"

"Yes."

"It made me proud!", he said. And his eyes glistened. "I was so proud I hulled down and *cried!* Yesser, at my age! I didn't think that Pres-i-dent had it in him. But it come *out.* He from Texas."

"Yeah," I said. "So I've heard."

"Sure he is!" He gave me an amazed look in the rear-view mirror. "But he a good man. That speech!"

We banged around a traffic circle. In the center a long-dead general postured on his stone horse, forever doomed to the vengeance of pigeons.

"Do anything Russia or anybody *else* can. Like that nice space-shot trip today. Them boys down and safe in the water." He turned a knob to enlarge the miracle, and a quartet harmonized the glory of a hair shampoo.

"Walken in Alabama and flyen in space," the hackie said, laughing.

He double-parked between the Longworth and Cannon House Office Buildings. The Capitol loomed over us, frightening in its physical scope. *One day,* I thought, *it will get us all.* A girl in green crossed the street. She had good, tanned legs and her hair was blowing in a strong breeze. Soon she would be typing letters to pacify some John Bircher spooked by a Communist plot to control our thinking through fluoride in water. A blonde boy swaggered up the street, self-conscious in Sunday-go-to-meeting best, fingering his midget necktie. He reminded me of my own son, whom I had not seen since late July, and who had just turned seven. The stab was sharp: *"My son, where you were born the land is bloody and full of guilt."*

I asked, "How much I owe?"

"Uh . . . that's . . . that'll be . . . ninety cents." Honest cabbie. Right zone charge. I gave the old sport a dollar and a dime. Then, impulsively, I made it a more wonderful country by two-bits worth. The dark old man nodded and beamed benediction and babbled on: thanks for my generosity, something about the Pres-i-dent, a comment on my face-beard, all culminating in a cracked cackle. He was damn near toothless. I hadn't noticed before.

Frank McGee waited until I got involved in banging the dented door before divesting himself of intelligence: the Navy carrier La-de-da or Something-Something was now just X miles from the *Molly Brown*.

The old cab lurched away and the old man's voice rode back on the wind . . . "them boys outta that water . . ."

I had a meeting scheduled with an able Member of Congress, less a jackass than most, who had been slated to emote in my TV film, but who now wouldn't do because a fly-by-night Hollywood type had it in him to spread goose-grease to the folks out there in educational television land.

To hell with ole Hollywood. And the script. And the Congressman. *Without amendment, so ordered.*

I turned into the Congressional Hotel's curved walk. Plaster figures on the lawn. A donkey and, of course, an elephant. Too, too cute. Carefully bi-partisan. Grog at the going rate for all regardless of race, color, or political creed. All you need is the money.

The cocktail waitress gave me a warm hello. She stood brown and smiling and showing good teeth. (Could I borrow her teeth for my mythical Frank Merriwell-type Senator? Then if I could just find somebody with a Duke Wayne jaw . . .)

I said, "Miss Gloria. A Miller's beer."

She made for the bar, smiling. A Negro waiter togged out in gold jacket methodically wiped an ash-tray. The TV set, sans sound, offered a silent peek of the *Molly Brown* headed for outer space through the miracle of video-tape.

The bar was quiet, and lonely. I had two beers. I telephoned my wife to meet me after work. I telephoned the Congressman, explaining about the Hollywood fop and how the Hollywood fop had blown the script. The Congressman and I cursed in concert, he without spirit—more as a duty. I telephoned my wife again and said "I love you." She said, "Me too." I said: "You mean we both love you?" We laughed, I hung up, and felt immeasurably better.

Back in the bar I made notes for this piece on a napkin, my pen catching in the rough paper. Much solitary munching of potato chips and peanuts. Now and then a great, restive sense of loss beyond any inventory. *I recollect lotsa changes* . . .

A congressional aide stood in the door blinking into the interior gloom. When his orbs adjusted we exchanged pleasantries, and I hand-signaled him into a chair.

He flopped down. "Waiting for somebody?" One hand dived for the peanuts.

"Anybody," I said. "Right now I'd enjoy the company of Bruce Alger."*

He laughed, but not for long. Soon he started to fume about the goddamn nuts and kooks who write letters to their congressmen, and all the time wasted answering them. He griped because he couldn't get new D.C. car tags until he settled some unpaid traffic tickets—a precious accumulation of them, it seemed. About a hundred dollars worth. He swore, with feeling and *in absentia,* at Oregon's Senator Wayne Morse. (Morse doggedly insists that each "fixed" traffic ticket in Washington be reported to him personally. He passes the info on to the press. The publicity, Senator Morse feels, discourages ticket-fixing. He's right.) The aide drummed with his fingers on the polished table.

Gloria had been out of the bar. Spotting the new customer she put urgency in her walk. She paused at our table, impassive now and thoughtful.

"Decision, decisions," my friend said, eying the bar.

I said, "We maken progress. Things changen. We walken in Alabama and flyen in space. Ya dig me, Sweetheart? Ya dig me, Baby?"

He flicked his eyes at me before glancing up at the silent TV screen. A reporter mouthed into a microphone, the White House his backdrop.

I said, "We ken do anything. I give that Russian boy credit. He got out and turned flips in space . . . Another one these here champagnes of bottle beer, Miss Gloria. This a wunnerful country. . . ."

My friend stirred uneasily. He said, "Vodka martini, I guess."

When she was half-way to the bar he called, "On the rocks. And with a twist of lemon."

* Then a Republican troglodyte in Congress, from Dallas.

CHAPTER 11

Joe Pool of HUAC:
McCarthy in the Round

There is really very little that is funny about the demagogue. He is too much a reflection of what our society is in the moment of his dark power, or at least that part of society where he holds sway. Yet, I am always bubbling some dark mirth on contemplating the demagogue. Maybe it is because I simply enjoy the fantastic free show that some of God's clowns offer from this earthly sideshow. Perhaps deep in my viscera are tender sensibilities so shocked by the audacity of demogogues who ask us to accept their preposterous propositions as Gospel (Dwight D. Eisenhower as part and parcel of the Communist Conspiracy, for instance, or the idea of Medicare destroying "the sacred doctor-patient relationship") that laughter flows so that tears cannot. Or possibly my sense of humor is out of joint.

I did not laugh at Hitler, but the late Senator Joe McCarthy did provide me with one uncontrollable spasm of mirth. McCarthy, by the time I struck up a fleeting barroom acquaintance with him, was just another spookless old ghost with a bad liver. His censure by the U.S. Senate in December of 1954 occurred only some six weeks after I arrived in Washington as the round-eyed assistant to a freshman Congressman. McCarthy never amounted to a tinker's damn after that. Oh, periodically he rose in the Senate to bawl that John Foster Dulles had 150 men frantically working to censor the Yalta papers so America would never know the truth of "the sellout to Communism," or to call Sherman Adams a "pinhead politician." But by this time Senators who had once quaked in McCarthy's presence walked out of the chamber rather than monitor his brayings, and the newspaper men who had largely "made" him with the headlines he reveled in had taken to throwing the Senator's mimeographed news releases into the handiest trash can.

It was during this period that I met Joe McCarthy, though "met" makes it sound a lot grander than it was. One afternoon in mid-1955 I was in the Carroll Arms Hotel bar, a watering hole on Capitol Hill where McCarthy often lubricated his tubes, when the Senator entered with two companions. They took a nearby table, McCarthy glancing around as if to check the room for Reds and perverts, nodding and smiling to two or three persons who presumably had passed the test. This was my first flesh-and-blood look at Joe Mc-Carthy from close range, and I confess that I stared at him shamelessly. Politicians fascinate me, and the bigger the demagogue the greater the fascination. My frank eyeballing seemed to disconcert Senator McCarthy. Several times our eyes met, and we would both look immediately away as if what we had seen was too gross to be dwelled on. Suddenly, without a word to his companions, he rose, plunged across the eight or ten feet separating our tables and said, "I'm Joe McCarthy." There was no smile on his face, no frown, nothing. There was just this big, beefy man who looked like a sackful of doorknobs in a rumpled suit which in the dim artificial light could have been brown or may have been gray, and there was a hand hanging in mid-air about six inches from my nose. I shook the hand rather awkwardly, half-sitting and half-standing, mumbling my name, not knowing whether I would be charged with contempt of Congress on the spot or whether Heaven might send a lightning bolt to rescue me. The Senator asked was I new on the Hill. I said yes. He asked who I worked for and where was I from. I told him, though I had an insane desire to plead the Fifth Amendment. We gawked at one another like two embarrassed enemy generals who had unexpectedly encountered each other before either had drawn up a battle plan. Abruptly the Senator muttered something in the nature of "gladtameetcha" and I responded in the same verbal shorthand, still in a daze and wondering what the exercise was all about. He returned to his table as abruptly as he had left it. Periodically over the next few months I saw Joe McCarthy in the same bar. Generally he would nod, or maybe wave in a curious, sweeping gesture that showed you the back of his hand, and a couple of times he said, "Hello, Texas."

Most of the time, though he was a political zero by this juncture, McCarthy would be in the company of one or two or three men— rarely, however, the same ones. There had been a time when he swept into the Carroll Arms with an entourage so full of bustle you might have thought they were fleeing the gypsies. There would be Roy Cohn and David Schine, the hottest second-banana politicians on the circuit, an admiring coterie of Super Patriots preening themselves before the Presence, and, inevitably, several of the dozen newsmen (self-named "goon-squadders") assigned to take down his every headline-making pronouncement. In those days the sight of McCarthy lordly marching ahead of his legions sent waiters scurrying to his table with heel clicks that might have appeased Mussolini, and I am told that tourists in the cocktail lounge sometimes burst into spontaneous applause.

But the glory left Rome, and ultimately it left Joe McCarthy. One post-adjournment afternoon, with Congress gone home to fence-mend and things slow on Capitol Hill, I lingered in the shadows of the Carroll Arms cocktail lounge morosely contemplating my future. Of which, it seemed, I had none. For a year I had worked terribly long hours on the Hill doing the ditch-digging work that a combination office manager-speech writer-political backstop soon learns is his lot in life, and yet the frantic motions seemed without purpose. I was not making enough money to stay ahead of the financial hounds, things were about as pleasant in my household as in Dante's Inferno, and nowhere was my name writ large in the stars. I had, in the previous six months, become a compulsive eater—tearing at chicken breasts and great cheesy pizzas and downing oceans of beer as if to smother all my frustrations under a sea of suet—and had ballooned 960 ounces above my normal weight to a king-sized 250 tubby pounds.

Only one other table in the room was occupied, and I could have done without even that dubious companionship. A middle-aged woman at the other table had drunk a hearty lunch that put her on a crying jag. Between great, wind-gulping sobs and saying things like "I can't hardly *stand* it" or "But why did he do it, Norman, *why?*" she blew her tomato-red nose with a great series of honks into, of all things, a polka-dot bandanna. Norman, a timid-looking bit of protoplasm with receding hair and worried, darting eyes, was the sort of bread-pudding fellow who had learned early that life has too many riddles ever to be solved, so he merely shook his head at the lady's wails as if to say: well, that is the way things are on this mudball, kiddo, and if you can't adjust to it, then you had damn well better carry a generous supply of polka-dot bandannas.

Into this setting, so dismal that Edgar Allan Poe himself might have fled it, stepped—Joe McCarthy! Alone.

Senator McCarthy surveyed the room, turned as if to leave, spotted me at about the halfway point of his turn, pivoted, and hesitated. Would he attack or retreat? With a quick flash of his practiced politician's smile, one that lived so briefly you wondered whether you had imagined it, he galoomped over and asked if I'd mind a little company. Without waiting for an answer—indeed, even as he asked the question—he plopped into a chair and turned toward the bar, twisting his short, thick neck on invisible swivels, intent on inciting the bartender to action.

Now, you must understand this: if ever there was a politician—nay, if ever there was a *human*—that I detested more than I despise snakes, lapdogs and thunderstorms, it was the rude fellow who suddenly sat across from me about to bellow for booze. Inconceivable! Utterly impossible! Fantastic! There he *was,* so close that I could have picked his pockets and then maybe have told the world whether it was really 57 or 81 or 203 "card-carrying Communists" we had over in our State Department.

And here was I, who only a year earlier, back in the living room of my crackerbox $70-a-month apartment in Odessa, Texas, had watched the televised Army-McCarthy hearings in revulsion and sometimes with slack-jawed disbelief as Senator Joe McCarthy thundered how General Zwicker was "unfit to wear the uniform"; as he grew so reckless with men's reputations that Special Counsel Joseph Welch asked, "Have you no shame, sir?"; as McCarthy repeatedly demanded to know "Who promoted Peress?" and made Army Secretary Bob Stevens cringe, crawfish and appease—here was I, seventeen hundred miles away from my native desert, where I had often been in trouble with my right-wing newspaper publisher during the McCarthy Era because I had a tendency to hint that the Wisconsin witch-hunter was less than a major God; yes, here was I, nursing all my physical fat and internal hurts over grog while fretting over the future of mankind and myself, suddenly sitting at the *same table with*—yes, on the verge of *drinking* with—Joe McCarthy Himself!

Well sir, I started to laugh, and I couldn't have stopped even under the threat of a court order. It was wild laughter, bubbling up and spilling over and booming out, and no doubt I looked like a young Sydney Greenstreet suddenly gone mad, hoo-hawing and pounding the table that-a-way, unable to do anything but shake like jelly and gasp "Oh, God!" and "Oh, Christ!" and then offer another great braying burst of crazy laughter.

Joe McCarthy could not believe it. Here *he* was, minding his own business in the middle of the afternoon, shopping around for a drink or two and maybe a little companionship with somebody who could talk with him about the good ole days, and here was a fat man going all-the-way coo-coo before his very eyes. He gave one long oxlike dumb stare as if to say: Good God, boy, you are more a menace than John Foster Dulles and Alger Hiss rolled into one big round ball of conspiratorial Red twine. Then the man everybody had so feared jumped up and hauled the hell away from there, knocking over a chair as he went. My little concert of hysteria aroused a dozing waitress who knew me to be harmful only in a minor key, so she hurried over to ask was everything all right? I just kept on gasping and wheezing and carrying on until little bread-pudding Norman steered the crying-jag lady toward the door with such haste you might have thought he was hunting the bomb shelter.

That ended my association with Joe McCarthy, and while it is not enough to make the history books it is enough to make my point: maybe I would have laughed at Hitler, if I'd ever gotten to know him. Once in the newsreel he danced this real neat jig.

The first cousin of the out-and-out demagogue is the Philistine: one who opposes culture or progress, or whose interests are wholly in the present. He may have little understanding of the past and no concept of the future. It is this type of know-nothing politician who holds a grand potential to be tomorrow's demagogue or fanatic. Whether he goes the whole route depends on a combination of his character, his ambition, his intelligence (or a lack of these qualities), plus the breaks of the political game.

Such a man, I think, is Congressman Joe Pool of Texas. Pool burst upon the national scene in mid-1966 as chairman of a sub-committee under the parent House Un-American Activities Committee. Some months earlier Congressman Pool had introduced a bill that would have provided criminal penalties for persons who dissented with the Vietnam war to the extent that they "aided or comforted" the enemy. The bill was vague and blowsy, begging the question of where honest dissent stopped and sedition set in—if it did set in. As Pool saw it, public demonstrations against the Vietnam war were enough to border on treason. He knew, certainly, that his position would be acceptable to his right-wing Dallas constituents, but I honestly think Pool *is* of the opinion that if you aren't willing to march on Hanoi with bayonets, no questions asked, then you are not "a good American"—never mind all that jazz about not being "officially" at war with the Viet Cong just because Congress hasn't declared war like the Constitution says it should if we are to fight; never mind whether we have any business in Vietnam or not, or under what authority. Such logic leads people like Joe Pool to the conclusion that if one is not "a good American" then one is an enemy of the State and should be dealt with harshly. It is a dangerous philosophy, of course, a narrow and frightening one, but Pool is not alone in holding it.

As chairman of the subcommittee to which his bill had been referred by the House parliamentarian, Pool was in an excellent position to advance its cause. In mid-1966 he called it up for hearings. These were the hearings that ended in as tragicomic a wrangle as the stormy House Un-American Activities Committee, never known for purveying sweet reason, has ever produced. There was the spectacle of Arthur Kinoy, a Civil Liberties Union attorney, being hauled out of the Committee room by several beefy cops who had choke-holds on his 135-pound frame. There were bearded types parading around in Revolutionary War costumes and other attire that defied description, cursing the Congressmen and hissing them and giving them that old vulgar gesture of the middle finger standing erect from the balled fist. There were the Congressmen themselves, braying like so many jackasses locked out of the barn, and Pool banging a gavel until it broke, and huffing and puffing along between two uniformed policemen even when he went to the House Restaurant for lunch. And there was everybody being injudicious, as Pool was when he snapped (to a hostile witness who had claimed identification with the American Revolution), "I know another man who identified with it. I think his first name was Benedict." There was, it later turned out, a "friendly" Committee witness once part of the anti-war movement (publicly identified as "a rat-fink son-of-a-bitch" by "unfriendly" witnesses) who had gone on HUAC's staff payroll for a $1,000 chore —a bit of information unknown to the public, the press, or even to some of the harassed, confused Congressmen participating in the farcical hearings. The subtleties of liberty seemed to escape both sides. People at the Washington *Post* and *The New Republic* were horrified at Pool and HUAC; the Dallas *Morning News* and Bill Buckley's *National Review* were predictably aghast at the conduct of the bearded protesters. Watching, I could not help but adopt a "plague on both your houses" attitude. And, may God forgive, I laughed a lot.

It was with this sideshow as background that I went forward to write of . . .

JOE POOL OF HUAC: McCARTHY IN THE ROUND

Until a certain hectic week in August, Joe Pool was just another junior Congressman. His pet legislative scheme would have turned a Texas mountaintop into a National Park—provided, Pool made clear, that a major oil company retain drilling and mineral rights. True, he had got his name in the paper a few months previously when the House Un-American Activities Committee investigated the inner tickings of the Ku Klux Klan. He also had been the subject of Page One stories when his $30,000 fund-raising "Appreciation Dinner" in Washington coincided with Drew Pearson's revelations in the Dodd Case, causing suspicious reporters to show up and count the lobbyists, contractors, and professional gladhanders among Pool's official appreciators. But roly-poly Joe Pool remained, until late this summer, slightly less anonymous than the Unknown Soldier. He was also having reelection troubles from a Republican in his new Dallas district.

Then came his House Un-American Activities Committee hearings. A week after the storm broke he proudly told a cheering Dallas crowd, "Little Joe has been catapulted into a very prominent spot in American history overnight." The Dallas *Morning News* rhapsodized: "The [House Un-American Activities] Committee, since the day of Texas' Martin Dies, has been the people's last resort against those in Washington who are lenient on rats in our midst. In protecting the function of this Committee, Mr. Pool is protecting the voice of the people." A woman wired: "AN AMERICAN HERO WAS BORN TODAY." A Grand Prairie, Texas, man resorted to special delivery and a special form of Latin to advise: "NON CARBORUNDUM ILLEGITIMI!" ("Don't Let the Bastards Grind You Down!") The Veterans of Foreign Wars told Pool that if he would get up to their national convention in the New York Hilton, they'd lay a special award on him.

When Congressman Pool flew home for the weekend, some three hundred Dallas boosters jammed a hotel ballroom to sing "For He's a

Jolly Good Fellow." Placards said, "Give 'Em Hell, Joe!" Spokesmen for the Jewish War Veterans, the American Legion, and the VFW variously gave Joe the nod in impromptu eulogies over Davy Crockett, Sam Houston, and Douglas MacArthur. An ancient warrior represented as being eighty-eight years old and a veteran of San Juan Hill, garbed in a Rough Rider's outfit, paused to give the Congressman a palsied salute. A woman shouted, "You're my next President, Joe Baby!" Others took it up.

It was too much. Joe Pool wandered around the ballroom shaking hands, as he told me, "bawling like a baby." "When all that happened it—well, it just got to me. I felt *humble,* you know whatta mean?" Pool recovered from his attack of humility long enough to tell the throng, "Most Americans live for the day when they can do something for their country that will go down in history. I feel like I did exactly that last week." That started them singing again.

Writing in a national magazine recently, historian Arthur Schlesinger, Jr., suggested the approach of a new "McCarthy Era." Pointing out that witch-hunting traditionally reaches its peak during wars, Schlesinger wrote, "If history repeats itself—and history sometimes does—the war in Vietnam ought to produce something roughly comparable to the McCarthy phenomenon. The Vietnamese war is just as frustrating as the Korean war and a good deal harder for most people to understand. . . . As the war increasingly dominates and obsesses our national life, we can look for the appearance of associated symptoms: the oversimplification of issues, the exchange of invective, the questioning of motives and loyalties, and the degradation of debate."

If we are to have a new McCarthy Era we must, by a small extension of logic, have a new McCarthy. Does Joe Pool qualify? What manner of cat is he?

It was World War II that opened Pool's eyes to the joys of "investigative work." His biographical sketch notes that he served as "special investigator with Air Corps Intelligence." Pool says that "when a plane crashed we'd cordon off the area and try to reconstruct what happened, figure out what went wrong." For a time he was a Provost Marshal's gumshoe, looking into thefts, frauds, larcenies, and crooked crap games in a half-dozen Southwestern states.

He was elected to the Texas Legislature in 1952, and in time became Chairman of the House Investigating Committee. During this period the state government was rocked by major scandals involving insurance companies, loan sharks, real-estate schemes, and the Veterans' land program. Attendant explosions sent a few folks to jail (including the Texas Land Commissioner and a State Representative), inspired at least one prominent suicide, and caused another public figure to seek the better climate of Brazil. Joe Pool's Investigating Committee had nothing to do with any of this. It did, however, war on lewd and horror comic books.

To this day Joe is intrigued by intrigue. Some months ago I chanced upon the Congressman in a Capitol corridor. Perhaps I eyed him a bit warily, for I had just written in the *Texas Observer* of his voting record, and in less than complimentary terms.

Pool jovially hailed me in the thick accent of our common habitat. "Yew ole Liberal thang, yew! Lemme buy yew a cuppa coffee. Ah wanta talk *turkey* to yew."

What Joe wanted to talk turkey about was the upcoming HUAC hearings into operations of the Ku Klux Klan. Joe had a scheme. We would go, the two of us, in tandem and incognito, into the seedier traps of deepest Dixie—into snooker parlors, roadside honky-tonks, cheap hotels, stock-car race tracks, hillbilly dance joints, fishing and hunting clubs—there to infiltrate the Klan, during the annual adjournment of Congress, until we knew its spookiest secrets by heart. "You gotta have undercover work to get anywhere on a thang like this," Joe assured me. "We'll wear ole clothes. Khaki britches and short-sleeved sports shirts and thangs like that. I betcha we can crack 'em."

"Godamighty, Joe," I said. "We'd probably get killed!"

Pool acted as if he hadn't heard. He said, "We can get the evidence. I don't have any doubts about that. You can get you some good stories that'll sell, and as far as I'm concerned you can keep all the money. All I want is the publicity." He stared at me over his coffee cup there in the hushed splendor of the House Restaurant. "A-course," he said, thoughtfully, "you'll have to shave that shaggy ole beard off."

As Harry Truman once said of Stalin in an unguarded moment, "I like Ole Joe." He is a jovial companion at libations, quick to pick up the tab for his table, and maybe the neighboring one as well. He is good to his employees, paying them well and smiling away mistakes.

He makes easy jokes on himself. Only five feet, six inches tall and admitting to 235 pounds, he likes to tell of being introduced as the Congressman-at-Large to a lady who cracked, "Well, you durn sure look like you qualify!"

Somebody over at *The New Republic* wrote that Joe would have to be seen to be believed, that he looks like "a frog on a lily pad," and that "he is not very bright." It *is* true that you can relax beside Pool without feeling like he may steal your girl. He may not be much prettier than Elizabeth, New Jersey, and he will never bore you with a lot of small talk about Dostoevski or the later plays of T. S. Eliot or prevailing economic conditions in Peru. One should not deduce from this, however, that Joe Pool is without resources.

Some months ago I was in Pool's office when a staff member told him of a Dallas newspaper story to the effect that his GOP opponent was having trouble gaining meaningful financial backing from the Republican National Committee. Pool looked up from signing his mail and drawled, "I thought that never *would* get printed. Planted that rumor nearly two weeks ago." He led the laughter.

There is sometimes a sort of blurted, barstool frankness about him that makes you wonder whether he ever kept a secret. Asked why he was the only member of the House to vote against the Wilderness Bill (to preserve certain wooded areas in their native state) when it passed 388 to 1, he said, "Well, I figured I could throw my conserva- tive friends an anti-Lyndon vote and at the same time not do much damage." In the summer of 1963, Pool rather curiously announced to the world that he would sleep in his Congressional office "until the demonstrators disperse." He did, for one night, which was the announced duration of the March on Washington anyway. Two years later, when I pressed him for an explanation of what he had expected to accomplish by the theatrical act, Pool said candidly, "Tell you the truth, I'm not sure I could explain it to myself. It just seemed like a good idea at the time."

Perhaps Pool is most appreciated in professional circles for his ability to walk the political chalk line well enough to keep the Presi- dent's goodwill even while voting against most of the President's programs. There is nothing especially mystic about why Joe Pool has so much unexpended coin in Lyndon Johnson's piggy bank.

A few years ago LBJ wanted to appear on the Texas ballot both as a candidate for U.S. Senator *and* on the national ticket. This required a May, rather than a July Democratic Primary (as was customary) if

Johnson hoped to go to the July Democratic National Convention in 1960 with his Senatorial renomination locked up. Technical points were involved, some requiring an amendment to the Texas Constitution, but the main goal was to allow Johnson to hedge his political bet. It was Joe Pool, then a member of the Texas Legislature, who rushed forward to sponsor the necessary bill and gain its enactment.

Having served his political apprenticeship in the boondocks, Pool was elected to Congress in a manner that seems to have been preordained. He was one of two dozen candidates, all so obscure they might have profitably robbed liquor stores without wearing masks, to vie for the Congressman-at-Large seat vacated by Martin Dies. An El Paso County judge led the first primary from here to Iwo Jima, Pool barely qualifying for the showdown runoff thirty days later. Within a week the leading candidate had been indicted (and was ultimately convicted) of income-tax evasion; he had not filed an income tax in ten years. Pool got to Washington virtually by default. He immediately asked for his seat on the House Un-American Activities Committee.

I called on Congressman Pool in Washington the Monday following his hero's welcome in Dallas. A uniformed Capitol Hill policeman, eyeing my beard, asked what he could do for me. Jean Jones, Pool's executive secretary, the sight of whom will almost automatically make you think of Girls, has suffered everything on Capitol Hill from bearded prophets to cocktail-hour proposals of marriage. She spoke to the nervous cop in tones meant to assure him that I carried no bombs.

The walls were covered with Washington Wallpaper: autographed photos of the mighty (HST, JFK, LBJ) and the obscure (booted Texas oil barons, a 4-H Club champion who had probably raised the fattest hog, mink-clad matrons giving Pool, or perhaps receiving from him, some certificate or scroll of special merit). There were oil paintings by student Rembrandts at Southern Methodist or Texas Christian. Just inside the Congressman's private chamber is a partition shielding him from a view of the sink where his staffers brew mildly vile pots of coffee. The partition was festooned with colorful record jackets advertising the triumphs of certain hillbilly or rock-'n'-roll music men. A neat, hand-lettered sign said, "These Records Made in Texas!"

Behind his executive desk Joe Pool came off like the lean, loose-jointed Texan of legend the same way R. C. Cola comes off as Châteauneuf du Pape. He filled the padded chair, horizontally speaking, though you had the notion that maybe under the desk his feet didn't quite reach the floor. "Come on in," he said, grinning. "Hail, I put up with lots worse than you, lately."

We both enthused over his new prominence. Pool lovingly described his Dallas homecoming, and how the salute of the old Rough Rider had moved him to tears. Art Cameron, a young Capitol Hill lawyer assisting Pool with "Constitutional questions," relaxed on the couch with a fat *Constitution Annotated*. Behind the partition Jean Jones ran water and clanked a coffee pot.

"You're a writer," Pool accused me, suddenly. "Tell me somethin'. Few days ago I was interviewed by a kid from the school paper up at Harvard. You know, Harvard College?" I said I knew. "Anyway, he promised he'd call back today," Pool said, "to let me check my direct quotes out. But he didn't call. You reckon he will?"

I said I had no way of knowing.

"I doubt it," Joe judged. "He tole me he didn't see eye-to-eye with me. Which didn't come as too big a surprise. He probably went off and wrote it like he wanted to." He toyed with an ashtray. "A-course," he said, elaborately casual, "I had Art here, and Jean, with me all the time *he* was here. They can be my witnesses . . . if I need 'em."

The prospective witnesses went with us to the Capitol Hill Democratic Club across the street when I volunteered to buy post-work drinks. "The thing about this man," Art Cameron said, once we'd claimed a table, "is that he handled himself so *beautifully* during all those outbursts. He had to make quick decisions time after time after time. And he *always* made the right one." Pool dropped his head and said modestly that, well, *some* people might not agree with that, but he'd done the best he could and he knew *one* thing about it: he'd sure earned his money *that* particular week. Miss Jones said, "It was a real education. I learned that a reporter can paint any picture he wants just by being selective—by writing *some* things and leaving out *other* things. That damn Washington *Post!* You read the actual transcripts and you'll find a different hearing than the one you read about in the papers." Pool said, philosophically, that well, you can't fight City Hall, and Art Cameron said that was for sure.

I remarked that Pool's GOP opponent, who a few weeks earlier had been judged capable of winning, must have suddenly felt as if the moon and the stars had dropped on him.

Pool grinned. "I dunno. . . . He jumped on me in the papers. Said I'd did the same thing as all those street rioters when I ignored that court order. I don't think anybody very smart's gonna see it like that. A-course, you never can tell . . ."

"Hell," I said, "the only way you can lose this election, Joe, is to get caught in bed with a live man or a dead woman."

Pool boomed with laughter. He poked his finger at me in a stabbing motion, gasping mirth: "*You* . . . said . . . that! *I* didn't."

A Congressional staffer in a bow tie paused to wring Pool's hand. "You really got after those nuts," he said. "I'm proud of you, Congressman." Pool thanked him and noted that "they really got after *me,* for a while there, didn't they?" He offered to buy his admirer a drink but the fellow explained about a waiting wife and dinner.

Two or three other people stopped to congratulate Pool as he sat basking in his new glory, smilingly mumbling something about how "the Commonists" probably didn't agree but *he* sure as heck did appreciate it. Pool stopped Arizona Democrat Morris "Mo" Udall, who happened by with three constituents in tow, and through gasps of laughter, his broad belly shaking uncontrollably, he repeated my crack about being "caught in bed with a live man or a dead woman." Udall smiled as if his feet hurt and moved on.

Soon the crowd thinned, shuffling away to the bar or in search of dinner. I asked Pool what he thought the HUAC hearings had proved. "I think," he said, "it proves the Commonists are behind all this treason. They showed their true colors. Lot of 'em admitted being Commonists, or Marxist-Leninists or Progressive Labor, or whatever it is." Suddenly, he beamed, turning to Jean Jones: "Say, Jean, my opponent says he's a *Progressive* Republican. Think we can make anything out of that?" They laughed like winners who own the dice.

Why, I asked Joe, had he abruptly ended the hearings—even when two witnesses, who had been officially called, clamored to testify?

Pool said, "We thought we'd proved what we set out to prove. They *said* they was Commonists! And then, too, we wanted to be sure we gave those two boys—the ones who didn't testify—their Constitutional rights. Give 'em time to prepare their defenses. Get lawyers." He explained that the two had been represented by Arthur Kinoy, the American Civil Liberties Union attorney who had been bodily carried to jail. "You know," Joe confided, leaning across the table, "that

Kinoy thang had me worried for a while. If that judge had found him *not guilty*—Lord God! Well, I'da been *in* for it!" (Kinoy was fined $50 on disturbance charges by a judge in the District of Columbia.) Pool felt another seizure of confidential information coming on. He said in a conspiratorial tone, "You know the luckiest thang we ever done? Hold those Klan hearings! Yessir! Now we can say we got the Klan and the Commonists after us at the same time!" His eyes twinkled over such twin good fortune.

I said there was a rumor that the White House, as well as the Congressional leadership, had soured on the stormy HUAC hearings and had instructed Pool to stop them. Anything to it?

"Not a thang in the world," Pool said, heatedly. "A-course, I guess a lot of people might like to think so!"

I mentioned the Johnson Administration's opposition to the bill. The Administration had taken the position, I said, that no new legislation is needed; that the demonstrations are a long way from treason; that since Vietnam isn't officially "a war," Congress must move slow in legislating punitively against dissenters. Could Pool account for the Administration's logic?

Pool said that maybe I'd better ask the President; he couldn't tell *him* what to do. Then he added, "Some of those Administration witnesses didn't stand up too well to the Committee. That Army General—the one that testified that all these demonstrations don't hurt our troop morale? Well, when we pinned him down he admitted it might help the *Vietcong's* morale! That's the same thing, now, don't you think?"

Art Cameron said, "Oh, Congressman Ichord got that out of the General *so* beautifully. It was just . . . well, *beautiful!*"

Pool said that you sure couldn't put much past ole Dick Ichord. Then he told Cameron, "We got ole Ramsey Clark comin' up here to testify tomorrow."

"He'll be pretty tough," Cameron predicted.

"I dunno," Pool said. "I heard he said he wouldn't hurt us much."

"He's an Administration witness."

"Well . . . I *heard* that, anyway."

"You just wait," Cameron warned. "I'll bet he throws you some real Constitutional toughies."

"That right?" Pool asked. He gazed into his glass, discouraged.

"Joe," I said, "some people see you as 'the New McCarthy.' You have any comment?"

Pool's laugh seemed genuine. "Boy! If I ever heard one to quit on, that's *it!* Waiter, brang me the check for this table!" While he signed the check, dismissing my halfhearted efforts to pay, he shook his head: "Yew ole Liberals! I dunno. . . ."

I told the Congressman I hoped to see him later in the week. "Make it before Thursday," he said. "I'm goin' to Vietnam."

To *Vietnam?*

"Yeah," he said, offhandedly. Then he grinned. "Reckon what my Republican opponent's gonna say about that?"

I mumbled that I didn't even know what to say. When had this come about? And for what purpose?

"I'm on the Post Office and Civil Service Committee, too," Pool reminded me. "Chairman's asked me to go over and investigate our boys' mail service. We've had a lotta complaints that the mail's been slow gettin' there, and thangs like that." He added quickly that the assignment had been given him "before all this notoriety."

Would he talk to the troops about their morale, or whether antiwar demonstrations hurt their cause?

"You betcha! You just betcha! And I'm takin' a whole shoebox full of letters people have give me since this thang come up. I'm gonna show those boys over there fightin' Commonism that America's backin' 'em up! And that all these dadgummed Vietniks and beatniks and whatnot with their beards—" He trailed off, momentarily abashed.

I said, "Joe, you sure do make it sound personal."

"Aw," Pool said, "I didn't mean *you!*"

Joe told me to take it easy, moving away. Somebody at the bar yelled, "Hey there, Statesman!" as he walked by. Somebody else called, where was his police escort? Another barstool comedian asked didn't he know that the Communists might be waiting for him out there in the dark, right out there in front of the Congressional Hotel? Joe Pool waved and laughed and performed a little series of bobbing half-bows, thinking, maybe, what a friendly bunch of guys hung around Washington once you got to know 'em and the notion struck you that maybe you were catching the world premiere of McCarthy in the Round. He pushed against the thick glass door and bounced energetically down the hall that, if you just followed it far enough and made all the right turns at the right places, would take you straight to Vietnam.

CHAPTER 12

Making the Scene at Mailer's

I have always believed that F. Scott Fitzgerald was many times over more intelligent than Ernest Hemingway. Fitzgerald loved feather beds, soft lights and all pleasures accruing to the Great Indoors; probably he would have had the good sense to bolt in panic from the presence of a single lion. Hemingway, on the other hand, tracked lions down in prides and enjoyed parking his one-man sleeping bag in the mud.

All writers may have in common the secret certainty that immortality will claim their persons ahead of rigor mortis, but they sharply part company in seeking out life-styles. William Faulkner was content to nurse his isolation on the ancestral acres in Mississippi; Robert Ruark loved roaming Spain; John Steinbeck likes to tool around the country in a camper with his dog, Charley—and if Mrs. Steinbeck is happy, who am I to suggest anything peculiar in the arrangement?

Not counting those of us whose annual scramble for the rent requires us to go wherever our next magazine assignment points, writers roughly fall into three distinct geographical categories: (1) the expatriates who flee with their loot to foreign shores, returning only to plug their latest best seller or to fight with tax agents; (2) the "isolationists" who hide out in small, back-water, root-America towns so as to avoid the frightening hurry and glitter of New York; and (3) the "in crowd"—those urbane, successful men who comprise the writer's wing of the Literary Establishment and who, almost to the last in number, consider themselves hopelessly lost in the horse-latitudes when out of Manhattan's sight.

One of the latter is Norman Mailer, a simple, barefoot Brooklyn boy whom fame reached out and dragged around the world when he wrote his magnificent war novel, *The Naked and The Dead,* some twenty years ago. I became a Mailer fan then and I am a Mailer fan now that his hair has grayed and mine has thinned. I believe that much of Mailer's work belongs to the very first rank of American letters.

I do not pretend to know Norman Mailer well, having engaged him in tepid conversation at only two of the thousands of cocktail parties he must by now have graced, and having once—as the following story indicates—crashed a party at his Brooklyn Heights home, which has a much better view of Manhattan than William Buckley does. I have wanted to know Mailer, however, for I have often felt a kinship of anger with him. I had also been intrigued by Mailer's "bad boy" reputation: how could he cuss and drink and make love all night and still face the typewriter by day? Just as fascinating was his ability to worry seriously over his struggles with "The Beast" within himself; his tendency to berate himself, like a Puritan father, for moments when The Clown had overcome The Artist. And, above all, I have wanted to know Mailer because he has talent and the guts of a daylight burglar.

To drop a few names, the first time I met Norman Mailer was at a George Plimpton party. Bud Shrake of the *Sports Illustrated* staff, taking me there, warned of the evening's perils. "Not everybody's had pleasant dealings with Mailer," he said. "He's unpredictable. He may offer you money or he may box you about the face and ears." As we were being introduced I mumbled to Mailer that I would take the money, if it were all the same to him, which may have been a factor in our not forming any fast friendship.

Not that there was any trouble. In spite of all I could do, Norman Mailer would not be roused from a gentlemanly lethargy. When I remarked on the time he'd gotten drunk and challenged Sonny Liston to a fistfight, Mailer mumbled apologetically into his highball that he sure had made an ass of himself that day. ("I don't want to come off as a character," he said, seriously.) When I mentioned another top-ranked writer, known to be Mailer's blood enemy, he said softly that he hadn't seen that fellow in a long time. We exchanged chitchat on the weather (Mailer said it was damn cool for the time of year; I agreed), our surroundings (I said Plimpton's apartment sure looked comfortable; Mailer agreed) and a young actress' cleavage (we said the obvious). Then Mailer plopped down on a couch to listen to an improbable, impromptu concert (Jose Torres, then light-heavyweight champion of the world, singing love ballads; David Amram, composer-in-residence for the New York Philharmonic, playing piano*) as if it

---

* Torres had the weight on him, but Amram was quicker.

were the most normal thing in the world. He kept sneaking glances at his wristwatch and yawning.

I *know* Mailer Swings. My bones tell me so. Besides, I have read it in the newspapers. Proving it got to be a big thing with me: I had these dreams in which I caught Mailer with a left hook, somebody else's wife, and in night court. Not that I wish the man any bad luck, you understand: it's just that I know these two literate Texans, see, and everytime I go home the both of them always ask if I know Norman Mailer. When I say "yes" they ask what I think of him. Then I say that he seems like a pretty nice guy, and they sit back all hurt and disappointed and accusing. It gets to be damned embarrassing.

Not so very long ago I again was at liberty in New York. My book-editor promised to take me to a party Mailer was himself hosting. Like many of this particular editor's midday promises, it somehow remains undelivered. Don't ask me why: I stood on the designated corner so long that I joined the Salvation Army and was offered a bargain in eight pounds of hashish. Ultimately I withdrew to a place where the lights were dim enough to hide my shame, and took on about a year's supply of antifreeze. Some few hours later I found myself in a cab, solo, headed for Brooklyn Heights and intent on . . .

MAKING THE SCENE AT MAILER'S

These were Norman Mailer's friends and admirers, so the story line ran, come to an after-theater party celebrating the opening of his new play based on his old novel, *The Deer Park.*

There was this stairway chock-full of folks, one group possessed of knowledge that all the action was Upstairs, and those in the other lane of traffic convinced that Downstairs was the source of magic. A lot of rude pushing and shoving went on, but since it was all in place you didn't get any points for it. Nobody could move.

After we'd guarded the stairway until our mouths were dry a fellow with a high voice, a sweet smile, and a gold jacket that glittered in the light and was festooned with spangled do-dads, asked: "Are you a friend of Norman's?" "Well, ah, not exactly," I said. "You might say I'm a friend of a friend. Are *you* a friend of Norman's?" He said, "Well, not exactly. I'm sort of a friend of a friend, too." Within five minutes everybody within earshot had been forced to confess, with blushes and stammers, to being friends of a friend.

When that little game was over I said to the guy in the trick jacket, "You see the play tonight?" This question was somehow outside the rules: nobody answered, several people frowned, and one lady (whose purple hair was piled up the way Madam DuBarry wore hers) arched some orange eyebrows and said, "How *gross!*"

Up at the top of the stairs the host was stationed at a door leading into a large room where the action was, either greeting guests or demanding to see invitations. I hoped it was the former. A New York newspaperman whom I'd known for about two minutes said aw hell, don't worry about it, Ole Norman and me are thick as runaway slaves; I'll vouch for you. When we reached the door my new friend whooped and gargled his joy at seeing ole "Norm," thwacking him on the back with such force that I would not have blamed our host for counter-punching. You could see Mailer did not know my friend from Madame Chiang Kai-Shek. I ducked behind a fat lady and thus passed Mailer unseen.

No more than two hundred people, not counting the rock and roll band, were milling around in Mailer's spacious study. A pert young thing with long hair and in bell bottom trousers, whom I almost swear was a girl, grabbed me by the elbow and demanded my name. When I told her she said "Never *heard* of you, man" and went on about her mischief. Somebody told somebody else that Pamela Tiffin, the actress, was over there on the couch and that my dear she looks *divine,* just *groovy,* a real *gas.* Everybody within earshot chose to surge toward the couch on a course passing directly over my shined shoes. The celebrity hunters kept stalking around asking people their names. Everytime I gave mine it drew accusing stares, so that ultimately I found myself saying in tones of abject apology, "I'm sorry, I'm just Larry King," until a lady with a faint mustache told me that I should be ashamed of myself; I was, without ever knowing exactly why. For awhile I alternately posed as people named Chicken Gumbo, T. Ashley Goodfellow, and Rex Whoopee the Singing Cowboy, none of whom got really first-rate respect.

The hefty ole chick I'd used for protective covering when I crashed the gate hemmed me in after she'd picked up an advanced case of glazed eyeballs and began to complain that this was a shame and disgrace: all these nobodies and hangers-on had piled in here to ruin Norman's party—prize fighters and coffee house poets and deadbeats on Welfare, she said, and none of them had invitations, for God's sakes, and how could people *do* that? I agreed that Class was getting tougher and tougher to come by. Anybody who was *really* anybody, she said, had gone home—and she'd be gone as soon as she could find her chauffeur.

I said that Pamela Tiffin was over there on the couch.

"Pamela *Tiffin!*", the old gal snorted. "What does *she* know?"

Well, Arthur Schlesinger, Jr., was across the room.

"Arthur *Schlesinger!* What does *he* know?"

Jose Torres?

"*Jose Torres!* What does *he* know?"

"Larry L. King's here, too," I said.

"*Larry L. King!* What does *he* know? All those people are pompous asses. Frauds and fakes. Do you *know* those dreadful people?"

I said that I knew one of them, whereupon the old gal moved off shaking her head in disgust and her ample hips in what she thought was in tempo with the music, not having noticed that the band was enjoying a ten-minute break.

There was a long line at the comfort station. While I waited my turn this young man in faded blue jeans, sideburns, and a sort of paisley smock played the name game with me. When I gave him my true name he professed to have heard it someplace. Well, I said, I'd been calling it out about every 37 seconds all night, so that they'd probably heard it over in the Bronx. "No," he said, "*really*. Who are you?" I said that anybody who was *really* anybody had gone home and that I was going as soon as I could find my chauffeur. "You're putting me on," the young man said, his face tortured. "I just *know* you're famous as shit and I'm making an ass of myself!" Later on I saw him sitting cross-legged on the floor, desperately searching in *Who's Who*.

Three or four swingers tried to buck the comfort station line, only to be roundly jeered and thrown out, save for one happy young lady who explicitly and quite graphically described what would happen to her in the way of an accident of nature if we insisted on enforcing our pecking order.

A sweet little ole lady soon approached, marching resolutely down the hall, seemingly intent on bucking the line. I gently detained her and said in my best Southern Gentleman manner, "Ma'am, I'm sorry but some of us been waitin' 32 minutes. You'll have to go to the end of the line." She gasped, shook off my grip, announced that she was merely passing through to the cloakroom, and besides, young man, she was Norman Mailer's *mother*. She was, too.

Back upstairs the pace had quickened. The band was making more noise than a Democratic caucus and a bevy of pretty girls in funny costumes were climbing about on rope ladders leading to a spiffed-up nautically-motifed loft where, somebody said, Mailer writes his prose. Some frantic dancing was going on, people jerking this way and that in the steps and motions that always reminded me of the Holy Roller seizures of my childhood. What had happened to Mailer's carpet should not happen to the two-dollar bleacher seats in Shea Stadium, and there was a little air in the smoke.

Publisher John Cowles, Arthur Schlesinger, Jr., a young lady once related by marriage to the Gimbel department store folk, and a fellow wearing a purple turban and proclaiming himself to be from the Sudan were deep in some urbane conversation. Cowles introduced me all around, Schlesinger providing the evening's biggest thrill by saying he knew my work from the *Texas Observer* and *Harper's*. But the Lord giveth and the Lord taketh away: "I haven't read your novel yet," Schlesinger confessed. I said this put him in league with 195 million other Americans, or however many we have, and we morosely rattled the ice in our glasses.

On the way out I realized that I had not seen our host since crashing in, and was consoled by the thought that this probably meant he hadn't seen me, either. I winked at Pamela Tiffin as I passed the couch, she turning her head away coolly as a proper lady should. "Pamela Tiffin!" I said to nobody in particular. "What does *she* know?

In a cab a block away from Mailer's pad the driver said, "You been over to that party where that famous writer lives?" Yeah, I said, I had been making the scene at Norman Mailer's.

"You know," the driver said, "about an hour or two ago that Mailer cat come out and got in this cab and had me haul him up the avenue. He got out and bought all the morning papers. And you know what he *did?* Like, that cat just tore out *one page* from all them papers and threw the rest on the sidewalk and went off and left 'em!"

I explained that Mailer's play had opened that night and he was checking to see what his reviews were like.

"Yeah, man, but why didn't he take the whole *paper?*"

I said it must be a tradition or a Teamsters' Union rule that playwrights rip out their reviews and dump the rest of the papers on the sidewalk; that I'd seen it done in the movies several times.

The cab driver shook his head and said, "Man, this town drive you crazy! I'm going back home to North Carolina. *Everybody* nuts up here!"

"How long have you been here?"

"I ain't been here only twenty-one years," he said, seriously.

I laughed and whooped and coughed all the way to my hotel, no doubt ratifying the cabbie's suspicion about mankind in general and New Yorkers in particular. Maybe I made it up to him with my generous tip, however, for I figured he had it coming: he hadn't once asked my name.

CHAPTER 13

Notes of a Native Son:
An A-B-Z Primer of Texas

The last thing a Texas boy should do is poke fun at Texas in print. I never would have done it if it hadn't been for the money. Even this explanation probably won't satisfy some people. Look at the way they knock Judas.

One midday an editor from *Venture* magazine telephoned me in Washington to say that he was bringing out an issue devoted to my native state. "We are calling it," he said, " 'Texas Without Clichés.' It's been several weeks in the making." Apparently at the eleventh hour the editor decided that Texas without clichés made pretty grim reading, for he almost pathetically begged a 2,000 word "humor" piece within twenty-four hours. I consented to turn on Texas only after withstanding many moving pleas, though in a rare moment of insight I later knew that was less because of my strength of character than because I enjoyed hearing the music an editor makes when he begs.

It takes a monumental ego and damned little judgment for a writer to promise a "humor" piece on such scant notice. "Humor" is the hardest kind of writing. The word "humor" is itself intimidating enough to strike melancholy in the hearts of clowns. You might be able to get off a rich crack or two when the office Christmas party is about one slipped inhibition away from wrecking several careers or marriages, but just sit down at the typewriter and think "I am going to be very, very funny because I must, and if I do not, then they are going to shoot me," and see how many Ha Ha's the scene plays for. I tapped and banged and spoke to my typewriter in soothing tones for some six hours. At the end it had produced a joyless document that Stalin could not have presented to the Politburo in the hope of getting one honest chuckle.

What was wrong was that the piece could not be written in Washington. This was suddenly and startlingly obvious; it became imperative to get out of town. Somewhere, over a distant hill or in a hidden valley, lay the funny place I simply had to be in order to write "humor." My wife could not fathom this urgent need. Four hours later she was struggling with the unfamiliar knobs of a strange stove in the kitchen of my friend Bob Novak's summer beach cottage in Ocean View, Delaware.

Summer had not yet arrived, it being the rawest part of early April. I spent a fruitless three hours trying to master the pilot light on the gas heating system while brushing up on my cursing. The best I could understand the girl from the gas company they did not make wintertime house calls. Meanwhile, my wife shivered by the electric kitchen stove, muttering in her mother tongue. Night came, the radio spoke cheerfully of frost, howling winds roared in off the Atlantic which crashed only ten feet short of the back door. With driftwood and small boards appropriated from an absentee neighbor's picket fence, we built a fire in a wood-burning contraption with four open, screened sides and an impressive stovepipe running through the roof.

I have never understood flues, drafts or dampers. Somehow I got crosswise with the mechanical parts of the wood-burning vessel. Within twenty minutes we had our own smoke factory. We fled to the beach, huddling in blankets on the wet sand while the fire burned itself out and acrid, noxious fumes boiled from the windows and doors. When we returned, a light gray coating of ashes, not much more than one inch thick, had settled throughout the interior. We finished our housecleaning at 2:10 A.M., my wife not locking the bedroom door behind her until she said, "Well, this sure has been a lot of laughs, Charley. Knock 'em dead, now."

Bundled in an overcoat, imagining each windy tug at the dark, isolated cottage door to be the bloody hand of Jack the Ripper, and wondering who "Charley" was, I grimly wrote humor until dawn. Then the bed had sand in it. Arising at mid-morning I saw through the blood that my little masterpiece was worse than what I had come to think of as the Stalin script. Deadline was now four hours away.

One hour was lost addressing the gas system in vulgar tones and unavailing ministrations. The second hour was spent on the phone begging a $10 road call from a wrecker, the better to pull my darling wife's car from the beach sand where the sweet precious angel had stupidly bogged it to its axle. The third hour was given to a shouting

match between bride and groom. That left me half-deaf and one hour
in which to come on funny. Laugh? I thought I'd die! I mailed in a
hybrid script lifted in part from each of the two dreadful earlier
manuscripts, then sat back to await complaints.

Through the miracle of modern communications they were not
long in coming. I know not how well-rounded are the editors of
Venture as a group, though they do have one who is awfully adept at
sarcasm. He began by reading me the definition of "humor" from the
dictionary in a way that Captain Bligh would not have spoken to Mr.
Christian, and concluded with observations that may have been bio-
logically inaccurate. He also gave me another shot at the thing, only
this time he put a twelve-hour time limit on it. I have never felt more
awkward thanking a man.

I am not sure how a passable "humor" piece came to be written.
Some days I think it was seeing how much fun my wife got out of
learning that the pilot light wouldn't work because I had forgotten
to turn the gas on, and other days I think it was seeing the funny
way her legs crumpled when the brick hit. Anyway, the words came,
I made the deadline, and the *Venture* editor mailed a check if not a
note of apology. That's how and why I put Texas on, Governor, and
I feel simply terrible about it, but you've got to remember that Ocean
View, Delaware, is a mighty comical place in which to live.

NOTES OF A NATIVE SON: AN A-B-Z PRIMER OF TEXAS

The first Texas tourist was Cebeza de Vaca in 1528. Shipwrecked off
the southeast coast he almost drowned, was captured by Indians,
bound, gagged, and prodded on long hikes. His hosts hit him to claim
his attention. This, along with a solid diet of war whoops, grass-
hoppers, and rain dances, may have inspired his escape. With no help
from Duncan Hines or AAA maps he wandered around for several
years wondering where he was. This was altogether embarrassing to a
famous explorer. Cabeza de Vaca fretted that if word got out he
would suffer by comparison with Columbus, besides which his fees
would go down and his children forced to attend integrated schools.
The weather rusted his armor, things growled at him in the dark, he
caught chills, fevers and everything but Chautauqua shows. En-

countering Spanish soldiers near the Gulf of California, he almost immediately consented to be shipped home to Spain. He arrived nine years tardy and daring the Spanish Court to call him Tex. Nothing of record indicates that Mr. de Vaca ever again vacationed in Texas.

Texas is my home state, my mother digs Lawrence Welk, I blow myself kisses when passing mirrors and those are the last confessions you get from me without I consult a lawyer. This personal A-B-Z primer of Texas is offered in the hope that its secrets will pass the weary stranger through my native bogs with less painful diversions than our first tourist encountered.

Alkaline: A condition of certain Texas water that puckers the mouth, sickens cattle, and does in movie Black Hats in the deciding reel. Also the name of a major league baseball player. (Al Kaline, get it? You'll encounter an awful lot of native wit in Texas.)

Borders: Texas provides borderlines for Oklahoma, New Mexico, Arkansas, Louisiana and the Republic of Mexico. Borders provide markers for fugitives to flee across. Borders permit us to doll up the Texas Rangers in cowboy boots, whoop a state song, and honor the bluebonnet without having to apologize. Borders give us Okies and Arkies to look down on. Borders are our little friends and we should all protect them.

Chamber of Commerce: One in almost every town, but then India has trouble with elephantiasis. Sam Rayburn once said that any town big enough to have a Chamber office was beyond saving. But that was before penicillin.

Democracy: The Texas Legislature once rejected a bill requiring trucks hauling migratory workers to (1) have operable windshield wipers, (2) provide a tarp or other covering against inclement weather, and (3) make rest stops every four hours. Explaining his negative vote, one legislator said, "Well, I tell ya, ya git somethin' like that started and no tellin' *whur* it'll all end." Next thing you know they'll want four wheels, right?

El: Very common Spanish word meaning "the."* Often used by pretentious Texans to advertise their multilingual abilities. Example: "Hay, *garçon,* brang me *el glasso* uh bourbon and branch water over cheer raght quick, will yew?"

Faux pas: Texas opposite number of hind paw. (As "The dawg got a sandburr in its fo' paw.")

---

* Never to be confused with the pronoun "Thee." Thee is *tu.* Also, avoid confusing *tu* with the English "two," which in Spanish is translated *dos.* Look, *amigo,* maybe you better stick to English. *Muy bien?*

Governors: They reside in Austin in a neo-antebellum mansion across from the State Capitol grounds and serve two-year terms. It only seems longer. One of our governors was a hillbilly-singing flour salesman, one was a woman, one was publicly caned, one was impeached, one died in office, and one was shot. We just can't seem to get the hang of it.

Honesty: Indigenous to Texas. Signs proclaim it: Honest Joe's Insurance for the Blind, Honest Ed's Kwality Kar Korner and Square Deal Wig Shoppe. Though honesty is second-nature to Texans, beware a certain shortchange artist working a cantaloupe stand on the Pecos outskirts. (Two blocks south of the Billie Sol Estes Homestead. Honest.)

Isleta: Name given to the first Spanish mission in Texas. Later, because of difficulty in pronouncing and spelling the name, this was changed to Ysleta. The difficulty cleared up almost immediately, especially when we got Zip Codes.

Jokes: Texas Aggie jokes are big. How many Aggies does it take to pop popcorn? Five: one to hold the pan and four to shake the stove. Then there was the Aggie who found a pile of empty milk bottles and fled screaming that he'd discovered a cow's nest.

Knife: The Bowie knife is named for Jim Bowie. So is a Texas town, and countless schools. Bowie has been so honored because he gave his life for Texas. I have been offered the same deal, but turned it down.

Legend: The bravery of Texans at the Alamo is legend. Sometimes, however, I wonder if the Texans gave enough thought to strategy. The Alamo's surrounded by all the Mexicans in the world, right? And where do our guys look for help? Gonzales.

March 2, 1836: Texas declared its independence of Mexico. Statewide celebrations commemorate this event each year. Mexico does not openly celebrate this holiday, but then the Mexicans are a courteous people.

Navy: The one ship in the Texas Navy is retired in dry dock. Still, visiting V.I.P.'s are almost always commissioned Texas admirals. Only a small minority take offense.

O. Henry: His home has been preserved on Austin's East 5th Street, though a local banker refused to help because, "I do not understand this sudden excitement. I knew the man called O. Henry —Will Porter that is—very well, indeed. Worked with him, in fact. He was a very indifferent bookkeeper."

Palestine: A town in East Texas. Many are the native tots who presume this to be the biblical city of the same name. The day they question this particular geography is traditionally a sad one for their families. Everybody knows they will probably grow up to be writers or pickets, and live in racy places like Omaha.

Quaint: Former Governor Jim Hogg named his twin daughters Ima and Ura. He thought this quaint. What Mrs. Hogg and the daughters thought apparently didn't matter.

Rainfall: Texas has a mean average rainfall. Just what the exact figure is escapes me, though I reckon it's mean enough to get by. I wouldn't trifle with it.

Spain: Texas has survived six flags. One was Spain's. Such were the Spanish noblemen's proprietary instincts that when the first American, Phillip Nolan, came to Texas in 1799 to catch wild horses he was ridden down and killed. This led people to wonder whether the Spanish were very much fun, though nearly everybody predicted they would do well in the oil business.

Taciturn: Yep. Someofus.

Ulcers: "I don't get 'em," Lyndon B. Johnson once said, "I *give* 'em." We think a lot of that boy down home.

Vice: We've got a few games of chance on Galveston Island, a dirty book store in South El Paso, and a chain of real swinging massage parlors I am not at liberty to discuss. We get by.

Wet goods: Liquor laws are a morass of local options. Mixed drinks are sold only at private clubs. This may entail checking into a motel or paying $5 for a "guest locker number," but you've got to know where the action is. Some places they look at you funny if you order anything stronger than Tex-A-Cola. Package stores will sell you anything science can ferment and labor can bottle. In some spots, however, hard stuff is out and beer only is in. I doubt whether the governor himself understands it. If you bring your thirsty uncle, don't forget his flask.

Xenophobia: What raises its ugly head when Outlanders crack tired jokes about the Alamo lacking a back door.

Yas (Pronounced Ya-Yus): a three-letter word signifying consent in a four-letter circumstance.

Zealot: A Texan who wears cowboy garb in his home state, prefers greasy barbecue plates to roast Long Island duckling with orange sauce, and ranks the oil depletion allowance above free love or football. This group currently controls the Democratic Party.

CHAPTER 14

Everybody's Louie

It is simply torture to be interviewed. I have seen the pain and confusion of those subjected to examination by another of the species, their eyes almost universally resembling those of a deer stalked and now trapped with no hope of evading the hunter. On a few occasions I, personally, have been considered "copy" by some reporter or critic on a slow news day and so learned at a terrible price how the other half lives.

No matter how open, free and candid one presumes himself to be—nor how much one has assured the mirror that it has little or nothing to hide—there comes a sinking moment when one realizes the cards are stacked to the benefit of the fellow across the table. He has the pen. He will make the judgments. If he is at all accomplished in his craft, he will select the questions, guide the conversation, extract those comments that put you on record in matters you might think better unexplored. Granting that the inquisitor is an honest man who will tell it as he sees it, there are still moments of unease. Who knows what another man will see—or think he sees? One realizes in such moments that a writer is not just another hail fellow who has stopped by to toss a few pots with you and give you some nice publicity, but is an agent of Truth sent to plumb your soul, note your face moles and expose the whole sorry mess to the world. The next thing you know you are sitting at a certain stilted angle that cramps your neck so that it will not be written how your nose is too big, or you evade mention of the Hottentots because the Hottentots are sensitive folks who will not buy your books ever again if once offended.

There are persons who insist that some answers not be directly attributed to them or who (and politicians are particularly guilty here) beg to go "off the record" anytime they find the conversational bogs getting a bit sticky.* "Off the record" time is almost invariably spent by the interviewee in trying to convince the writer why a certain question is unfair to him, his heirs, and possibly to our free Republic. Then there are those who immediately retract any spontaneous comment they may have let slip. Such people are prone to answer questions by referring to their old speeches, ancient writings or yellowed news clippings—all carefully selected and culled in advance and guaranteeing to contain all the freshness of yesterday's fish.

The most dangerous game is the subject who demands to see your copy before it is published. No responsible writer or publication will hold still for such a request, for though it is always founded on "guaranteeing factual accuracy" the interviewee is really worried about what the writer will say of his jug ears or the way he broke his mother's last will and testament, if not her heart. His true purpose is to gloss his image over and above what the objective writer has.

Submission of copy prior to publication leads only to clumsy attempts at censorship and, eventually, to wrangling writers, agents and editors. I made this most obvious of discoveries the hard way as a cub reporter some twenty years ago. A New Mexico mayor with oil-slicked hair and a toothy smile—which in my ignorance I took for personal charm—persuaded me to agree foolishly that any copy about him or about the city's official business would be submitted in advance. With unctuous biblical quotes and serpentine smiles he told of his interest in seeing that I got off on the right foot in the newspaper dodge and of his great desire to see that the public be served in matters of information. After this little lecture, he handed me over to a young blonde whose primary duty in City Hall seemed to be that of exposing great, velvety stretches of female leg when such exposures seemed in the interest of Good Government. I blush now to recall how quickly the young lady convinced me of the correctness of the mayor's position. Within a few days, however, I realized that my newspaper could dismiss its editor in the interest of economy, since the mayor himself was blue-penciling my copy with gusto and devotion. When I reneged on our one-way agreement Hizzhonor raged, the blonde cried, the sky fell. Hizzhonor circulated word in City Hall that

---

* Governor Nelson Rockefeller of New York, for example, seldom yields to a private interview unless the writer agrees that *everything* is off-the-record.

I was not to be given so much as the time of day off the city clock from that moment forward. I confess in vanity that it was a great day for Freedom some six months later when I could write of the mayor's being kicked out of City Hall and charged with an amazing variety of rascality. Since that time I have never fully trusted men who want to audit my copy in advance or who have engaged as their secretaries blondes in short skirts.

Thus I approached an assignment to do a story about Louis Armstrong with certain trepidations, for his long-time business manager and friend, Joe Glaser, requested through my agent that my copy be submitted in advance "to guarantee factual accuracy, of course." Of course. When I refused there followed an ominous silence. On the day Armstrong arrived in Washington and I contacted his traveling manager, Ira Mangle, I thought that his initial response was decidedly cool. My one great ally in the story, however, was Louis Armstrong himself. "Don't pay them people no mind," he airily instructed me of his protectors, and then proceeded to grant great gobs of time. He did not stop in mid-sentence anytime I reached for my pen, nor did he keep going "off the record" or worrying about the shape of his nose. He was perhaps the most natural, open man that I have interviewed to date and for that reason he is my favorite.

For a man on the brink of his septuagenarian years, Armstrong is astoundingly energetic and enthusiastic. He trembles with life, interest, opinions. There is a robust vitality in everything that he does, whether blowing his famed trumpet or "telling it like it was" about the old days in Storyville and Chicago when he was on his way to becoming perhaps the most celebrated jazz musician of them all.

I can see him now, hopping about some strange hotel room at dawn, eyes round and brown and popping, hands waving like semaphoric equipment, his dark, diminutive body tugged this way and that by the tides of some tense excitement building in him and spilling over unrestrained. His talk is often colorfully profane, yet not offensively so, and I hope that in recreating his speech patterns on paper I have not made him sound vulgar or somehow gross. He is a rarity that should be preserved and if possible perpetuated: an American who does not stop to weigh his every word out of fear of dissent or of what the neighbors might think or because he is overly concerned with that dratted, overpolished, and overemphasized thing we have come to call our "image."

EVERYBODY'S LOUIE

Perhaps you have not heard of my singing with Louis Armstrong. Nobody reviewed us for *Downbeat* and we didn't get much of a crowd —just the two of us. This impromptu duet with Pops (also Satchmo, Louis, Dippermouth, "America's Ambassador of Good Will") took place last July in his suite at the Chalfonte, a resort hotel on the Boardwalk in Atlantic City, around five o'clock of a groggy morning.

For several hours we had been "stumbling over chairs"— Satchmo's euphemism for serious tippling—while he reminisced, smoked an endless chain of Camels, and poured with a quick hand. This mood carried him back almost sixty years to New Orleans' Storyville section where as a boy he delivered coal to the cribs of certain available ladies, lingering to monitor honky-tonk and sporting-house bands until "the lady would notice me still in her crib—me standing very silent, digging the sounds, all in a daze—and she would remind me it wasn't no proper place to daydream."

Storyville was wide open in those days. Liberty sailors, traveling drummers, cotton traders, and assorted bloods in hot pursuit of fun mingled with prostitutes, pickpockets, musicians, gamblers, street urchins, and pimps. It was located directly behind Canal Street and touching the lower end of Basin in the French Quarter, and it had everything from creep joints where wallets were removed from the unwary during sex circuses to Miss Lula White's Mahogany Hall on Basin Street with its five posh parlors, fifteen bedrooms, and $30,000 worth of artfully placed mirrors. Miss Lula hired "none but the fairest and most accomplished of girls," and Jelly Roll Morton played piano for her. In 1917 the Navy Department sent in a task force to clean up the district after too many sailors turned up robbed, drugged, or dead. Preachers railed against this sinkhole, but it was the place where jazz was born and where Daniel Louis (pronounced "Louie") Armstrong, literally before he was out of short pants, learned to play a little toy slide whistle "like it was a goddamn trombone." The boy strolled behind brass bands at street parades, funeral processions, or in horsedrawn bandwagons to tout their appearances at local clubs. "Two bandwagons would park head-to-head," Armstrong remembers, "and blow until one band was reduced to a frazzle."

The Armstrongs lived in a cement-block house on Brick Row. Armstrong's grandmother bent over a tin tub and corrugated washboard to scrub white families' clothes and his father, when he was around, attended turpentine boilers. There was a decrepit neighborhood tavern called the Funky Butt, which Armstrong remembers for its bands and its razor fights. A detective grabbed Armstrong for celebrating New Year's Eve with a "borrowed" revolver in his thirteenth year, and he was banished for eighteen months to the New Orleans Colored Waifs' Home. At nineteen in Storyville he chose the first of his four brides. One night she caught Louis with another doll and chastised him with a brickbat. "I ain't been no angel," Pops confessed that morning as we lounged in the Chalfonte, "but I never once set out to harm *no* cat."

Louis Armstrong's marvelous memory took me back to the night he arrived in Chicago in 1922, up on the train from New Orleans to join King Joe Oliver's Creole Jazz Band as second trumpet for $50 a week. "I was carrying my horn, a little dab of clothes, and a brown bag of trout sandwiches my mother, Mayann, had made me up. Had on long underwear beneath my wide-legged pants—in July. I am just a kid, you see, not but twenty-two years old, don't know nothing and don't even *suspect* much. When we pull into the old La Salle Street station and I see all the tall buildings I thought they was universities and that I had the wrong town. Almost got back on that rail-runner and scooted back home."

He spoke lovingly of old pals: King Oliver, Jack Teagarden, Kid Ory, Bix Beiderbecke, and a hotlicks bass drummer everyone recalls only as Black Benny. ("All dead and gone now, them swinging old cats—and I've took to reading the Bible myself.") Between dips into his on-the-rocks bourbon Armstrong hummed or scatted or sang snatches of his ancient favorites. "Hotdamn"—he would say, flashing his teeth in that grand piano grin—"you remember this one?" and out would pour *Didn't He Ramble, Gut Bucket Blues, Blueberry Hill, Heebie-Jeebies, Black and Blue.*

Just how I presumed to sing with him remains unclear and possibly indefensible. Earlier, in a noisy penny arcade on the Steel Pier in Atlantic City, I had proposed to his traveling manager, Ira Mangle, that I perform on stage with Armstrong at one of his three-a-day shows. Mangle, a stoic man of generous figure, ate peanuts, staring, while I explained. I would describe both the elation and the dread of appearing with the most celebrated figure in a field wholly alien to my talents, a man who has been called "an authentic American genius" for his contributions to jazz. Paul Gallico and George Plimpton had done the same thing in sports, I recalled to Mangle, boxing Jack Dempsey and Archie Moore, golfing with Bobby Jones, pitching to Mantle and Mays. Their first-person stories permitted the average sports fan to consort vicariously with champions. Out there on that stage, moving into the spotlight to join Pops in *Blues in the Night* or perhaps even *Hello Dolly,* I would represent all my peers.

Ira Mangle has been in show business almost as long as pratfalls. He is neither easily rattled nor easily amused. When my special plea was done Mangle gazed into my face, chewing all the while. When the peanuts ran out he smiled and walked away.

Now, days later, sitting at a table holding the wreckage of our midnight snack (sardines in oil, Vienna sausages, Chinese food, soda crackers, pickles, beer) Pops and I somehow cut into *That's My Desire.* My uncertain baritone mingled with the famous voice that has been likened to a "cement mixer . . . rough waters . . . iron filings . . . a gearbox full of peanut butter . . . oil on sandpaper . . . a horn wailing through gravel and fog."

Once—when I came in on the break behind him at precisely the right point—Pops gave me some skin. He reached out his dark old hand just as he does on-stage when Joe Muranyi has ripped off an especially meritorious stretch on clarinet, and I turned my hand, palm up, as I had seen Muranyi do. Leaning across sardine tins and cracker wrappers Pops lightly brushed my open palm in a half-slap, the jive set's seal of approval, the jazz equivalent of the Congressional Medal of Honor. And there was good whiskey waiting in the jug.

We had already siphoned off generous rations, waving our arms a bit much, gently boasting and exaggerating. "Hey, Pops," my host said (it is his all-purpose salutation, as well as what friends call him, and saves everybody memorizing a lot of troublesome names), "this is the way I get my kicks. Having a little taste . . . talking over the olden times in Storyville and Chicago . . . remembering all the crazy sounds that always seemed to be exploding around you and inside you. *Everything* made music back then: banana men, rag-pickers, them pretty painted street walkers all singing out their wares—oh, *yeah!* Everything rocking and bobbing and jousting and jumping." He grinned that huge, open grin again. "Ya know, Pops," he said, "my manager, Joe Glaser—Papa Joe, bless his ole heart he's *my* man, we been together since we was pups, why to hear us talk on the phone you'd think we was a couple of fairies: I say, 'I love you, Pops,' and he say, 'I love *you, Pops'*—well, anyhow, Joe and Ira and all them people don't like for me to talk about the olden days. All the prosty-*toots* and the fine gage and the bad-ass racketeers. But hell, Man, I got to tell it like it was! I can't go around changing *history!"*

(Often one gets the feeling that Pops prefers those "olden days" to the frantic existence that has become his life. He once told writer Richard Meryman, "I never did want to be no big star. . . . All this traveling around the world, meeting wonderful people, being high on the horse, all *grandioso*—it's nice—but I didn't suggest it. I would say it was all wished on me. Seems like I was more content, more relaxed, growing up in New Orleans. And the money I made then—I lived off it. We were poor and everything like that, but music was all around you. Music kept you rolling.")

Though two weeks earlier Louis Armstrong wouldn't have known me from any other face in the multitudes, we had reached a stage of easy friendship—all thanks to him. For though I have known three Presidents and two wives, I sat down to face Armstrong that first night in Washington with a head full of wind and dishwater. There seemed nothing I was able to ask or say, not even banal comments about Washington's dreadful humidity, for on the couch beside me sat a living legend, a talent so long famous and admired that I considered him of another age and so was struck dumb in his presence— as if I had come upon Moses taking a Sunday stroll in the Gaza Strip or had encountered Thomas Jefferson at a Democratic National Convention.

Downstairs, I knew, Shriners offered hotel bellboys five-dollar bribes for Louis Armstrong's room number. No telephone calls were put through to him from the Shoreham front desk unless you knew a special secret. In Armstrong's suite (a palace of curved glass, rich draperies, soft carpets, and pillows of psychedelic hues) he sat wrapped in a faded robe. A white towel around his neck soaked up juices from the last of the evening's two one-hour shows, while Pops accepted photographs of himself from a thick stack presided over by his hovering valet, Bob Sherman. On each he scrawled "Hello, Louis Armstrong" in a round, uneven hand. Ira Mangle asked his star if he would like a drink, a snack, another pen, a crisp handkerchief. Mopping his brow, Louis declined with grunts and headshakes. "You go ahead," he said as I sat there tongue-tied and witless. "Ask me anything you want. Won't cramp my writing style. Just doing the bit for a few of my fans." Out of the silence Ira Mangle suggested that Armstrong discuss a recent TV tape cut with Herb Alpert and the Tijuana Brass: perhaps Armstrong would compare the two generations of music and judge the younger man's artistry. "Oh, yeah," Armstrong said. "He blows pretty, all right. Nice young cat." Mangle then prompted him to say something of his popularity with the public, his friendships in show business, the world figures who have toasted him. "Everybody's been real nice," Pops said.

Mangle's helpless shrug left me on my own. Finally I said, "Well, I seem to have come down with a bad case of buck fever or hero worship. Can't think of a damn thing. Maybe I'd better run along and return another night." Quickly Armstrong cast aside his pen. A look of pain passed his face. "Aw, naw!" he said. "It ain't like that! We'll just loaf and chew the fat and have a little taste of bourbon and if we feel like stumbling over chairs—well, hell, we all over twenty-one! Ira, get my man a little taste." Then he launched into a story, and the generous act got me functioning again.

The men who handle Armstrong thought we got a little too chummy. Valet Bob Sherman, a dapper middleweight with a heavyweight's torso and a Sonny Liston scowl when one is needed, nailed me backstage at the Steel Pier. "You'd better cut on out tonight after about an hour," he said. "Otherwise, you're gonna wear Pops out. He needs rest." Later, when I tried to leave at a decent hour, Pops protested. "Man, I'm just starting to *roll*. Won't be hitting the sheets for some-odd hours on. Here"—he splashed liquid into my glass— "relax and have another little taste." Waiting in the wings for his introduction one matinee, mopping his face and carrying that golden trumpet at trial arms, he waved me over: "Where'd you go last night, Pops? Had to stumble over chairs all by myself. Ira and them people keep you away from me?" Well, yes, I admitted. "Aw, they ought not to do *that!*" Armstrong said. "They *know* Pops is still gonna be unwinding when first light comes. Don't pay them people no mind."

Armstrong's associates can hardly be blamed for their vigilance: he is a most valuable commercial property. Last spring a two-month recuperation from pneumonia cost more than $150,000 in bookings. His sixty-seven years, his respiratory ailments, and his grinding travel schedule—Ireland, England, Denmark, France, Spain, Tunisia, New England, the Midwest, the West Coast and two major TV bookings in August and September alone—cause concern for his health.

He is not the world's most docile patient. He walked around with bronchial pneumonia for two weeks last spring before anyone knew it. His trombonist, Tyree Gleen, was one of his first hospital visitors; Pops coaxed him into rehearsing a duet he wanted to put in the show. Nurses managed to clear the room only after a one-hour concert. The Washington booking was the first to follow his illness. Yet he stayed up all one night reveling with me, another with old musical world cronies (Duke Ellington and Clark Terry turned up at the Shoreham on July 4th to lead the midnight-show crowd in singing *Happy Birthday* to him), and on his night off he dropped by Carter Barron Amphitheatre to catch Ella Fitzgerald's performance—and ended up doing several numbers with her. Pops played two shows of his own each night and one two-hour benefit for wounded Vietnam veterans at Walter Reed Hospital.

A week later in Atlantic City he stunted and cheered at a nightclub until dawn, and the following night railed—in vain—when he learned that Ira Mangle had wired a second club expressing regrets that Pops would not catch the late show as promised. "Dammit!" he complained. "All them cats over there live and *breathe* Louis Armstrong. They *love* Pops! If I go back on my word to them people, it's like— why hell, it's like the United States Marines losing a goddamn *war!*"

Armstrong has a zealot's faith in certain old nostrums. He is quick to offer his medical opinions: "Man, a heart attack is nothing but so much *gas* accumulated and bubbled over." Armstrong on cancer: "Nowadays it has come in fashion to die of it. What they call cancer is merely the bodily poisons fermented because people is so full of fevers beating and working in the blood." Germs: "I always carry my mouthpiece in my hip pocket—never pitch it around where germs can crawl over it and into its parts." To rid himself of possible heart disease, crawling germs or malignant tissues, Armstrong recommends the removal of "bodily impurities." For this he relies on a purgative called Swiss Kriss. It is his old reliable among an assortment of wonder-working products. One dawn he gave me three Swiss Kriss sample packets. The following night, as we blitzed another midnight snack of sardines and supporting embellishments, Pops asked, "You take your Swiss Kriss yet?"

"Ah . . . well; not yet."

"Get my man some Swiss Kriss," Armstrong instructed Bob Sherman. "Be just the thing to clear him all up. Flush out the bodily impurities." Sherman didn't move a step. He dipped into his pocket and produced a thin packet of olive-drab substance that looked to be a cross between thyme, marijuana, and sawdust.

"Lay it on your tongue," Armstrong said. "Take it dry, then send some beer chasing after it. Beer all gone? Well, bourbon do it too." I turned the thin packet in my hands to stall for time. "Active ingredients"—I read aloud—"dried leaves of senna. Also contains licorice root, fennel, anise, and caraway seed. Dandelion, peppermint, papaya, strawberry and peach leaves. Juniper berries—"

"Oh yeah," Pops broke in. "Got all *manner* of elements in there. Lay it on your tongue."

"—Juniper berries, centaury, lemon verbena, cyani flowers, and parsley for their flavoring and carminative principles."

"Here's your chaser, Pops." Armstrong nudged the bourbon glass over while I frantically searched for something more to read. "Modern Products," I said. "Milwaukee, 5, Wisconsin." Bob Sherman celebrated my discomfort with a grin as Armstrong, hooting and exhorting like an evangelistic witch doctor, urged the treatment on.

I know not what Swiss Kriss tastes like on the tongue of Louis Armstrong. In my mouth it registered flavors of creosote, licorice, and sheep-dip with slight overtones of Brown Mule chewing tobacco. It neither improves bourbon nor bourbon it. Just as the main body of agony had passed my host reproved me: "Looka here, Pops! You left half it in the bag!" He poked the dose under my nose. "Don't never do nothing halfway," Pops said; "else you find yourself dropping more than can be picked up."

"Take off your shirt" he ordered, suddenly.

"Beg your pardon?"

"Gonna teach you another little trick. Now this"—he grabbed a brownish bottle from a nearby table—"is called 'Heet.' H-e-e-t. Swab myself down with it when I come off stage all sopping wet. Cools me down and dries me out and steadies the skin. . . . You ain't got that shirt off, Pops." Armstrong circled me like Indians attacking a wagon train, crying a sales pitch as he daubed my chest, ribs, back. "Don't that cool you like rain?" he said. "Ain't that a goddamn groove?"

"Now you take a man's eyes," he said, ominously. "You ever have any trouble with your eyes?"

"No . . . not really . . ."

"Must have trouble, else you wouldn't be wearing them eyeglasses! This little remedy gonna pull all the blood-shot qualities right outta your eyeballs." He brandished a new bottle. "Witch hazel. Now, I take these"—he was ripping into a package and extracting two gauze pads—"and I dab a little on there, like this, swoggling it all around. Now I put them babies on your eyelids and it won't be thirty seconds until you feel it cooling up all the way back inside your *cranium!"* He marched about, rattling on, while I sat in darkness feeling like a man who has stumbled into Mayo Clinic by mistake. "Take them pads off in another three minutes and you can feel heat on the underside like you had fried an egg there! So, quite *nat-ur-ally*—you gonna see clearer and sweeter and cooler than you ever did see before."

"You use all sorts of nostrums, don't you?" I said.

"Use whatever *helps.* You know, it wasn't long ago I believed in all kinds of old-timey remedies like the voodoo people. Yeah! Various dusts and herbs and junk like that." He laughed to think on days when he had been so medically unschooled. "Now I just use things do me some good, ya dig? And it works, Pops. Do you know I am the only one left from the olden days in Storyville still blowing? Oh yeah, lotta cats lost their chops. Lips split and god*damn* the blood spurt like you had cut a hog and the poor cats can't blow no more. Now, I got this lip salve I'm gonna expose you to. Keeps my chops ready so I don't go in there and blow cold and crack a lip like I did in Memphis so bad I lost a chunk of meat."

Armstrong snatched the pads away and leaned forward with his face almost against mine, pulling his upper lip outward and upward, trying ineffectually to talk under the handicap. I leaned in, much in the manner of a man judging a horse's teeth for age, and saw in the middle of that talented lip a sizable flesh-crater. "My poor damn chops would be tender as a baby's bottom," Pops said. "Oh, *no way* to tell you how them chops could throb." He poked a small orange tin at me. "I order this salve from Germany by the caseload. Bought so much the cat that boils it up named it after me. See, it says 'Louis Armstrong Lip Salve.' You write something nice about that cat for Pops, ya hear? Aw yeah, he's *fine!"* He reached for my pen: "I'll write it down so's you don't forget."

He selected a cocktail napkin and printed in large, undisciplined letters: ANZACZ CREME MADE IN MANNHEIM GERMANY. He turned the napkin over and printed BY FRANZ SCHURITS. "That cat saved my lip," he said. "Reason his salve's so good it draws all the tiredness out. So—quite naturally—your chops rest easy. You oughta try some . . . only you don't blow so it wouldn't benefit you." He daubed his own lips with the wonder potion. "Oh, *yeah!* I got this other little tidbit here! I see you got weight problems—now no offense, Pops, 'cause most of us go around bloating ourselves up with various poisons which—quite naturally—causes some heavy stomping on the scales. All the sweets and sugars a person eats just goes right down there and hangs over your belt and *looks up at you!* Fat is made outta sugar more than anything else—you know that? Yeah! Why, a year ago I weigh two hundred and some pounds and now I'm shed off to a hundred and sixty-some and feel retooled. Between my Swiss Kriss and this Sweet 'N Low—it ain't like real sugar, you can eat a ton of this—I got no more weight imbalances which throws the body off center. Here"—he again sprang across the room to produce yet another packet—"it goes groovy on grapefruit. You want to try it? I got plenty grapefruit."

When I demurred, Pops looked somehow betrayed. "Well," he said, "you come on back tomorrow night. I'll lay it on you then, Pops."

"Quite naturally," I said.

Louis Armstrong is sophisticate and primitive, genius and a man-child. He is wise in the ways of the street and gullibly innocent in the ways of men and nations. After four marriages, reform school, international fame and personal wealth, there is still a fetching simplicity about him. (Of his friend Moïse Tshombé, kidnapped and facing a return to the Congo, he says, "I pray each night they won't kill him. When I played Africa in '59 that cat was *so* nice to me. Kept me in his big palace and all . . . fed me good . . . stayed up all night gassing. I had this little tape recorder had cost me several big bills and Tshombé dug it so much I laid it on him. They ain't gonna kill a sweet cat like that are they? So maybe he hung out with the wrong cats—that any reason to *kill* a man?")

The on-stage Louis Armstrong is all smiles and sunshine, almost too much the "happy darky" of white folklore. When he has finished *Hello Dolly* in a spasm of body shaking, jowl flapping, and gutteral ranges, and has the joint rocking with applause, he sops at his ebony, streaming face with his white handkerchief and rasps, "Looka here, my Man Tan's coming off!" Maybe his white audiences break up, but they no longer laugh at such lines in the black ghetto. One soon learns that this "happy" image is not all stagecraft; privately Pops is often full of laughter, mugging, instant music, irrepressible enthusiasms, and vast stores of colorful misinformation.

He is not all Old King Cole merry-old-soul, however; his waters run much deeper. I have seen Pops swearing backstage between numbers, his face wrinkled and thoughtful and sad only seconds before he burst back on stage, chest out, strutting, all teeth and cutting the fool. He can be proud, shrewd, moody, dignified—and vengeful. "I got a simple rule about everybody," he warned me one evening. "If you don't treat me right—shame on you!" Cross him or wound his pride and he never forgets. My innocent mention of a noted jazz critic set off a predawn tirade: "I told that bastard, 'You telling me how to blow my goddamn horn and you can't even blow your goddamn nose.' " When he was young and green somebody gave him fifty dollars for a tune he had written called *Get Off Katie's Head*. "I didn't know nothing about papers and business, and so I let go all control of it." Pops did not share in the money it made under another title. He has never performed the tune in public and never will. Of his father, Pops said, "I was touring Europe when he died. Didn't go to his funeral and didn't send nothing. Why should I? He never had no time for me or Mayann."

He is big on personal loyalty. "Frank Sinatra—now there's a man carries a lot of water for his friends. A *most* accommodating gentleman—if he digs you. My wife, Lucille, she's another one that when she's with you she's with you one thousand percent.* And my mother, why she would work with you—laugh, cry, or juice with you. Oh, what a sweet and helpful girl Mayann was. Only tears I ever shed was when I saw 'em lower her into that ground."

He is generally a relaxed man, able to take a quick nap in strange rooms or on buses. "I don't like nothing to fret me," Pops said. "You healthier and happier when you hang loose. Business I don't know nothing about and don't want to. It must have killed more men than war. Joe Glaser books me, pays my taxes and bills, invests me a few bundles. Gives me my little leftover dab to spend. And that's the way I want it. Don't want to *worry* all time about that shit! I don't even know where I go when I leave this pier until today I overhear Ira say something about Ireland and France and such places. I go wherever

---

* Lucille holds the record as Mrs. Armstrong. They have been married twenty-five years, and live in Queens on Long Island.

they book me and lead me." (Both Armstrong and Joe Glaser are wealthy men. Armstrong commands top money—$20,000 to $25,000—for guest shots on television. He accepts eight to ten such jobs each year.)

Nothing worries Louis Armstrong for long. "Mama taught me," he says, "that anything you can't get—the hell with it!" This philosophy may be at the root of Armstrong's rumored differences with militants of the Black Power generation. Nobody has flatly called him Uncle Tom but there have been inferences. Julius Hobson, a Washington ghetto leader, said during Armstrong's Shoreham appearance last July, "He's a good, happy black boy. He hasn't played to a black audience in ten years. I'm glad I saw him though, but I wouldn't come here if I had to pay. He's an interesting example of the black man's psychology but if he took this band '—two whites, three Negroes, a Filipino—' down on U Street it would start a riot." Armstrong, who remembers that not long ago everyone cheered him for having an integrated band, is genuinely puzzled by such comments.

He was not eager to talk civil rights. When I first mentioned the subject, as he dried out between shows in the dingy dressing room at Atlantic City, Pops suddenly began to snore. The next time he merely said, "There is good cats and bad cats of all hues. I used to tell Jack Teagarden—he was white and from Texas just like you—'I'm a spade and you an ofay. We got the same soul—so let's blow.' "

One morning, however, he approached the racial topic on his own. "When I was coming along, a black man had hell. On the road he couldn't find no decent place to eat, sleep, or use the toilet—service-station cats see a bus of colored bandsmen drive up and they would sprint to lock their restroom doors. White places wouldn't let you in and the black places all run-down and funky because there wasn't any money behind 'em. We Negro entertainers back then tried to stay in private homes—where at least we wouldn't have to fight bedbugs for sleep and cockroaches at breakfast.

"Why, do you know I played ninety-nine *million* hotels I couldn't stay at? And if I had friends blowing at some all-white nightclub or hotel I couldn't get in to see 'em—or them to see me. One time in Dallas, Texas, some ofay stops me as I enter this hotel where I'm blowing the show—me in a goddamn *tuxedo,* now!—and tells me I got to come round to the back door. As time went on and I made a reputation I had it put in my contracts that I wouldn't *play* no place I couldn't *stay*. I was the first Negro in the business to crack them big white hotels—Oh, yeah! I pioneered, Pops! Nobody much remembers that these days.

"Years ago I was playing the little town of Lubbock, Texas, when this white cat grabs me at the end of the show—he's full of whiskey and trouble. He pokes on my chest and says, 'I don't like *niggers!*' These two cats with me was gonna practice their Thanksgiving carving on that dude. But I say, 'No, let the man talk. *Why* don't you like us, Pops?' And would you believe that cat couldn't *tell* us? So he apologizes—crying and carrying on. Said he was just juiced and full of deep personal sorrows—something was snapping at his insides, you see—and then he commenced bragging on my music. Yeah! And dig this: that fella and his whole family come to be my friends! When I'd go back through Lubbock, Texas, for many many years they would make ole Satchmo welcome and treat him like a king.

"Quite naturally, it didn't always test out that pleasurable. I knew some cats was blowing one-nighters in little sawmill stops down in Mississippi, and one time these white boys—who had been dancing all night to the colored cats' sounds—chased 'em out on the highway and whipped 'em with chains and cut their poor asses with *knives!* Called it 'nigger knocking.' No reason—except they was so goddamn miserable they had to mess everybody else up, ya dig? *Peckerwoods!* Oh, this world's mothered some mean sons! But they try such stunts on the young Negroes we got coming along now—well, *then* the trouble starts. Young cats, they ain't setting around these days saying 'Yessuh' or 'Nawsuh.' Which I ain't knocking; everybody got to be his own man, Pops. No man oughta be treated like dirt.

"If you didn't have a white captain to back you in the old days—to put his hand on your shoulder—you was just a damn sad nigger. If a Negro had the proper white man to reach the law and say, 'What the hell you mean locking up MY nigger?' then—quite naturally—the law would walk him free. Get in that jail *without* your white boss, and yonder comes the chain gang! Oh, danger was dancing all around you back then.

"Up north wasn't much to brag on in many ways. Not only people put your color down but you had mobsters. One night this big, bad-ass hood crashes my dressing room in Chicago and instructs me that I will open in such-and-such a club in New York the next night. I tell him I got this Chicago engagement and don't plan no traveling. And I turn my back on him to show I'm so *cool*. Then I hear this sound:

SNAP! CLICK! I turn around and he has pulled this vast revolver on me and cocked it. *Jesus,* it look like a cannon and sound like death! So I look down that steel and say, 'Weeelllll, maybe I *do* open in New York tomorrow.' That night I got every Chicago tough me or my pals knew—and it must have been eighteen hundred of 'em—to flock around and pass the word I wasn't to be messed with. And I didn't go to New York. Very very shortly, however, I cut on out of town and went on tour down South. And the mob didn't mess with me again. They never wanted me dead, wanted me blowing so they could rake in my bread.

"You was running a very large risk to buck them mobsters and all the sharpies. They controlled everything. Cross 'em just so far and— BLIP! Your throat's cut or you're swimming in cement with lumps on your head. You needed a white man to get along. So one day in 1931 I went to Papa Joe Glaser and told him I was tired of being cheated and set upon by scamps and told how my head was jumping from all of that business mess—Lil, one of my wives, had sweet-talked me into going out on my own to front some bands and it was driving me *crazy*—and I told him, 'Pops, I need you. Come be my manager. *Please!* Take care all my business and take care of me. Just lemme blow my gig.' And goddamn that sweet man did it! Sold his nightclub in Chicago where I had worked and started handling Pops.

"Sometimes Joe Glaser says I'm nuts. Says it wasn't as bad as I recall it. But then Papa Joe didn't have to go through it. He was white. Not that I think white people is any naturally meaner than colored. Naw, the white man's just had the upper hand so long—and can't many people handle being top cat.

"Passing all them laws to open everything up—fine, okay, lovely! But it ain't gonna change everybody's hearts. You know, I been reading the Bible this last little bit and them Biblical people had wars and riots and poverty and bad-asses among 'em just like *we* got. Nothing new happening!

"It's much the same they talk about making marijuana legal. They think they're gonna do that and say, 'Everything's cool now, babies, it's all right and set square.' But how about them poor bastards *already* been busted for holding a little gage and have done their lonesome fifteen and thirty and fifty years? My God, you can't *never* make it all right with them! Many years ago I quit messing around with that stuff. Got tired looking over my shoulder and waiting for that long arm to reach out and somebody say, 'Come here, boy.

Twenty years in the cage!' BLOOEY! Naw, they can't undo all the years of damage by passing a few laws." After a moment's brooding he said, "That's why I don't take much part in all this fandangoing you hear about today. All I want to do is blow my gig."

Louis Armstrong's first professional gig—as a substitute cornet player in a Storyville honky-tonk—brought him fifteen cents. He was fifteen years old. "But I sang for money long before I played for it," he says. "When I was around twelve we formed this quartet— me, Little Mack, Georgie Gray, and Big Nose Sidney. We'd sing on the streets and in taverns—pass the hat; might make six-bits, a dollar. Good money. After hours all them prostitutes would be juicing, having a little fun, and they would offer us big tips to entertain 'em. Carried their bankrolls in the tops of their stockings. Some would hold us on their laps and we would sniff the pretty scents and powders they wore."

Though he had taught himself to play the little toy slide whistle and a homemade guitar, Armstrong really familiarized himself with musical instruments in the New Orleans Waifs' Home. He began with the tambourine, then the snare drum, then ran through the alto horn, bugle, and cornet. Soon he was the leader of the Waifs' Band, playing picnics and street parades. Old-time drummer Zutty Singleton, a boy then himself, was so astounded at hearing Armstrong's horn that he moved closer to see if the boy was actually playing those fabulous notes. When he was released from the home, Armstrong took one-night jobs filling in with bands until a few months later he landed a regular job at Henry Matranga's in Storyville. "I wasn't making no great sums so I kept on delivering coal, unloading banana boats, selling newspapers—though there never was any doubts I would follow music at that point. Had to work for extra bread, you see. For when I am sixteen I start hanging out with the pretty chicks and need operating money."

King Joe Oliver took Louis Armstrong under his wing. "He was the best," Pops says. "Laid a new horn on me when mine was so beat I didn't know what sounds might come out of it. Advised me . . . took me home for red beans and rice feasts. Taught me about blowing trumpet, too. Lotta claims been made that Bunk Johnson put me wise to trumpet—Bunk hisself helped that story along. No such thing. Joe Oliver was the man."

When King Oliver left Kid Ory's brass band to go it alone, seventeen-year-old Louis Armstrong took his chair. In the eighteen months he played with Kid Ory at Pete Lala's, Armstrong's reputation grew. He was with the Tuxedo Brass Band in 1922, when King Oliver called him to Chicago—then the center of jazz as New Orleans once had been. In 1924–25 Armstrong was with the Fletcher Henderson band but quit because "The cats was goofing and boozing—not blowing. I was always deadly serious about my music." From Henderson he joined Lil Hardin's group (she was his second wife) and also worked in Erskine Tate's pit orchestra at the Vendome Theater in Chicago. Then he went to work at the Sunset Club for Joe Glaser—who immediately billed him as "The World's Greatest Trumpet Player." This title had been generally conceded to Joe Oliver—and King Joe was playing at a rival club nearby. It came down to a head-on contest between the two great trumpeters. "I felt real bad when I took most of Joe Oliver's crowds away," Armstrong says now. "Wasn't much I could do about it, though. I went to Joe and asked him was there anything I could do for him. 'Just keep on blowing,' he told me. Bless him."*

Armstrong first played New York in 1929, fronting the old Carroll Dickerson band at Connie's Inn in Harlem. He arrived there with four carloads of sidemen, ten dollars, and after two car wrecks en route. "Blew four shows a day," he remembers. "Wild stuff. Knocked myself out—blowing crazy and carrying on. Going in with cold chops. Wonder I got a dime's worth of chops left." In mid-1932 Armstrong made his first swing through Europe—and Europe flipped. By 1935 few disputed that Louis Armstrong was the king of jazz.

Though with the advent of television and smash hits like *Hello Dolly*† Armstrong became more popular than ever, jazz purists say that he is no longer inventive, that he is too commercial, too much the clown. A decade ago Raymond Horricks wrote that his trumpet playing "in recent years . . . has declined as a creative force on account of the contact with unsympathetic supporting musicians and of Louis' own increased exploits dressed in the cap and bells of a court jester." Even a dust jacket plugging a record Armstrong made with Ella Fitzgerald carries this curious advertisement: "Unfortunately, of late, Louis has confined himself almost exclusively to

---

* Years later, when Joe Oliver was on the financial skids, Armstrong several times helped him.

† "The best-selling record of all time"—Ira Mangle.

remaking the blues of an earlier age and pedestrian popular songs so that each impression was but a fainter and dimmer carbon of the original talent."

He is impatient with this criticism. "Aw, I am paid to *entertain* the people. If they want me to come on all strutty and cutting up—if that makes 'em happy, why not? For many years I blew my brains out. Hitting notes so high they hurt a dog's ears, driving like crazy, screaming it. And everybody got this image I was some kind of a wild man. Joe Glaser told me, 'Play and sing pretty. Give the people a show.' So now I do *Dolly* how many times? Six jillion? How ever many you want to say. Do it every show. And you got to admit, Pops, it gets the biggest hand of any number I do.

"There's room for all kinds of music. I dig it all: country, jazz, pop, swing, blues, ragtime. And this rock 'n' roll the young people believe is a new sound—babies, it comes right outta the old spirituals and soul and country music and jazz. Like I have said, 'Old soup warmed over.'

"Each man has his own music bubbling up inside him and—quite naturally—different ones will let it out in various ways. When I blow I think of times and things from outa the past that gives me a image of the tune. Like moving pictures passing in front of my eyes. A town, a chick somewhere back down the line, an old man with no name you seen once in a place you don't remember—any of 'em can trigger that image. Or a certain blue feeling or a happy one. What you hear coming from a man's horn—that's what he is! And man can be many different things."

Pops is right: if the critics have soured the people have not. "Can't even go to a baseball game," he said one night. "Went to one Dodgers-White Sox World Series game and cats was climbing all over my box seat. Some the players asked what in hell was all that commotion up in the stands. Sometimes them big crowds can spook you. Get to pressing you and grabbing your clothes. You get a funny feeling they might trample on you. Especially in Europe. I draw a hundred thousand people over there blowing outdoors. And they go crazy."

Each afternoon and evening a limousine with Pops and Bob Sherman in the back seat made its way slowly along the Boardwalk; police and firemen walked ahead to clear the massed crowd. "Hey! That's Louis Armstrong!" someone would shout, starting a stampede of old women, small children, bald-headed men. ("Hey, Louie, looka me!" "Satchmo—over here!") They clawed at the car, knocked on windows, snapped cameras in his face, tried to poke their hands inside for handshakes. Pops smiled and waved in return, seldom missing anyone, though he might be chattering away about Storyville.

Through the entire Atlantic City engagement a wizened, aged little man in hand-me-down clothes haunted the backstage area. After each show Pops courteously received him in his dressing room. "You really got your chops tonight, Pops," the old man would invariably say. Armstrong would beam: "Aw, thank you, Pops. How you been?" After a few moments the old fellow would go away content. I later learned that he is known to Armstrong's entourage as the Clipping Man. "He lives in Philadelphia," I was told, "and anytime he sees Pops' name in the paper he clips it and mails it to him. If Pops plays within a hundred miles of Philadelphia he makes the scene and hangs around for his two or three private moments after each show." The Clipping Man was around so much that for days, seeing him standing patiently in the wings or sitting on a bench backstage, silent and pensive, I had presumed him to be a stagehand. One night he encountered me in the alcove outside Armstrong's dressing room. "You know Pops long?" he asked. No, only a few days. "I been good friends with him for thirty years," the Clipping Man said.

One night near the end of Pops' ten-day Atlantic City run we dallied in his dressing room long past midnight, having a little taste, while on video-tape heavyweight contender Joe Frazier repeated his brutal knockout of George Chuvalo. Freshly toweled by Bob Sherman, wearing a faded robe and a handkerchief tied around his head so that he resembled Aunt Jemimah, Pops bounced around the cramped room, grunting and grimacing as gloves thudded against flesh, sucking in air and occasionally throwing an uppercut of his own.

After he dressed we walked along the Steel Pier, dark now except for a few dim lights on the outer walkway. The noisy crowds had been dispersed and the gates locked; a few sleepy night watchmen prowled the shooting galleries, fun-house rides, and endless rows of concession stands. Strolling the walkway, we could hear the ocean boiling beneath us. Pops peered up at a tall tower from which a young blonde on horseback plunges into a giant tank of water three times each day. He shook his head. "Ain't that a hell of a way to make a living? And them cats in there fighting on the box—beating each other crazy for the almighty dollar. Pops, some people got a hell of a hard row to hoe."

We paused at the end of the pier jutting into the Atlantic; Pops lit a cigarette and leaned on a restraining fence to smoke. For long moments he looked up at the full moon, and watched the surf come and go. The glow from his cigarette faintly illuminated the dark old face in repose and I thought of some ancient tribal chieftain musing by his campfire, majestic and mystical. There was only the rush of water, gently roaring and boasting at the shore. "Listen to it, Pops," he said in his low, chesty rumble. "Whole world's turned on. Don't you dig its pretty sounds?"

CHAPTER 15

Epilogue: The Obscure Famous Arthur Grows Older

This collection has skipped along like a flat rock bounding across some great placid pond, changing directions and doubling back, and, no doubt, shall shortly sink from view without making a splash. If it has any one central theme, however tenuous, then that theme addresses itself to the mingled joys and sorrows of writing for a living in a society that honors disk jockeys over poets and pays them better to prove it.

This admission alone should limit sales to roughly 300 copies, even without help from my dear friends the critics or relatives who beseech Heaven for a cheaper version in paperback. Since the suspicion already exists that my publisher is bringing this work out as part of some vague, fuzzy tax dodge the author stubbornly insists on a curtain speech.

In its terminal rattlings this voice may be raised in one last, awful hoot of anger; may grow petulant or whine or blindly accuse. It may get embarrassingly personal, even to the point of edging up on telling just how little money my special Art brings in, or how achingly lonely one gets depending for companionship on a typewriter that speaks only when spoken to. The instinct to blurt all is, however, overpowering—for if my wretched confession steers just one wholesome American boy away from the shoddy path of the free-lancer, then my pride shall not have died in vain and will have cleverly killed a potential competitor on the edge of the grave.

On a cheerless spring morning in May, 1964, waking in an acre of bed unwarmed even by a temporary helpmate, I advised the ceiling that the United States Congress could go pleasure itself. And, for the first time in ten years, could do it without my standing by to hold one or more coats. By late afternoon I had filed off my chains, cleared my

desk of a decade's accumulated trivia (free passes to the Washington
Wax Museum, Stevenson campaign buttons, letters from loan sharks,
rodeo clowns and one-gallus parsons especially gifted at instructing
their Congressman in affairs of state), had lashed my car round and
about with books and personal mementos judged worth preserving,
and then in one great, umbilical severing had cut loose from a
$16,000 position as top wiper to a Texas Congressman. Through a
goodly portion of the night I prowled favored Washington hangouts
in search of a few bittersweet good-byes.

That proved to be a truly humbling experience. For though I
poured my heart out to old friends and rank strangers alike (saying
how I was chucking this sick goddamn freak society with its high-
finned cars and fixed quiz shows and tasteless TV dinners, and was
going off to write myself into a Famous Arthur) the only reactions I
drew were from a former secretary of mine who advised that I
shouldn't take any wooden nickles and from a citizen on a neighboring
barstool who loudly predicted that I would, and, what's more, would
probably need them. Though our altercation was short-lived, old-
timers still remark on its ferocity. Around midnight, no longer struck
dumb with sorrow over quitting town, I pulled out for my native
Texas.

It is terribly embarrassing to tell you why. A deep depression
dating from the Kennedy assassination and a collection of $2 woes
amounting to a small fortune played their parts, sure. But I really cut
my ties and paychecks off because I had—well, decided to take a
year out and write a novel that would win the Nobel Prize. Unlike O.
Henry, I do not specialize in pulling surprise endings so you are here
directed that I did not win it.

I thought the Nobel Prize lay right out there at a given point on
Route 66 the night I started for Austin. Had I not only a few weeks
earlier sold (on the basis of one thirty-six-page chapter and the promise
of much more) a novel to a major publishing house? And was not all
that remained (1) a few joyous months of inspirational creative
bursts after which (2) the manuscript would be forwarded to New
York by Brinks truck while (3) I spent a few weeks on Miami Beach
enjoying my movie money, granting interviews alternately to Granville Hicks and Dorothy Manners before (4) flying off to Czechoslo-
vakia or some such seaport to pick up my medallion along with its
incidental stipend of $50,000?

That was the way it was planned, though I hear for the record the

Nazis had planned the Sam Hill out of the Battle of Stalingrad. Those inspirational creative bursts I had counted on arrived as erratically as nonscheduled airlines and soared not half so high. My three children were with me in Austin for the summer; while they are extraordinarily sweet children of staggering talents, they also disturb the peace with great skill and a consistency to astound. The chick next door wore tight white shorts and stooped over all day in a garden perfectly viewed from my writing table, looking north, which is the direction she generally looked, too. Somebody was always giving a swinging party, I discovered a barrelful of old World War II *Esquires* in the attic, my attention span peaked out at seven seconds. Say no more of that wasted summer other than it was very interesting, indeed, and that it ended one night when a lady of prior associations beat me up in front of witnesses. Packing the nine pages written in a mere four months, your agent re-retreated to Washington City. Where, it dawned, he had no job. Or much money. And no living quarters at all.

Only God and the landlord know exactly when my earlier abrupt flight from Washington had been discovered in real estate circles. As soon after discovery as local laws permitted, my abandoned furniture was dumped on the public sidewalk (within view of the Capitol's dome) to the music of some nameless official chanting enough legal cadenzas to give the rude act a requisite amount of grace in the eyes of General Sessions Court. Less than twenty-four hours after I retook Washington a majority of Capitol Hill's hirelings, approximately one fourth a free nation's elective pooh-bahs, and two blind beggars sang out that they had personally witnessed those high ceremonies amidst the wreckage of my former home. It was not the kind of thing a budding Nobel Prizer would have wished for his past.

Somebody knew a Nice Greek Lady with a houseboat for rent. It was not a houseboat, as fate and the Crisscraft Cabin Cruiser folks would ordain it, but she rented it to me anyway. For months I bached and wrote on the twenty-three-foot *Pres,* docked on the Maryland side of Chesapeake Bay, living off a dwindling checking account, potted ham, and faith in the Nobel judges. The Nice Greek Lady cleverly turned up to rent-collect on weekends, thereby assuring that her many gregarious friends could join in spilling gin-and-tonic on my manuscript, asking why I wanted to write a book anyway, and taking my house out to sea.*

---

* It later developed that this was the N.G.L.'s way of courting me. Many first-generation Americans retain the quaint customs of the Old World.

One morning the *Pres* cupboard was as bare as my bank account and as the Nice Greek Lady was in my better dreams. An old political crony with connections in the Governor's office pledged to help. In no time at all this man of power and influence secured me a series of positions that broadened my scope. I delivered produce to Annapolis markets from the bed of a gas-fumy truck. Installed seats in the new Naval Academy football stadium by hand—and in August. Discovered, janitoring a truck stop, that Teamsters do not necessarily mix well with poets. For a while I wore an eye-patch and trick britches while busboying a dank watering hole named something like "The Pirate's Cove." (I quit when the owner, who insisted that the help call him Long John Silver, ordered that I double one leg up behind me at the knee and affect a wooden peg.) Thereafter, my writing was done between hunger pangs. Some days I wrote around the clock.

Came the morning when I couldn't pay the boat rental. The Nice Greek Lady and I, by this time friends, conferred about our mutual problems. Mine was that I had no place to hang my seabag, and hers was that she absolutely could not live without me. We settled my problem by stowing my gear in her Washington apartment, and hers by getting married, though it could be I have the order mixed. There, under more commodious conditions than I had known in some years, I finished *The One-Eyed Man*. That was about mid-1965, or eight deadlines and one full Nobel Prize behind schedule.

Do not think my book failed to create a certain stir. Visions of sugar plums danced in my editor's head and laughter was heard escaping the executive washroom. One of America's leading writers —critically acclaimed *and* a Big Seller—on reading an advance copy wrote a page of praise so fulsome Lyndon B. Johnson might have blushed to hear it said of himself. Unfortunately, the Famous Arthur added, it was his policy not to give quotes on the public record. Therefore, we could not use his letter in promotional campaigns. The letter got less interesting from that point on, though he was terribly nice about it; even friendly. I understood his position very well—even sympathized with it. I liked and admired him and his work. Still do. And, of course, every time I think about the whole damn deal it makes me sick.

Now for a little sneaky mid-story O. Henry. Several Famous Arthurs whose high principles did not collapse in a heap at the friendly exploitation of their names (among them Richard Condon,

John Kenneth Galbraith, David Weiss, Vance Bourjaily) said flattering things of my novel. Such trade publications as *Publisher's Weekly, Library Journal* and *Virginia Kirkus Reader's Service* warned bookstore owners and librarians that here was A Big One. Wham! Literary Guild Book Club bought my novel! Bam! My publisher sprang for a full-page ad, my book sharing co-billing with one by 007 creator Ian Fleming,* in the Sunday *New York Times.* Then my publisher threw me a swanky party to which 500 of Washinton's most literate free-loaders were attracted at a cost of only $33 per head. I was given my own booth to sign autographs and smile from at a posh hotel hosting the National Book Sellers' Convention. I signed a contract for a second novel on terms considerably less niggardly than those associated with the first. Somebody Big in the movies was reportedly doing a jig-dance all the way from Hollywood to my bank, pirating editors eager to lure me to their own publishing houses told me the usual promissory lies, literary agents vied to act as middlemen between me and my royalty checks for a token 10 percent, and magazine moguls stood me lunch.

I went off from fame to Florida and rented a glass house along a stretch of the Gulf of Mexico where the sunset looks like a million dollars and the rental fees match the view. The better to draft my Nobel acceptance speech, you see. ("The creative writer is, above all, a carpenter. The pen, the language, the hours of his life are the only tools in his kit. How well he uses his tools determines whether he builds a birdhouse or a cathedral. To you who have generously decided that I built a cathedral, let me say from a full heart bla bla bla and wasn't that silly?" Continued Next Nobel.)

I didn't win any Nobel Prize. Not even a Pulitzer or the National Book Award.† There are many laugh-proof reasons for this. The first of which is a human entity, one R. Z. Sheppard, whose name will live in infamy as long as there are Kings to be hounded for credit. Mr. Sheppard does mischief under the auspicies of *Book Week.*‡ He is paid to criticize Literature and I am here to testify that he is a zealot on the job. His views roughly were that I should join the plumber's union and possibly needed a little frontal lobotomy work. This first

* Who was, I later recalled, then dead.
† Trailways Bus Company is, however, considering me for its Travelingest Author Award.
‡ Or did, until it folded recently, which should tell you something right there.

critical word to the world of my novel was flashed four days before my solid-gold publication party and two weeks before my book would be officially published. It tended to put a damper on things. I will say for Mr. Sheppard that he sure is fast coming off the blocks.

A good lap behind, I launched a twenty-three-day promotional campaign in four states and the District of Columbia: TV interviews, radio talk shows, bookstore autograph parties, author-critic luncheons. One highly advertised author-critic luncheon consisted of the author and the local critic grabbing a corndog at a sidewalk stand. On a mid-morning TV show I followed a gynecologist who, with the aid of color charts, came out against cancer of the uterus. A Washington columnist promoted an old Marlon Brando film in mistakenly identifying me as the author of *One-Eyed Jacks*. In one Texas City, after I'd rushed across 120 miles of burning desert sands to claim a precious half hour of TV time, the station blew what obviously was the keyest of fuses; due to conditions beyond our control there was neither interview nor air conditioning. Resuming the tour, I appeared on the Texas Department of Public Safety's private radar screens for the duration of one blip, at a speed in excess of seventy miles per hour, and at a personal expense of $23 and costs. In my hometown of Odessa, Texas, some 300 revelers came to a whing-ding thrown by my friend and lawyer, Warren Burnett. Half of them recalled "when you couldn't write your name," one-third asked whether my mother was ashamed of my vocation, six actually came to my bookstore autograph party the next day (four of them buying books), and one, leaving, smashed into my car in his dumptruck.

To tell the truth, we had hoped to do a bit better in Odessa. No really memorable event had occurred there since a falling meteorite carved a crater outside the city limits. Though I do not recall exactly when the meteorite hit town, I can tell you the exact day that Dean Martin did. On the day of my bookstore huckstering. Martin teed-off in the Odessa Pro-Am Golf Tournament at the exact hour I waited on the steps of the bookstore for my fickle public.

I would almost bet that Dean Martin could come to New York or possibly even Miami without knocking anybody out of a solitary book sale. In Odessa, however, Dean Martin's arrival set off more celebrations than Lindbergh's return. Loyal company men walked off their jobs; dowdy housewives bought $50 permanent waves. Floral shops sent him blossoms and I have heard it said that some modernist parents offered their daughters. The Odessa Country Club looked like a modern version of the Oklahoma Land Rush. Gallery Score: Martin 7,000; King 6. One of my callers was the golfing equivalent of a double-boogie: a minor bank executive who came bearing an old promissory note of $300 in his favor, which I had forgotten sooner than he had.

In Midland, Texas (another community where I once numbered among the resident citizens), the day after I had appeared on TV, radio, had my picture displayed in the local weekly newspaper, and was welcomed in lights on the marquee of the Holiday Inn, I was strutting to coffee with a high city official, feeling so famous I wondered why somebody wasn't running ahead to strew rose petals, when I encountered an old school chum I had not seen in twenty years. "Hi, Larry!" he called out. "You still workin' over at the post office?"

My car broke down in a part of rural Louisiana that has not yet been named. The Nice Greek Lady glimpsed a garden snake on the road near Greenville, Mississippi, and fainted dead away. As luck would have it she was driving at the time. So much for the promotion tour save for thanking my publisher, who, drawing on years of experience, cleverly promoted my pro-Civil Rights novel almost exclusively in the Old Confederacy.

Meanwhile, Up North, the folks at *The New Yorker* indicated that where my novel was concerned they preferred streptococcus. A gentleman at *The New York Times* devoted approximately twenty lines to my two years of labor, and I wish publicly to express gratitude for his brevity. The *Texas Observer* (to whose pages I had for three years contributed, for shamefully low wages, and with whose editor I had for many more years frequently shared the Chair of Philosophy at Scholtz beer garden in Austin) broke in a young and dyspeptic reviewer anxious to catch R. Z. Sheppard at the quarter-pole. To quote a Great American, it was "the ugliest thing I ever saw." Later my friend the editor-philosopher presumed to make amends with a second *Observer* review, in which he said my book was too funny for his taste and, besides, I probably didn't have much imagination. After this classic example of literary overkill, *Time* varied the script by doing a glowing, yard-long story on the New Novelists of 1966. They mentioned for good or ill every first novel coming off the press in that given year, except, of course, mine.*

Then the heirs of a long-dead politician threatened to sue because

---

* No, I don't know why and at this point I don't give a damn.

a character in my book happened to bear his family name. Literary Guild Book Club, which often drumbeats its offerings for a year or more, apparently experimented with subliminal advertising in my case. To the best of my knowledge they stuck my book in one ad that appeared in *Ladies Home Journal* before somebody caught the error. Whoever it was probably got a raise.

For fear you'll think my novel was as bad as the record indicates, I now attempt to muddle the issue with statistics. My favorable reviews *actually outnumbered* the unfavorable ones, by the most honest count available, and by a score of 43½ to 7½!* And they didn't just love me in Oshkosh. Learned critics in such sophisticated cities as Washington, Houston, Cleveland, Miami, Chicago, New Orleans, Boston, Atlanta, Louisville and Casper† came out foursquare in favor of *The One-Eyed Man*. And as of noon yesterday it had sold eighty-six copies.

Well, now, we all know that I am putting you on about the number of copies sold. Because the law considers it aggravated assault for any adult male publicly to humilate his spouse, I am statutorily barred from naming exact sales figures. I have heard it claimed by a certain editor that my maiden effort sold "much better than the average first novel" (which mythical volume sells, according to current lore, about 5,000 copies) although he only insists this when called before the Board re: Certain Judgments of Purchase.

In retrospect, I am less ashamed of my record than perhaps a decent family man should be. Experience has taught that success in the book business, as in the banditry profession, is often a matter of timing, luck and imponderable vagaries. Anyone can have the misfortune to write a book that backfires or to hijack Macy on the same day Gimbel waits on record trade. So I have learned to do my sentence at the typewriter one word at a time, no longer thinking a Nobel Prize ahead, expecting neither pardon nor parole; hopeful only that I never again will telegraph Frank Sinatra that he is my personal choice for Protagonist while still drafting the plot, and remembering always that it is bad form to write off for a Nobel Prize Entry Blank, c/o Contest Editor, *New York Review of Books*, New York City, New York.

Humility and patience is what I have learned. When Mother for-

* I split down the middle the vote of the small-town Ohio critic who described me as "horribly talented."
† Well, strike Casper.

warded a clipping headlined CRITICS SAY NOVEL DEAD, on which she had written in the margin, "Son, do they mean yours?" I simply wrote, "It is not dead, Mother, only sleeping; my love to Dad," then mailed it back. Two years ago I would have enclosed a stinging scorpion.

So having endured, one survives. And surviving, works. And working, learns. And learning, grows wise. Wise, now, I shall know when *The One-Eyed Man* appears in paperback some three months from this writing to expect no sudden riches, no boatloads of glory, no sounding of trumpets. Unless, of course, they happen to establish a Paperback Division in the Nobel competition this year.

Throughout this confession I have shown a high fidelity to Truth, exaggerating only when the pale facts wouldn't do, and otherwise heaping honor on my art form. You may, however, have noted that certain cheery optimisms expressed in the opening salvo have turned to quincelike cynicisms. This is directly traceable to the passage of one year's time. Another 365 days of observing the currents has made me less confident of the swim; I am no longer a svelte thirty-eight but a thickening thirty-nine, both in years and circumference.

Yes, neighbors, many a black-bordered letter has arrived in the box since Page One. They have had their cumulative effect: I no longer lapse into unknown tongues at the prospect of speaking to a New York editor, nor lead strangers by the sleeve to marvel at my name blinking from the magazine rack. More and more one worries less and less about his Nobel competition and more about what they are paying for 3,000 words these days over at *Sadistic Detective*.

Writing has been described as the search for Truth, though possibly this was first said by some fellow well in the jug and who wasn't any too stable to begin with. I have caught up with twin Truths and here the rascals are: my prose just won't sing to me from the page like William Styron's does, and I couldn't sell as many units as John D. MacDonald sells* if I owned a penicillin factory. These are painful lessons. But, like those teaching that Santa Claus is nobody more important than Daddy and that the stork rarely flies, there comes a time to admit them and move resolutely toward the next disappointment.

Spelled m-o-n-e-y. I don't honestly know how to discuss money and at the same time preserve the public fiction of my wealth. Maybe,

* Thirty-odd *million* at last count.

however, the myth that writers no longer starve in garrets, but own vast estates staffed by liveried footmen and Harvard-tooled accountants, is not worth preserving.

For years the average nonwriting American has lived in the illusion that publication of a single book amounts to inventing Instant Money. Possibly the trouble started when Congress voted Dwight D. Eisenhower a capital gains arrangement on *Crusade in Europe,* or maybe the fiction was promoted by writers' ex-wives. Surely it is among the least creditable of our national myths. Yet I have heard it said on good authority that I, personally, made one million dollars or a quarter-million dollars or one of those fantastic Irving Wallace sums on my first novel. Just how this money accumulated or where it is presently stashed my friends do not tell me; they merely know that it exists and, like the Baptist God, need not be seen to be believed. Though I have taken pains to deny promptly all rumors of personal profit exceeding $100,000, this myth of wealth lives and grows. Oddly enough, those friends who toss the higher figures around in juggling my wealth are the exact same friends who have yet to come into the prideful ownership of my book. When I ask them where in the world they think an author gets money if not through royalty sales, they just wink and grin like I had weighed my elbow with the lamb chops when the customer wasn't looking.

Possibly one reason the myth of authors' affluence persists is because writers are such terrible hands to lie about money. I, personally, have lied shamelessly about each story sold or any contract signed—seldom failing to double the sales price in the first telling and on a good day quadrupling my money before the stock market closes. A man of such sinful pride will not reveal the whole truth even here or under torture. I do, however, promise from this point on to tell you no out-and-out falsehoods.

I propose to cite the example of a contemporary writer's earnings, with the stipulation that I am permitted to make unspecified brags in advance about making more money than he does. The other writer is Dan Wakefield. In his collection, *Between the Lines,* published last year, Wakefield confessed, with that addiction to veracity that makes the rest of mankind shudder, that he has never made more than $8,000 in any one year at the keyboard.

Mr. Wakefield is one of the better and more perceptive writers now slowly starving. His name is respected by top editors, he has received critical acclaim from the right corners, he is serious about his craft;

presumably he works hard. And yet in his best year Dan Wakefield has earned less than many bus drivers and no more than some custodial engineers guarding the bowels of nameless Federal Buildings. Somehow it does not seem altogether fitting and proper, though I don't know what to do about the financial plight of work-a-day writers short of asking you to send in your dimes and nickles.

A wife hoping to cheer her writer-husband on a day when he refuses to come out from under the bed, or an editor trying to buy him cheap, may philosophize that one's character is vastly improved by a little frantic struggling en route to the noose. Reliable sources at the National Institute of Health, however, report a paucity of scientific data supporting the theory that starvation is the surest path to Art. Still, even if the quality of the Art isn't improved by financial jitters, the quantity often is. Like Gloria Steinem, or anybody else with all the equipment Heaven intended, I do not enjoy writing so much as having written. ("Writing is easy," Red Smith once said. "You just stare at the keyboard until little drops of blood appear on your forehead.") Let yourself stand about a hop, skip and jump away from the poorhouse, however, and you will write you some prose. It may not sing a note but it sure will weigh heavy. The day you cannot see five magazine assignments ahead is the day your agent gets the little pep-talk that begins with curses and ends with threats.

Short of receiving a Guggenheim Fellowship or some similar grant (and these aren't exactly forced on you), there are two ways the writer living hand-to-typewriter may survive while he architects the Big Book. He may, if he owes no debts or owns no dependents, live in an open field and eat bush-berries while devoting full labors to his masterpiece. If, however, his name is known to the retail merchants and he has a retinue rivaling that of the late Nizam of Hyderabad,* he will find himself traipsing the sidewalks of New York more frequently than a street mugger. I can recite the exact distance from the front door of the *Saturday Evening Post* to the steps of *True* thence to the holy halls of *Harper's Magazine*. The only rule you need to remember to be a free-lance Artist is this: you get out and get the work or the bill collector gets you. ("Free-lancing," Hemingway once said, "is like playing sand-lot second base—the ball can take some awful hops."†)

If you think we do not have us a word factory at our house look at

* Mourned by 3 wives, 42 concubines, 200 children and 300 retainers.
† What did Hemingway know of privation?

the record: in one recent week newsstands blossomed with the by-line of your Obscure Famous Arthur in *Harper's Magazine, Saturday Evening Post, Dissent, The Washingtonian,* and *The Texas Observer.* Even as they appeared I was finishing another *Harper's* piece, one for *The New York Times* Sunday Magazine, beginning the initial interviews for a *True* article, doing one book review for *Book Week* and yet another for *Time.* In spare moments I worked on the marvelous tome now in your hands. Meanwhile, my agent was bugging editors all over America about next week's production schedule.

The foregoing will likely cause the legendary little ole housewife who is eternally threatening to "sit down one day and write a book" to think that she will sit down one half-day, maybe, and rip off about sixteen tons of magazine articles. It shouldn't. For although five of my articles did come to flower on the newsstands in a single week, several months had been devoted to getting them there.

The next time you hear some self-made tycoon whoop of how only businessmen have guts enough to hump it alone, or express the thought that God wishes the world's control for those who have fearlessly met payrolls, you invite him to get his rugged-individualist carcass over here in the deep end of the pool with us Artists. We do not have a 27½ percent oil-depletion raft floating slickly under us at tax time, nor will the government pay us not to write five acres of stories this year, nor the All-State insurance folks to come running to settle ninety cents on the dollar if we call to say a disaster has befallen our manuscript. The free-lance writer can teach you more about pure Free Enterprise than Harvard Business College or all the pious editorial hirelings of all the safely monopolistic newspapers in the world. My sweetest vision is to get one day one of the Rotary Club species in a poker game and watch his eyes as he learns just what a mean, money-grubbing S.O.B. a Bearded Dreamer can be.

Now to deal harshly with Glamor. Unless I have misjudged thirty-nine years of living evidence, the nonwriting citizen sees more Glamor in the Writer than he does in 007 multiplied by Perry Mason times Bart Starr. I don't want to destroy any helpful illusions, but just submit yourself to the following exercise and then come tell me about Glamor:

Take one human body and lock it indoors for a minimum of two weeks. Sit it at a typewriter with stacks of blank paper in near repose. Cause its fingers to spasm involuntarily on the keyboard no more than once a day. Let it wander around, make instant coffee, mutter to itself, and expel huge sighs. Make it scrub the bathtub, paint bricks, goggle the television tube, reread old passages of Poe, cereal boxes, and its Domestic Relations Court citations while hoping to be sneaked up on from ambush by some hairy Great Thought. Give it absolutely no thought not currently expressed in *Reader's Digest.* Smoke it five cigarette packs per day, pour assorted juices down it, and jump it in response to sudden noise. Forget to wash it or feed it and rub carbon paper all over its face. Have its wife weep because it won't communicate, throw its wedding-gift cut-glass ashtray at it, and say in its presence that she admires a current best seller by Another. Overflow its waste baskets and lose its background files. Just as it begins to write effectively have it get telephone calls saying it has won $20 worth of free studio dance lessons toward the $3,000 beginner's course, that its best suit has reacted strangely to a new cleaning fluid, that it has thirty seconds to remove its car from the fire lane, and that its central charge account begs immediate attention. Cause it to sleep fitfully and to cry out in the dark for its mother. Send it gratuitously a seventeen-year-old freshman from across the hall, home for the holidays from Vassar, to exchange lengthy views with it on the Writer's Role in Contemporary Society and then leave it a shoebox full of original free verse to read and report on by tomorrow. Keep it well shaken-up at all times and ample heat on it. Repeat cycle until all signs of life are gone.

Now that you know the recipe, how many do you want, and will you eat them here or take them with you?

Yes, it is a rat race and justice nowhere in it and I expect with luck to ghost a few pieces from Heaven for a travel magazine generous in its expenses. Though I have wept these many paragraphs and called out scorn, I am not about to quit writing for the good reason that I own no other skills. Many of my former professions are no longer open to return, bridge-burning having a way of creating chasms, and as a former politician I am too proud to take honest work. My knuckles are thus sentenced to a life of flashing fat and pale on the keyboard even as they do now, while the brain behind them is forever mindful of new deadlines, old bills, and that in this moment Mother and Dad are somewhere clutching each other while asking what went wrong when the *other* children turned out so well?

Even if Congress passed an anti-writing law, many of us would break it. The sooner society discovers that the compulsive writer can no more help himself than can his cousin with the bottle problem, the quicker we will return to you as healed men. Why don't they cut down on some of this wasteful foreign aid and build us more institutions?

It is customary at this point in so personal a recitation to offer up thanks to all the good spirits and old associates who have helped to make one what one is today. In the instant case this might come off as blame-placing. So we shall reserve that little ceremony for the next collection, though if nothing has happened to my career by then we will print their names and the Devil take them.

ABOUT THE AUTHOR

*Larry L. King is a contributing editor
to* Harper's Magazine *and* The Texas Observer.
*His articles, essays, and book reviews
have appeared in more than twenty-five
periodicals. His novel of politics,*
The One-Eyed Man, *was published in 1966
by The New American Library and was a Literary
Guild Book Club alternate selection. It has
recently been issued in Signet paperback.
A native Texan who now lives in Washington, D.C.,
King has worked on newspapers
in New York, New Mexico, and his home state.
From 1954 to mid-1964 he served as
Administrative Assistant to two Texas
congressmen. He is currently at work on
a second novel and a book of nonfiction.*